Heal Your Self

BOOKS BY JANET GREENE

HEAL YOUR HEART:
A JOURNEY TO FIND YOUR SOUL MATE
©2002

A SMILE FOR THE CHILDREN
©2002

THE LITTLE BOOK OF SECRETS
©2002

Author's Website
http://GreenesRelease.com

Please appreciate that since it can be difficult to express the Non-Physical ideas and concepts that Janet discovered with physical English words, she sometimes uses words in new ways in order to express unique views of life.

Heal Your Self

A Journey to find

You

JANET GREENE

HEAL YOUR SELF: A JOURNEY TO FIND YOU
Copyright © 2003, 2007 by Janet Greene

Cover design by Christina Mårtensson

All rights reserved. No part of this book may be reproduced by any mechanical, photographic, or electronic process, or in the form of a phonographic recording nor may it be stored in a retrieval system, transmitted, or otherwise be copied for public or private use - other than for "fair use" as brief quotations embodied in articles and reviews without prior written permission of the publisher.

The author of this book does not dispense medical advice nor prescribe the use of any technique as a form of treatment for physical, medical or physiological problems without the advice of a physician, either directly or indirectly. The intent of the author is only to offer information of a general nature to help you in your quest for physical and mental good health. In the event you use any of the information in this book for yourself, which is your constitutional right, the author and the publisher assume no responsibility for your actions.

Library of Congress Control Number: 2008903949
ISBN: 1-4382-1020-5
EAN-13: 978-1-4382-1020-9

Inspirations Books
Custom Books Publishing
Scotts Valley, CA

Printed in the United States of America

Contents

INTRODUCTION — ix
WHAT I BELIEVE — xii

SECTION 1 - TOOLS & TECHNIQUES
- THE PLAN — 1
- FEELING — 21
- ENERGY — 33
- HELP I'M OVERWHELMED — 37
- FEAR — 43
- LIFE LESSONS — 54
- TIME FOR SOME FUN — 61

SECTION 2 - RELEASING — 69
- A PERSONAL INTRODUCTION TO GREENE'S RELEASE — 70
- SUMMARY - GREENE'S RELEASE — 83
- A GREENE'S RELEASING SESSION — 86
- WHAT AM I? — 92

SECTION 3 - PULLING IT ALL TOGETHER   105
- STUMBLING BLOCKS   106
- A NEW VIEW OF LIFE   114
- LIVING CONSCIOUSLY   117

SECTION 4 - HEALING CHILDHOOD ISSUES   125
- REASONS/BELIEFS/WORKING WITH FEARS   127
- THE HURT CHILD   134
- ABUSE/INHIBITIONS   138

SECTION 5 - THE OUTSIDE WORLD   149
- PERCEPTION & FREE WILL   151
- LACK/LOSS/FAILURE   174
- THEM   182
- DIFFICULT LIVES   187
- FATHERS, MOTHERS & SIBLINGS   193

SECTION 6 - THE INSIDE WORLD - US   200
- WE CHOOSE HOW WE FEEL   201
- ITS ALL IN THE WORD   210
- EXPERIENCE   217
- TO CHANGE OR NOT TO CHANGE   230
- HOPES/DREAMS   244
- PASSIONS/HEART DESIRES   251
- THE FIGHT TO BE ME   256
- GRUMPY DAYS   264
- FAILURE & SUCCESS   267
- SELF IMPORTANCE   276

SECTION 7 - HEALTH & WELL BEING   294

SECTION 8 - THE NEW ME — 310

- WALKING THIS MORNING WAS VERY PLEASANT — 311
- ME — 317
- DARE TO BE YOU — 320
- WHAT I HAVE ACHIEVED — 322
- EVERYTHING IS CREATED WITH LOVE ENERGY — 324

- CONCLUSION — 330
- ABOUT THE AUTHOR — 331

Introduction

Imagine how many coats you might be wearing today if you put one on every time you've had an upsetting experience, every time your feelings got hurt, every time you were put down, and every time you put yourself down.

Imagine how difficult it would be to function, or feel, or even be seen with all of these coats on.

Now imagine how miserable you'd be if you thought you had to live the rest of your life buried under these coats, because you didn't know that you could take them off.

Heal Your Self takes you on a step by step guided journey to effectively take your coats off, and uncover the real you.

You will feel stronger and more like yourself as you work through the simple exercises in each chapter, which build upon the previous to create a journey of important stepping stones.

Every chapter will reawaken one specific aspect of the real you. The Feeling chapter allows you to experience deep feeling again without the restrictions of your painful emotions and fears, The Plan chapter awakens your logical reasoning and thinking that has been sabotaged by your belief that you are powerless, the Greene's Release chapter reawakens your innate ability to permanently release all that hurts, the Hurt Child chapter uses all of these skills to permanently heal your childhood issues that still affect how you think and feel today, and so on.

This workbook presents like a study course that enables you to build a firm foundation of skill, knowledge and ability to heal and self direct your life in just 30 minutes a day.

Take your time to feel and experience every single moment of this journey, because in the process of doing so, you *will* discover a new you that makes you smile from the inside out.

Just like you do in your everyday life activities, initially you may feel emotions and hear your self-talk *object* to the contents of this book. Know that every single negative thing you think or feel about yourself, your life or this book is in direct response to one of your beliefs.

By the time you reach the Greene's Release chapter you will be ready to learn about and investigate your own beliefs, their impact, how they were formed, and a simple technique to permanently remove and replace them with a new belief of your choice.

For now, to prevent their sabotaging your healing work while you get ready to address them, instead of listening and acting on their suggestions, try writing each thought and objection down in a notebook, recognizing that very soon you will have the choice to keep or permanently remove any of them. Thank them for their input, saying that you will address their concerns as soon as you are ready to undertake the work in the Greene's Release chapter. This is a technique that can be applied whenever you are triggered at inappropriate times.

Before You Begin

It is *very important* to write a detailed description of your current life so you have an accurate picture to refer back to. Read it in a month and *see* the changes, then write a new picture to review in another month, and so on. Include:

- Your current activities - work, relaxation, exercise, diet, habits, sleeping patterns etc.
- Your thoughts - the things you think/worry/stress about

- Your feelings - how you feel emotionally, upon waking, going to sleep, throughout the day, during interactions, your relationships
- What makes you happy, sad, and your thoughts of life

Hints and Tricks

I am including this quick reference guide to help you find answers to problems or issues you may have.

- I read half the book in one day and now I feel totally overwhelmed.
  Healing Childhood Issues refers to this topic

- I went straight to Greene's Release without looking at the earlier chapters, so now I am confused and don't think this book has anything to help me.
  Hints and Tricks in *The Plan* Chapter addresses this issue

- I feel so overwhelmed with emotions that I can't think or focus on anything, especially reading a book.
  Help I'm Overwhelmed has a technique to release overwhelming emotions.

- Something unexpected has happened in my everyday life which I need to focus on and resolve immediately.
  Living Consciously explains how this book can help you resolve everyday life dramas as they occur.

- The *Pulling it all Together* section includes tips and tricks to help with many areas including times when you are scared to let yourself feel, think too much about problems instead of doing the work to permanently resolve them, get stuck, or become overwhelmed by unexpected life challenges.

What I Believe

We Chose A Life Lesson

We each have a topic to resolve this lifetime. For some it is money, others health, having children, family, or finding a belief in self.

Each life lesson creates situations to push the person to discover the truth for themselves in order to resolve the issue and reach the goal. Money teaches people that they are valuable, health how to care about and for themselves, love that they are love.

Although my journey dealt with many topics, my life lesson was love. I desperately wanted to find love but could not because I didn't believe that I was lovable, and was filled with fears, insecurities and painful memories.

My journey led me to discover for myself that I am special, to form my own beliefs of myself, the world and my place in it, heal all of my fears so I could open and become love, and to follow my dreams because they are mine.

A life lesson journey is when people face and heal their fears and beliefs of themselves and in the process teach themselves how very special they are.

My books and teachings share what I discovered on my journey.

We Learn What to Believe From Our Family

When we were little children, everything was new so we didn't know what to believe about anything. Because a child's role is to learn how to live as a human being, we used all that we saw, heard and experienced to form a set of Inner Beliefs about who and what we are, the world and our place in it.

If mummy yelled at me then "I must be a bad person." If I am always getting into trouble then "I can't do anything right." If they don't like me then "I am not a lovable person."

We copied the behaviors and values of our parents, and began treating ourselves as they did. We even learned to judge and complain at ourselves just like they did.

"You are stupid." "You can't do anything right." "No you can't have a new toy because you don't deserve it." Sound familiar?

We Store Every Thought and Emotion

We can think of any event and feel the emotions of that time, as if experiencing it right now. Our stockpile of sadness and hurt is full and ready to be emptied, which is why they have been bubbling up.

We Grow Up Using These Beliefs

Our unique set of Inner Beliefs creates the foundation and rules of our life and living. We just know them to be true because they are the facts of life, the reality of life. We have no reason to doubt or question them.

"I am a lazy person." "I fail at everything I do." "Life is scary and hard." "I will always have to depend on myself and no-one else." "No-one can love me or is there for me."

We do grow up living and experiencing what we believe.

Beliefs are Temporary

We forgot one very important thing, and that is: The Inner Beliefs we took on as a child were only meant to be temporary, required so we could function in the world at that time.

They are temporary Inner Beliefs only to be used until we were mature enough to decide what to believe for ourselves!

Therefore, we can decide to change our Inner Beliefs at any time!

These Beliefs Are Not Our Own

Every single thing we believe about us is what someone else taught or said to us!

As a child we naturally accepted and believed what they said. When they told us "Your lazy and will never get anywhere in life" we believed this to be a fact of life.

Now that we are adults, we have the option to accept or deny anything we choose. If I told you today "Your lazy and will never get anywhere in life" would you believe and accept it as reality? I doubt it.

Every single thing you think of yourself, the world and your place in it is someone else's viewpoint, and NOT your own!

Do you wish to base your life on someone else's viewpoint? Or would you like to remove these foreign beliefs which cloud your thoughts and sabotage your life, so you can create your own special ones?

21st Century Personal Development

It is 40+ years since the New Age Movement first introduced the concepts of Personal Power and Co-Creation. Now 'doing what feels right', 'believing that we have the power to create' and 'the desire to take charge of our lives' are common place ideals.

Discussions of spirit, soul, reincarnation and belief in self are openly encouraged, even with children.

We who live in the 21st century have attained a freedom of mind, body and spirit that allows us to explore and grow far beyond what our parents and grandparents ever dreamed possible. This is clearly demonstrated by the fact that our quest to find inner peace often begins where theirs ended.

They perceived that thoughts *were* the Inner Beliefs; therefore forcing yourself to change your thoughts with affirmations changed your beliefs and your life experiences.

We now recognize that thoughts and Inner Beliefs are two separate things, so we can go directly to the source and treat the Inner Beliefs, which automatically creates the life changes we desire.

21st Century Personal Development is a direct reflection of this natural evolution of inner growth and ability.

Thoughts and Inner Beliefs Are Two Separate Things

For example: After going on a date I float around and dream of love, then snap myself back to reality with the thought "He won't love you anyway so stop being silly."

The thought "He won't love you anyway so stop being silly" is a reflection of something I know to be fact. "I am not lovable", which is my Inner Belief.

That is just an example of one of the many thoughts that would come from this single Inner Belief "I am not lovable."

Thoughts and words are not Inner Beliefs, but they do show us what we really believe from deep inside.

Taking this next step in Personal Development, we can use our thoughts and words as tools to become aware of our hidden negative Inner Beliefs, so we are then able to stop and decide whether we wish to keep this idea or remove and replace it with its opposite.

Affirmations

As affirmations aim to change thought alone, they do little to change our Inner Beliefs and life experiences. I can tell myself that "I am lovable and everyone loves me" repeatedly for days and days, even weeks, but unless I know it to be part of my truth (Inner Belief), it cannot make sense to me, nor fill my life with loving people and make it easy for me to express love as previously thought.

There are reasons why I am scared of love, why I took on the Inner Belief that I wasn't lovable, and why I am filled with sadness. Would you rather pretend to be happy by repeatedly telling yourself that you are, or actually be happy?

21st Century Personal Development goes directly to the cause of our unhappiness, the Inner Beliefs.

By changing our Inner Beliefs we automatically create new lives and experiences based on whatever we choose.

For example, a person who currently believes that "I am not lovable" can permanently change it to "I am lovable" using Greene's Release, which will change how they think, feel, view themselves, and act. They will immediately begin living the experience that matches their new "I am lovable" Inner Belief.

It is Not Hard to Change Our Beliefs
We Just Forgot That we Can

People often feel an emotion and talk about it, but don't go any further. I developed a relatively simple process called Greene's Release that allows anyone to access and change their subconscious beliefs by merely adding a couple of new steps to what people already do.

All we need do to go right to the subconscious belief is listen to what we feel, and follow the stories that come up. Then we can use a special technique to permanently remove any emotion, memory or belief and replace it with one we choose.

We Can Permanently Resolve Any Issue & Emotion

We can either spend our time in the drama of *wanting to escape* situations and emotions, or decide *to end* it permanently by *resolving its cause.* Use intent and determination to want every cause to surface, so you can permanently release them. Use each trigger to increase your determination to find and remove all issues.

Decide what you want. It is totally up to you!

The Plan

The aim of this chapter is to encourage a new mindset so you may go beyond merely reading a book, to discovering how you can take and apply its contents to yourself in a real life usable format. Hints and tricks learned while working with people are included to further promote your success.

It forms the groundwork, so you may successfully translate and apply all you read, into YOUR life, making this YOUR workbook, YOUR journey of self discovery. Please read the entire chapter first.

When you complete this chapter you will be able to:

- Take my ideas and apply them to you and your life
- Investigate and formulate your own ideas and concepts
- Make this your workbook to create the life you desire

We each are undertaking a very special experience of self learning and growth. While I may have discovered some of the answers you seek, they are mine, from my perspective and will have little relevance to you unless transferred into your world of experience and understanding. Therefore, I do not write of mere answers, I teach you how to create your own journey to find your own answers. You will read many of my thoughts and experiences as I traveled this same road you now take, and you will see how very normal your every thought and feeling are. We all have fears, doubts, desires, and pain.

Translating My Ideas

The first step involves learning how to translate my work and the tools incorporated within it. So you may be able to read my words, then bring them into and apply to your own world of feeling, thinking, experiencing and conceptualizing.

How many times have you read a book thinking this is the exact information I was looking for, the exact things I wish to learn how to do, then felt the disappointment at not being able to do so? How many times have you then gone on to think, they made it sound easy so why can't I do it? Am I too dumb?

There is a very simple reason why this happens. When we listen to other people's concepts/answers, while we may recognize them as making sense, unless we find a way for that same logic to be felt and experienced within us, it cannot be assimilated.

That was your answer, now do you know how to use it? Of course you don't. That was my answer, my logic, my expression of understanding formed by my experiences.

What if I shared concepts/experiences with you in a way that made you think, so you could try them out for yourself? Or that helped you remember your own similar experiences, encouraged you to feel those triggered emotions and feelings, then discussed what they meant and how to work with them?

Activity - Create Your Own Concepts

Perhaps this will help. Did you know that one smile can be shared with hundreds, even thousands of people? Try this. Spend 30 minutes in your local store smiling at every person you see, and watch the expression on their faces.

That one smile you gave that person, made them feel special and smile back at you, then the next person they met, and the next and the next. When they went home they smiled at their partner, and children, who smiled back. Then went on to smile at the next person they met and so on and so on.

How did you feel when they smiled back at you? Warm inside, happy? Just one little smile can change how you and hundreds of other people feel. Imagine that!

Those words about smiling were not mere words. I want you to go out and do it. Try it and see for yourself. Before you read anymore of this book, go find out about smiling. Take note of the reactions, notice how they makes you feel, how you then go on to relate to the next person you meet, then you will know how others feel when you smile at them. Think about how each smile will be spread far and wide, the implications. Feel the experience of discovering all about smiles.

Document your experience, findings and thoughts in your Journal, then discuss it with a friend or family member. Encourage them to do the exercise and see how it makes them feel. Then you can both enjoy a more detailed discussion on the merits of smiling, while you notice your naturally increased curiosity and understanding.

Activity - Journal

We speak without thinking about what to say, yet when writing, we consciously replace those thoughts with perceived logical wording, as we were taught to do in school. But thinking about what you are writing disables the flow of free thoughts.

Practice writing as if you are thinking or talking to someone, without thought or attention to what you are actually writing and you will amaze yourself at what comes out.

Writing is a wonderful way to clarify your thoughts and hear what you are really thinking and trying to tell yourself.

Most exercises ask you to write about your experience, conclusions, and thoughts to help you become more aware of them. This is a very important aspect of this program.

The more you ponder and write about your experiences, the more you encourage your insights to flow, and the more you will learn! Keep going with each exercise and concept until it clicks.

All it takes is awareness and practice then you will delight at your written or typed insights.

Practice - Intuitive Reading

The Smile exercise resulted in your taking my ideas and using them to form your own ideas, opinions, concepts and knowledge of smiling. You successfully achieved what you wish to do from reading this book by using intuitive reading skills.

It is one thing to listen to concepts, then think about them, but another entirely to live the experience of that concept, feel it so it becomes yours.

Now, go back to the beginning of this section on translating my ideas. Read it again, but this time think what it means. Remember a book you have read and had the experience I spoke of, remember how you felt. Think about that and you will form your own understanding of it. Open your memory banks to relate my words to your own situations.

Use this chapter as a practice ground to learn the tools of working through this book. So it becomes your book, your journey. Go back again and see what other thoughts come to mind from what you have read so far.

Do you now understand the paragraph described as relating to my answer, my logic, my expression of understanding formed by my experiences? Do you think this is a strange way to begin a book? Are you wondering what lay ahead? Is your mind beginning to think? What are you thinking? Are your own ideas and thoughts beginning to kick in? Are questions coming to your mind? That is the exact purpose.

For too long, we humans have gone about our days on automatic pilot, without any thought. How can we expect to unravel our lives without thinking?

Do not take my or anyone else's words on blindly. You and you alone know what feels right. Use others words to trigger you into thinking about things long forgotten, or perhaps for the first time. Churn them over in your mind, mix them with your own thoughts, and come up with your own conclusions. But, to do so you must firstly open to thinking.

With each paragraph you read, think how it relates to you, what does it mean to you? Think about every word you read, in relationship to YOU. In the process, this book becomes yours.

You may come up with more questions than answers, that's fine. Questions prompt further thought. But, by doing this, you will change as a person because you taught yourself a new perspective, a new way to view the world.

Activity - Concept Formation

The following excerpt titled 'How people relate to us' is from a chapter on Perceptions. Read slowly and think about each idea raised. Use your thinking and rationalizing, then experience from doing the suggested exercises. In the same manner you thought, experienced then drew conclusions about smiling, discover your own ideas/concepts about the topic that is discussed. Remember to write and expand your knowledge.

How People Relate To Us

Our beliefs create perceptions, which then dictate how we perceive, judge, accept and act towards ourselves, and all those we come into contact with. It is as though we put on a set of perceptual glasses, with which to view the world.

Let's take a look at how people's behavior relates to

us. Many of us go through life believing people do things 'to' us, and that everyone is out to get us. We often gauge our self worth and emotions by our perception of how others react to us.

Everything is from outside, continually aimed at and controlling our lives. But, we miss an almighty piece of understanding when we hold this belief. Every single thing only comes from within! There is nothing outside of us! But that doesn't make sense, I know they love to push my buttons, he did this or she did that. It is the people around me making me feel bad or fail, they prevent my success or happiness we say.

Think on this carefully then. We are in the grocery store and we see a good friend, we know they see us but then they bow their head and walk in the opposite direction. What would we think? They don't want to talk to us, or don't like us. We worry because we may have done something to offend them. We search for answers of what we have done wrong, automatically assuming it is our responsibility, our fault that they do not wish to talk to us. This is a very confusing situation. We truly do take everyone's behavior as relative to US, when in fact every behavior is only related to them. Their behavior relates to them just as our behavior relates to us. How can that be?

Activity - Comparisons

Bring this back to you. Think of several situations where you have not wanted to be sociable, perhaps avoided people, even canceling social invitations. Times when your worry and preoccupation about something has resulted in your being moody, unpleasant, or snappy with loved ones. Now list each one in your journal; noting the basics of each event, what was on your mind, how you were feeling, what you were worrying about and the eventual outcome. Become fully aware of why you avoid social interactions sometimes.

Were any of these events related to anyone outside you? No. They all related to how you felt about you, and how you reacted because of these feelings.

Now we can come back to our friend in the grocery store and think on more appropriate suggestions for their behavior, realistic ones. They felt unwell or unsure of themselves, were not feeling up to speaking to anyone, perhaps they still haven't the money to repay us the debt. For some unknown reason, this person felt completely unable to make contact with another human being. What a sad realization that people feel this way.

Do you feel different about them and the situation now? Can you feel compassion rather than thinking what is wrong with you?

We each act according to our beliefs and perceptions of the world, so of course it makes sense that everyone else does that too. Why is it we feel the right to act how WE feel, yet at the same time do not allow others that same right. We assume their actions are related to their perceptions of us. We literally make everything about us! It does not make sense to do that, and frankly, seems selfish to do so.

Activity - Concept Observations

Spend a day doing this exercise. Whenever people act in ways you normally assume are in direct relation to you, stop and think. Ask yourself these questions again, put yourself in their situation. But most importantly, remember they may be in real discomfort and need a compassionate friend. Their behavior is absolutely nothing to do with us!

Write down all you observe yourself thinking and feeling in response to their behaviors, your perceptions. Think of some possible reasons for their behavior.

Now pick 5 different situations and rationalize each out from beginning to end, coming up with your own reasoning of the entire event.

Read this entire How People relate to us excerpt again with your new found knowledge and understanding. Allow yourself to become even more aware, and think about then decide how you wish to react to these situations in the future.

Mind Set

Some chapters are written in a way to ask you questions, others to trigger your own thinking, and others of my experiences. Each chapter is relative to you the person. Do you think we don't all feel sadness, fear, and uncertainty? We all have the same experiences and emotions, merely from different perspectives and situations.

Feeling is another big factor of this book. I write of my own personal feelings, thoughts and experiences. They are common to all of us, so of course you will be triggered into discovering your own.

What of experiencing? You will think about things, come up with ideas and concepts, go about experiencing them to see how they feel, then draw conclusions, just as you did with smiling.

Everything you do is experiencing; thinking, feeling, knowing, all of it. Life is one big experience. You will discover for yourself along the way that to experience is not such a scary thing as you had thought.

And the last is learning. Think about the aftermath of your smiling experience. What conclusions did you draw, how did you feel, what is your new belief of how one smile effects you and the people around you?

I will share a secret with you. We keep hearing that all we need to know is inside us, but they don't say how to find it.

Feeling is the key. When we listen to what we 'feel', rather than what we 'think', stories are revealed. Then when we think and ponder concepts, experiences and feelings, we come up with our own ideas.

Now we develop our own knowledge and understanding relative to us, each piece adding to the previous. Just as the smile experience created new knowledge within you, as you add your experience of 'How people relate to us', and each new one as you progress through this book, your own knowing will blossom.

The second step is to present all you read in a way that stimulates your continual growing and learning, not only while you read. Just as the smile section brought my words into your physical world by having you go out and try, all you read will trigger further thought when not reading.

Use this book to encourage you noticing what you think and feel, your triggers. Then bring it into your physical world. Everything you react to becomes your key to locating areas to work on. Know that whenever you become aware of triggers, you are then able to decide whether the timing is appropriate for investigation, or to pack them away until a more suitable time. Making them settle.

The third step in this plan is to trigger you questioning your old belief systems. This book will certainly challenge them. If you were happy with your current beliefs you wouldn't be searching. You may read, agree with my logic, yet say no that is not so and feel very uncomfortable.

We each live in our own little safety net of familiarity and comfort, anything that challenges our stepping outside that can cause discomfort. It is that discomfort which shows where to focus. Feel it, listen to it, and learn what it relates to.

Hints and Tricks

As you work through each chapter, read it in its entirety. Then go back and start at the beginning. It is your workbook so take at least a week with each. With every thought and feeling you have, stop and ponder why and what is happening within you. Why are you feeling this? Which of your beliefs are being challenged? Every thought and feeling you have while reading is for a specific purpose, not to be passed by without attention. You will find most chapters progressively build on concepts, making it necessary to evaluate and grasp each new issue as it arises, so you are ready for the next.

Familiarize yourself with the set of goals for every topic, have some idea of the desired outcome. Spend time thinking what it will be like to achieve these new skills. Use this to motivate you through your work. Have a focused intent for the desired outcome of each section.

Keep dreaming of and feeling the person you CAN become, free of your fears and worries, free to be who and what you desire. Just imagine, and feel: Those hurts you feel so strongly, diminishing. Your feelings of hopelessness and lack of control, changing into confidence and self assurance. Happy experiences replacing those you currently dread. Your failures turning into successes. Feeling okay about you.

Develop a new success mindset as you are asked to stop and do an activity, create your own viewpoints on ideas and concepts, and write a journal of all that you discover, then talk to someone about it. This will further encourage more thoughts and ideas to flow and grow.

Make this your own personal life changing workbook. Don't loose focus and sabotage yourself by relating anything in this book to other books you have read, or working with another book at the same time. Put all outside thoughts and works aside for just a few weeks to give yourself a chance to experience being a doer, not a searcher.

Besides jumping from book to book, another self sabotage method people use is skimming and searching for specific topics within books. The problem with doing this is two fold.

Firstly, skimming isn't doing anything so it promotes the feeling of 'I can't do it', and secondly, you miss all the important bits required to grasp the later chapters, so they end up not making sense anyway and your more likely to walk away saying 'this is not for me'.

Yes, you are eager to change specific issues, but consider the following. The topic you think creates the situation is not always the one you need to work on.

Take love for example. A person continually searches for love, thinking that if they can just find someone to love them, everything will be perfect. But what if the painful memory of their last relationship keeps stirring up a fear of being hurt again?

How can they expect to be able to participate in an open and loving relationship while feeling these fears? So instead of being the topic to focus on, love becomes the trigger that pushes them to search for the real issue (past hurts to be released) that needs to be resolved so they can have love.

As the pieces all come together during your progression through this book, you will come to a point whereby you can easily stop, listen to an issue and feeling that is bothering you, know how to allow yourself to feel and find the real issue (above scenario: a belief that everyone will be unfaithful), listen to the story, then release the emotion and belief and replace them with a new one which creates the opposite experience. (Don't worry this will make sense to you very soon)

You will be amazed at how relatively simple the process becomes, and the profound effect it has. Work through each chapter slowly, take your time to really become it so it clicks in your mind, enjoy each new thing you experience and learn, and smile as you feel a new strength of self emerging.

Time to Start Planning Your New Life

The following 4 activities form the beginning plan for the wonderful future you will be creating for yourself while working through this book. After each chapter and section, reread and alter your plan and life goals to keep them up to date.

The Gift

I want you to get paper and pen, because it is time to make a

Heal Your Self

special list. Fold a plain piece of paper in 3 lengthwise, then cut into business card sizes. You will need 20. And a lovely small container to put the cards in when completed.

While you're writing the list, think of how each item can be done in a simple way. e.g. Happiness could come from stopping, and listening to a bird sing, or feeling love when we pat an animal. Think of the simple things that don't require anyone else to facilitate them.

Take your time doing this activity, feel the enjoyment your thoughts create. Do it with a friend, whatever.

1. Name 5 things people can DO that makes them smile

e.g. Smell a flower, feel warm sunshine, listen to their favorite song, take a long hot bath, watch the sunrise, sit outside and listen to a bird singing.

What are the things, just the mere thought of brings a smile to your face? Perhaps they are things you haven't done for a while and have forgotten of. Enjoy thinking of them all. Then get 5 of your blank cards, write one thing on each card, and set the pile aside till later.

2. Name 5 things people can GIVE SOMEONE else that they like receiving.

e.g. A smile, a hug, praise, a phone call to say hello.

Think how you would feel if someone gave these things to you, your smile, happiness. Then what it might mean, feel like for the person you give it to. Remember previous reactions, how it felt to see their smile, feel their warm energy.

Feel as if you are giving something to someone else right now. Enjoy the experience! Pick 5 that feel the best, and write them on 5 new blank cards, and put that pile aside till later.

3. Name 5 things people can GIVE THEMSELVES that would make them smile.

e.g. Time to themselves, patience, a treat, praise, yummy food, kindness.

How often do you even contemplate doing something for yourself? Is your life always too busy, do you have too many responsibilities, and think that other's needs must come before yours?

Well, now is the time to think of you for a change. What is it that you could give yourself that makes you feel warm inside, right now. Think of all different things, listen and feel each. Find 5 things that bring that special smile of yours to your face.

Get 5 blank cards and write one on each, then put the pile aside for later.

4. Name 5 things people can FEEL that makes them smile.

e.g. Happiness, hope, warm and fuzzy inside. They can be anything you like.

The last, but hardest to do for some people, don't stress if you only find 1 or 2. The thought is planted so you will think of more very soon. Include Happiness as one of your 5.

What feels good to you? Remember that warmth inside when you hold a new baby or kitten, the happiness when you see the smiles on children's faces at Christmas, the satisfaction of a job well done. Feel inside you for those special feelings which create a smile from the inside out.

Write your 5 on the last 5 blank cards, and put the pile aside.

You now have 4 piles of cards, with 5 activities representing doing, giving another, giving yourself, and feeling.

Pick up one pile and write on the blank side, which of the 4 it is (e.g. doing), then a short sentence about why you chose it, what it means to you. For example.

1. Doing: smelling a flower - Flowers are beautiful and I like their smell.

2. Giving another: a hug - Because hugs show we care. Hugs make me feel warm inside.

Heal Your Self

3. Give themselves: time to themselves - Because quiet peaceful time is special, we all need some of our own personal alone space to think and feel and be us without interference.

4. Feeling: happiness - Because it makes me smile and feel good about living and myself.

This activity can seem tiresome, please make yourself keep going because it fills an important step in reaching the end goal. With each, think about how this activity makes you feel.

Now We Come To The Fun Part

Combine all your piles into one, and as you place each into the lovely container, think of as many ways as possible to create an activity to allow you to experience this feeling. For example:

1. Doing - smelling a flower. What are all the ways you could do that, simply and easily, without needing another person to be able to? Walk around the neighborhood, pick flowers out of your garden, go to a florist, a park.

2. Giving another person - a hug. How many different activities can involve giving another person a hug? Visiting friends and hugging, taking the time to have a lovely long hug with your partner, hugging your dog or cat, sharing an energy hug with a dear one.

3. Giving yourself - time to yourself. How many different ways can you achieve quiet peaceful time alone. Taking a drive, sitting outside under a shade tree, cuddling up under the blankets, taking a long hot bath and locking the bathroom door.

4. Feeling - happiness. What are the things you can do that make you feel happy, really happy from inside?

Everyone is different, but we each feel a special warmth inside when doing something we feel happy about. Joy is a special sensation many people have forgotten along the wayside, it comes from doing what feels right, natural, the real you without restrictions.

Think laterally, come up with as many ideas how to achieve each activity as possible. Imagine doing them all, feel your smiles and pleasure. One by one, imagine doing each activity, feel your smile, then place the cards in their special container.

Each morning pick one card out. It is your gift to experience that day. Enjoy!

Each one picked is your theme for that day, or week if you wish. Say you pick happiness, your goal for the day is to feel happiness, in as many ways and as many times as possible. So think of things and do them, just to experience what happiness is. It's actually fun to see how many things you can come up with.

As you go along and learn the new experiences you like, think of all the simple ways they can be created. Write a card and place each in the container. For example: Doing something silly and not getting angry at myself, noticing how good I am at doing things, not being scared to feel, making choices, doing what feels right to do, understanding why I do things.

Build your own special container of life joys! Watch it grow and enjoy!

Your Life

Time to write a letter to yourself, telling you what you deserve and why.

Find a nice comfortable, peaceful spot where you can sit quietly for a while without being disturbed. Now write the words you dare not think, tell yourself what you have wanted to hear but haven't, be the adult telling you why you deserve a wonderful life.

Heal Your Self

I wrote my own letter 10 years ago and put it away. Unexpectedly, it surfaced a few months ago, even after moving 9 times and traveling across the world.

It was like a vision quest for my future. Speaking of 'all the things I deserve in my life, not might's or could be's, or wants or needs, but things I deserve because I, like everyone else on this planet was a unique and special person.' This letter told me these things. Include them in yours too!

My letter spoke of a soul mate, and what this person will be to me, the little girl within and her finding peace and love, of my personal needs, home and finances, finding success in any business venture I seek to undertake, and it finished with love, saying it will be love that surrounds me in my future world.

All these things written long before I had any interest or understanding of my own journey, yet what I wrote is what has become in my world.

Write your first thought, do not worry about spelling or editing. It is a letter from your heart. You may become tearful or smile, or feel nothing but peace. Whatever you feel is perfect.

Enjoy telling you what you think and feel. Enjoy hearing 'your' words. This letter is to put away in an envelope, somewhere special. With your name and private written on the front.

I would like to share an experience of this exercise in a workshop. Using the same forward as you have just read, I sent the group of to write their letters for 20 minutes, then after just 5 they started coming back to me saying "I can't stop crying, I feel it so strongly", "I feel this letter and don't understand why".

They went back to writing and I waited, putting on a CD and singing softly. "How could anyone ever tell you, you are anything less than beautiful, How could anyone ever tell you, you are less than whole. How could anyone fail to notice, that your loving is a miracle, How deeply you're connected to my soul." Elaine Silver 'Fairy Goddess'

20 minutes later, they came back all teary, but saying how good it felt. I formed a circle, and sat arms outspread, we all

held hands and felt love. And I talked softly. "Yes, even with the tears, comes much joy. Do you know why? Sometimes we literally feel as that child within us. We can feel sadness and pain, but as that of a child. Then we complain at her, saying how bad that ego part of us is. She cries inside even more.

Tonight you told her you love her. How special and perfect she is. You cared. And she cried the tears of joy. Of finally being recognized."

What was happening was an amazing experience. We sat in a circle, after feeling and sharing with our inner children, the ache of the inner child had been felt and acknowledged, the love shared with her, and her joy experienced.

The only words to describe the feeling, was peace. The deepest and calmest sense of peace possible. So we sat and shared, and floated in our own thoughts and feelings. Sitting quietly together. It was delightful.

It was a small workshop, yet it was the most beautiful experience I could have imagined. I could feel these beautiful beings, and their inner release from doing this exercise. We came together to share a moment in time and space. And we shared openly, and freely with each other. What more could any of us desire? Enjoy your letter experience!

Creating

There's a secret to creating that we humans have not realized. You can begin the process right now.

Firstly, the myths of creating. We think we need to create to 'escape' our situations. We think life controls and creates us, and what we think is merely reflecting that. Well, think again.

All those so-called dreaded experiences are so we may know their opposite! They are part of the creation process. Think of all that you currently experience, each sad situation one by one. Now imagine what it will be like to know and be their exact opposite. Feel that! Focus on that!

Feel being unwell, so you may truly know and appreciate the joy of health. Feel your lack being turned around to plenty. Feel and know your loneliness, and the understanding you will have during its opposite. Feel your unhappiness, self-hate, and anger, and just imagine what it will be like to have their opposite!

Whenever you think and feel the dismay of what you currently experience, stop and think again. Know these experiences are especially so YOU can become their exact opposite. Imagine that opposite, what it will be like. It will change how you view your life, and being trapped within it.

What we think IS the creating process. We literally tell ourselves what to create. So, next time you hear yourself saying what you expect to happen next, ask yourself this. Is what I am thinking what I wish to experience? If it is not, then think about its opposite happening. Smile and imagine the exact opposite experience occurring, feel and enjoy that fantasy. Forget about it really occurring, this is imagination and play to learn the creating process.

For example: I am driving to work and the traffic is heavy, so I complain how I will be late. I hear what I think and after acknowledging, think of another scenario. I tell the other drivers to please move over so I can get through and arrive at work on time. I smile as I picture them changing lanes right before my eyes, and I casually drive past the congestion.

Sounds silly? Are you sure? How much time do we spend in traffic, thinking and feeling stressed and upset? We think we have to physically do something so we won't be late. It really is all in our minds.

That scenario is one I use often, and it is the best fun to ask others for their co-operation in moving out of my way, then see them do it instantly! I smile all the way to work. We can literally play with our thoughts, recognize and acknowledge them, saying thank you for your input but I think I prefer another outcome to that one. Then think and enjoy experiencing it in our minds. Start with small thoughts, make it fun.

Now, write down and feel 5 future opposites for you to experience in your life. What are some simple things that would be nice?

For example: My office is an unhappy place, people always complaining and demeaning each other. My opposite to experience is working in a happy and accepting work environment, where people encourage each other and are kind.

My every thought is about my problems, I worry and feel fearful constantly. My opposite is to feel calm at knowing my problems will resolve, that there is more to my life than feeling the worry from them. I enjoy breaks from my life worries, with relaxation and calm feelings.

Cut one blank sheet of paper into 3 lengthwise, fold one of the pieces like a concertina back and forth, each section about the size of a business card.

When you have clarified your 5 future opposite experiences, on one side and leaving the top one blank, write one on each joined card (in pencil so you can replace with new ones as they are created).

If you feel opposition from within, know they are your gifts so you know exactly what needs attention, to create your future. Smile and put them aside until you begin that work. This current exercise is to create hope in feeling what your life will become.

Completion

Do each of the following steps one by one, prior to reading the next to do:

On one side of your joined/folded cards, you already have 5 things that will be part of your future, the things that will be created within it.

Get the letter you wrote to yourself, and using point form so you may easily read it, write what you deserve on the blank side of the folded cards, leaving the top one empty.

Write "This is MY LIFE!" on the top card. On the opposite side write your own words to represent " I do not wish to remain within this experience, so I make it a temporary one by calling forth my future opposite, and imagining what that will be like."

Now, fold and hold your joined cards in your hand. Feel what it is. (On one side you have your own words of what you deserve, on the other 5 things to be created within it) You hold your life in your hands. You hold your very own power of creation. You have claimed your life as YOURS!

This is the first day of the rest of your life. I wonder what magic you will create within it.

Feeling

What is feeling exactly? We all believe that we are thinking and feeling human beings, but is that really the case? Take the time to try the following activities one by one and find out for yourself.

They *will* change your life and your ability to experience life.

When you complete this chapter you will be able to:

- Experience deep physical and emotional feeling
- Use feeling as a relaxation tool
- Enjoy feeling
- Eliminate your event rating list
- Be a calmer and more relaxed person
- Be ready to apply true feeling in the upcoming chapters

What Is It To Feel?

Do you like showering? Why? Have you ever thought or felt any more than rushing through it and making sure you don't smell? If the act of showering is seen as a chore or merely one of those daily activities you have to undertake, you have indeed missed feeling this experience for its own sake.

We go about our days experiencing all manner of stimuli, from water on our bodies, the sunshine or wind, our working environments, interactions with people, yet we rarely feel any of them. It's like many of us have shut down our natural ability and delight in feeling. We all experienced it as babies yet we lost it along the way somehow.

Do you remember that first hold of a newborn baby, or puppy or kitten? Or, if none of these bring smiles and happy thoughts what about being in love, during that true ecstasy stage. How you felt it throughout your entire being, pure love? The warmth, tingly sensations, and the smile that couldn't leave your face. Think on this memory, how pleasant it was, picture it as if happening this very minute, and feel it yet again as you did at that time.

What I am trying to get you to find is one of those very remote situations where your emotions became highly charged with love. So you can, for yourself, remember deep feeling.

Activity - Feel

First, go run some warm water over your hand. Close your eyes and relax. Feel it! The sensation on your skin, and how that ripples through your very being. Enjoy it! Now go to a pet store and hold a baby animal, open your heart and feel your love for this tiny creature. Feel the warmth in your chest, and the smile on your face. Let it grow. That my friends, is what it is to really feel. Everything else is mind or thought feeling.

Spend a week opening to feeling again. Make a list of different things you can do to feel these sensations each day (at least 3 per day). You can find many ideas in this chapter. Take your time to enjoy and notice the sensory experience of each. Write about your experiences and come to your own conclusions.

Emotions

What of feeling emotions. Sure we say and think we feel them, but do we really?

Or have we become so very experienced at only allowing ourselves to feel what we perceive as good, that we have dulled all of our feeling.

Activity - Rating List Experiment

Did you know that within your mind is a list, a very powerful one that rates all events on a scale from good to bad?

Try this exercise and you'll see what I mean. Think of 2 things you may do next week, one good and one bad. Perhaps sitting outside in the sunshine reading a book and going to the dentist. Can you feel them?

Stop for a moment and think on each. Watch and feel your mind and body reactions. The dentist vision may cause you to literally shake, while the other relaxes you. One simple thought has created such strong mind and physical reactions within you, purely because of this rating list.

Is not feeling about an experience? Is it not something we won't know until the actual event? What are the implications of already knowing a feeling prior to experiencing it in reality?

We humans actually forgot to keep the act of feeling within the moment that we experience it. No wonder we don't feel, no wonder we've forgotten how, we haven't needed to feel anything because our minds have already determined what it would be like in its entirety and the judgment of good or bad already made.

That judgment dictates our expectations, mood and motivation to experience events. Why experience anything if our minds have already thought of, experienced and evaluated it? How could we have any real concept of what feeling is?

Removing the Rating List

What if we choose to scrap this mind-rating list and discover what it is to feel for ourselves? What might we find? Is that possible?

Yes it is very possible and a truly wonderful and releasing experience. When we understand this concept and consciously work to eliminate it, a whole new world opens up to us. One of wonder and joy. Keeping this mind-rating list inhibits all we are and experience; it is draining and depressing.

Let's do this gradually, step by step so we build a sound foundation of feeling in what will seem a new way, but which is really how we began as children.

Activity - Remove the Rating List

All unpleasant experiences are stored in our subconscious to be use as warnings to protect us from experiencing them again. Now you want to thank this internal protection system for its care, but tell it that you no longer wish to live by it.

For 2 days, consciously keep reminding yourself, every time you hear the list information pop into your head (because you are now aware you'll notice it), to thank it for its warning then say that you are safe and no longer need it. Making it shut down.

Keep bringing your awareness back to what you are feeling, experiment with things. Perhaps do this on a weekend when you can plan some specific time. When I did this exercise it was during a quiet time, at first it was hard to quiet my mind sufficiently to remain in the 'now' without wandering of as usual, and thinking about other things. But, I kept returning my focus to the experience at hand and within 2 days shutting down the list became mostly automatic.

I sat outside on my little veranda, dog at my side. I thought of how dear this little dog is, always faithfully by my side, like he smiles at me constantly. I patted him and he was happy. I felt myself smile from within and became aware of the warmth of our shared love for each other. As I looked around from my 2nd floor apartment, being at the same height as the birds in the trees, I smiled, so close to them. I listened to all the different songs, the cardinal, the mocking bird, and all the others I am still to learn the names of. I closed my eyes and listened as the music filled my ears. This lovely time is, as always, very special to me, being with nature and her creatures.

Finding and using something very pleasurable and dear to my heart as an initiation to bringing my feeling focus to the now made it so much easier, and was such a delight to experience.

Of course I wanted more, and I use similar experiences to begin each day. I walk with the sunrise and my dear little dog. We talk to the birds and squirrels and rabbits. I feel the trees and the earth below me. I allow myself to become one with the world of nature. I literally feel their energies around me, and of course always acknowledge such beautiful singing and the ways they greet us.

Then I return home to a shower, where I relax and allow my whole body to feel the warm water flowing, the smell and feel of cleanliness, the rubbing of a towel. Smiling at myself in the mirror as I greet a wonderfully clean new me, all ready for my day.

It's actually very interesting to spend some conscious time revisiting feeling. Washing dishes which I had personally never felt anything from except dread at having to waste the time doing it, became a fun time to play in the water, smells and smiles watching what began as a disaster turn into a sparkling clean kitchen. It is nice to feel satisfaction in what we do. Everything can be experienced in that light.

Activity - Take the Time to Feel

Plan some more feeling activities for yourself. Spend at least one more week experiencing some more each day.

You might decide to take time to becoming consciously aware of your children, feeling and enjoying their chatter, love of life and energy around you. Perhaps playing some games and feeling as a child yourself.

Anything you decide to try is fine, from the smallest event upwards. It is all feeling.

The Aftermath

Now that you have taken the time to re-experience real feeling, your perceptions may have changed. You may find it easier to give yourself a lift when tired or stressed, because you know that to feel without expectation or judgment is very enjoyable.

And you may now find yourself questioning the validity of your rating list's correctness also, as that which was previously viewed as negative was not so when you experienced it first hand. The list and the experience do not match.

Why don't they match? Why am I now confused as to which activities feel good and which feel bad? Why do I now prefer the actual experience rather than what my mind was telling me about them?

Of course they don't match and are now confusing, because our mind's perceptions were only from judgmental beliefs held in our subconscious.

They had absolutely no basis on our reality.

To want to feel the actual experience rather than think about it as we did previously, is a natural progression. To feel and live in the now of experience is natural to us, it is pleasurable, it is what we like to do. And most importantly it feels right!

Each day, as you expand your repertoire of experiences and feelings you'll notice it is rather difficult to compare them as you use to. They're not connected, nor opposing each other.

Experiences and feelings are just that, things to experience for themselves, nothing to do with anything outside the event.

Neutrality

If we take this one step further we may come to realize that all events and feelings are neutral. That it was only our mind's rating list, which we no longer rely on, that judged. If experiences and feelings can only be fully felt while remaining in the 'now' of that event, how and why would we even contemplate comparing them to others, which results in good/bad definitions? There is no longer any judgmental forethought on upcoming events, so we are able to sit back and watch and feel the event unfold, for its own sake.

I must say at this point, for I am hearing your cries. What of those horrible situations and experiences? What of the pain and suffering, they cannot be felt as neutral? Please tell your mind to put those events and thoughts away for now, for they are of past memories. They are discussed in detail within another section, then you will have the information to make clear evaluations on them. This chapter on feeling is necessary for you to begin your exploration of experience. Everything is one step built upon the last. You can't grasp or undertake the work in this book until you begin to allow yourself to feel again. So stay with pleasant feelings, enjoy them, and be comforted in being able to initiate them whenever you so desire.

During my personal work on neutralizing feelings and experiences, I had some very interesting times. I still smile at my first comparisons and the expressions and laughs when I discussed this with my peers.

I had spent my 2 days working consciously to feel the 'now'. This automatically led me to question how I compared and judged events and feelings as good/bad, so I put it to the test. As often is the case, my wondrous walks become my classroom. I decided to consciously listen to how I felt about each event that occurred. So I set off dog and plastic bags in hand. What I noticed was how I didn't seem to feel as emotionally charged from each occurrence as I had previously. I still enjoyed listening to the lovely songs and talking to the squirrels and rabbits, but it was less intense.

As I continued my walk the inevitable happened, my dog did his poop. This is usually my cue to sigh in dread, screw my nose up, as if that stopped me from smelling I doubt, and undertake this highly distasteful experience I had never encountered before moving to America. Cleaning up after a dog. (In Australia our dogs spend most of their time outside in fenced backyards, wandering in and out as they please. So walks are not an important time for bodily functions.)

Noticing the beginning of my automatic response to 'my list', I stopped myself and thought. This is merely another experience so let's see what it's like. I was very surprised that, when I had removed all expectations and judgment of this event, the intensity of it diminished. It felt very different and was just one of those natural things. The smell even appeared less and not offensive at all. Perhaps because I wasn't using the association of smell. I felt none of the angst or dread of having to do this, it was quick and easy, and actually, a kindness to my neighbors so I was pleased to leave their lawn clean.

By the time we reached home again, I had fully come to the conclusion that events and feelings are neutral in themselves. It is only our perceptions and beliefs that cause us to think the opposite. So I went about my days testing this theory, listening intently to my self-talk and keeping consciously focused in the 'now'.

It was hot in my car, so I opened a window. The traffic was heavy, so it took me a few minutes longer to reach my destination. More time to watch and experience the sites. I couldn't find specific groceries, then had a wonderful discussion with a kind lady who helped me. The market line was long, allowing conversation and interactions between people and a break. My son was grumpy so we shared some special time together, and I smiled for this opportunity to be there for him. A large bill came in the mail, what an opportunity to spread the wonderful energy money portrays.

These may seem mundane and insignificant events to

ponder, yet is it not these little events that comprise our lives? Do they not build upon each other filling our days?

Each day I found myself becoming more and more calm. The never ending jumping between happiness and sadness, which normally accompanied experiences, mellowed. There was no longer elation at talking to a bird or squirrel and the dread of receiving a bill. They were each individual experiences to feel for themselves. The feelings were neutral and pleasant.

Perhaps part of the issue has been that we think happy events occur so rarely, that we become more excited and charged when they do. Once we remove the judgment and expectations, and benefit from the calmness and pleasure of the myriad of experiences and feelings that fill our lives, we no longer crave the perceived good ones and value them too highly. Perhaps not only did our rating list exaggerate the negative experiences, but also the positive?

Anyway, now I feel much more at peace. When I am feeling ungrounded or stressed, its easy to bring myself back to the now and feel again.

I would like to share a sweet little story related to this topic, about a cardinal who came for a visit. But before I do, based on the personal work I have undertaken I do truly believe in being able to fully neutralize all of our days so we can live with peace and happiness. Yet I appreciate that reaching this reality is a gradual process which *will* come as you work through this book.

I have learned that along with events, individual feelings were added to our list of things to be avoided at all cost. Ask yourself this. How often, when you feel sad, or depressed or even angry, do you allow yourself to sit and become part of that experience, to feel it? Or do you focus on pushing it aside and continuing on with your day, perhaps telling yourself that you don't wish to feel them?

Why do humans think it is so bad to cry and so good to laugh? Both are amazing experiences to have. We say we don't like feeling sadness or other emotions, then why do we wallow in them? Why do we keep dredging them all up?

If you work to let go of the need to avoid and judge the various emotions as good versus bad, as you did with your mind list, then allow the emotion of whatever experience to surface, I think you will be pleasantly surprised.

To cry, scream, morn, or even to feel the power of fear sends an adrenaline rush through our entire body. You can actually feel it surging through you. It is our mind that has the fear of feeling, but there is nothing to fear. Try it and see for yourself.

Conclusion

Back to the story. One day I was sitting on my little veranda sharing the view with my little dog. I was not feeling good about myself at all that day, for I had failed to complete a task wanting and needing doing. I know this was due to a fear, but that didn't give me much comfort at that time.

Then I heard the most beautiful bird song coming from the sweetest little bird sitting on a nearby tree. I smiled and enjoyed coming back to the 'now'.

This dear little bird did not leave it with merely serenading me. As I sat, she flew very close and stopped for a quick chirp on the roof nearby, then skipped and flew over to the other side of me, then back to the other side, singing all the while. She flew around the side of the house and poked her head around to look at me, she then did this from behind a tree branch. This dear little bird sang and danced all about me, she was a pure delight. I felt our interaction, I felt her come to spend time with me, and I felt her happiness and joy of being alive. This dear little bird moved me greatly.

But I didn't know what breed she was, I knew what I felt from her but wanted to see what my 'animal speak' book said about this animal spirit.

I telephoned a nearby bird store and had a most delightful conversation with the lady there. She, like me was delighted and moved by this little bird's actions. After describing her I was

Feeling

told she was a female cardinal, who must be only having a very short break from her nesting duties. So our meeting was a chance one.

When I looked up messages of cardinal I beamed, for it is exactly what this little bird had shown me. It matters not what we do, for everything we do is important. Everything we, as human beings do as we go about our days has an impact on the world we live in.

Just as experiences and feelings are neutral, so is the act of actually selecting and undertaking them. Everything we do is learning, so how can it be more or less important to experience and feel the sunshine, a brush on our skin, drive to the mailbox, get a new job, or see a face light up when we smile at them.

They are each of value for themselves, yet we forget to value them. It is not more or less important that we experience poverty or wealth, that we lead quiet or hectic lives, that we are a success or failure. What is important is the experience, for it is that and only that which we continually grow from.

No I am not saying that to sit back and accept poverty as a way of life. What I am saying is that poverty in itself is a very important learning experience for some people (discussed in my Money book). Think of all the possibilities. What are the issues poverty is forcing us to face about ourselves, our environment, and our place in the world? It is an event to prompt growth. That is all.

Through experience we learn and grow. It is up to us to decide what experiences we do and do not want in our lives. If poverty is an issue we may choose to look into this topic, explore the reasons behind it, complete our learning and releasing, therefore ceasing the need to experiencing it and changing ourselves and our lives.

You could say work is more important than play. I ask why? Are they both not very different learning triggers? I am not saying we should do one in place of another. We have choices in everything. We are in control of what we want in our lives, as I hope you will come to believe.

Activity - Practice

Because the ability to feel is essential for all of the upcoming healing activities, take your time with this chapter.

Reread, plan activities, write of your experiences and findings, talk, discover and solidify your own concept of and ability to feel before you begin the next chapter.

Plan how you can include conscious feeling as an important aspect of every day.

Activity - Write

Start a feeling journal. Begin by telling yourself the story of feeling; what it is to you, what it is like to experience it, what it is like to float around in feelings.

Every time you have a new feeling experience, no matter what type of feeling it is, write about it in your journal.

Watch your experiences grow!

Energy

Energy affects how we feel and act every single day, often without our realizing. This chapter shows how to recognize, enjoy and benefit from this wonderful source of well being.

When you complete this chapter you will be able to:

- Experience 3 different forms of energy - Physical, Spiritual, Emotional
- Feel and know how to use energy
- Enjoy playing with energy
- Use energy to benefit your life
- Help other people feel better using all 3 energy types

Activity - Feel Physical Energy

Hold the palms of your hands about 2" apart, close your eyes and feel. You might feel a tingling or heat or cool. Move your hands closer then further apart, feel the difference.

Now, hold your hand over your arm or leg, can you feel warmth? What you feel is your body's natural energy field. This type of energy is very special, it is nice to use it for dis-comfort or when near another in distress.

Heal Your Self

When my son was little and had headaches I would tell him to feel the energy in his hands, then place one over the sore spot, it always removed his headache. He removed his headache with his own energy.

Building the skill and strengthening the feel of this energy is easily achieved with practice, no special learning or classes are required. Practice holding your hands apart, work to feel the energy stronger and stronger, to recognize feeling it, then as you progress you can move your hands further apart and begin to manipulate it. Make it into a ball, or change its shape, enlarge and surround your body with it, hold your hand over painful areas of your own or your friend's bodies. They will feel the heat and love you give them.

As you gradually become skilled with this energy, by playing and doing what feels right, you will find you can slowly move your hands along a body and feel differences, heat or cool, you will feel the need to hold your hand over certain areas, allowing your energy to be shared.

Enjoy this energy, enjoy discovering for yourself what it is, feels like, its power and uses.

Activity - Feel Spiritual Energy

Another form of energy is what I call life force or spiritual energy. We can feel our own and others, as well as natures.

Think of something or someone you love deeply, close your eyes and feel the sensations in your body. It is very hard to describe I know, but can you feel warmth or some sensation throughout your body or in your chest area? Many people have this experience without understanding who or what is felt. It takes time and practice, but very well worth the effort.

There are several ways to grasp the feeling of this form of energy and building recognition of it.

When you pat your animal, close your eyes and feel, when you walk with nature do the same. The more you allow yourself to become one with the now moment, the easier and more often you will feel this.

While showering, close your eyes and feel beyond the physical water, feel with your entire being, when you smile at a beautiful sunset, feel that smiles energy within you, when you pass a beautiful tree, touch and say hello to it, feel the trees energy, when you see your child sleeping, feel your love in your body. Enjoy feeling energy sensations within you.

We can use thought to share this energy with those we love. Sometimes when my son is unhappy or unwell, I close my eyes and quiet my thoughts, then picture him smiling and happy.

This is my focus attention. I usually see him very differently with added weight and an older face. My love energy I feel for him becomes magnified as I keep seeing him happy and well. I feel the energy strongly in my body and it go to him.

When loved ones are distressed the kindest thing we can do for them is feel love and send that, it is much more effective and better than pity. We do indeed see differences in them after this exercise.

Activity - Combine Physical and Spiritual Energy

Now you can begin to combine these two forms of energy. Place your hand on your animal, let the heat be felt from your hands, and think of the animal with love, feel the two energies combine and grow stronger. Watch the animal turn its head and smile at you, feel the animals love energy in return, for they certainly do feel yours.

What other ways can you find to use these energies?

Activity - Feel Emotional Energy

Whatever we feel becomes an energy force. Just like as you feel love for an animal that love energy radiates outwards from you. Remember that stage of romantic love, how you felt the energy bursting from your body, how it showed in your face and all that is you, how others noticed and commented as soon as they saw you? This is what I speak of.

If all our feelings become energy forces and are radiated outwards from our bodies, then our sadness, and anger and all the other emotions are sent out also.

Would you rather send pity or love energy to a sick friend? Become aware of your energy feelings as you go about your days, notice how other people react to them. Notice how your family reacts the minute you walk in the door, well before you have said anything to show your mood. Or when you visit another's house or a grumpy child's bedroom, you can feel the mood in the air, whether it be happy or depressed.

Activity - Play With Energy

Spend time exploring each energy type in more depth. Write of your experiences, feelings, responses. Develop your own thoughts, concepts and favorite uses of energy. Share what you learn with family or friends.

Activity - Write About Energy

So, what do you think about energy? Is it cool, is it strange, is it fun, is it like you have read about? Write your story of energy and create your very own concept from your very own experiences.

Help I'm Overwhelmed

We all have times when our emotions become so overwhelming that they take over. We can't think or focus or even act with a clear mind.

This chapter will show you how to easily release your overwhelming emotions, whether from current or past emotional shocks and when life just becomes too much to cope with.

Releasing overwhelming emotions involves the use of a simplified version of Greene's Release.

When you complete this chapter you will be able to:

- Release overwhelming emotions at will
- Let yourself experience uncomfortable feelings without being scared
- Remove yourself from the emotional impact of situations
- Help yourself feel better

We naturally have emotional reactions to all experiences. The more intensely we feel the experience, the more intense the reaction. Then, if we continually think about the event, our emotions continually build, reaching unbearable proportions that overwhelm us.

Overwhelmed by Life

It has been a natural reaction to bury our emotions because until now we didn't realize that we could resolve and release them and their cause.

The problem comes when our emotional storage bin fills then starts overflowing and interacting with everyday events, making each additional small stressor an overwhelming issue that we find ourselves unable to cope with.

How we deal with problems also causes our emotions to become overwhelming. The belief that the only way to resolve issues by rationalizing them in our mind until we find the answer means that we continually focus on the problem and build its emotional intensity until we become overwhelmed.

The answers to your issues cannot be found in logic as you will soon discover. All you need do is feel and let the answer come to you, so stop trying to find answers that are just not there.

Emotional Shocks

Emotional shocks come from any event that scares or shocks us. It is not the intensity of the event but rather how much it means to us, therefore emotional shocks can occur when making a dental appointment *or* watching our home crumble after a tornado.

Examples of singular emotional shocks include: Getting a large bill in the mail when you are broke, failing a test, going to the dentist, accidents, having an operation, physical or sexual abuse, or even seeing a huge spider (if you are terrified of spiders).

Examples of multiple emotional shocks resulting from a life event include: The death of a loved one - hearing the news, organizing the funeral, notifying relatives, changing bank account and utility names, etc.

Hurricane or natural disasters - the event, dealing without power, cleaning up the mess, seeing destroyed homes each time you go out, etc.

When not addressed at the time of the incident, every emotional shock is stored in the subconscious, ready to surface and compound with the next one that occurs during a repeated or similar situation.

For example: Seeing a large spider the size of your hand on the wall above your bed can be a real emotional shock. But does it make sense to have the same intense emotional reaction which leaves you screaming at the top of your lungs when a teeny tiny spider is seen a decade later?

Unresolved emotional shocks can cause post traumatic stress or panic attacks, result in emotional outbursts at the most inconvenient times, trigger repeats whenever we undertake a similar activity, and make our lives very miserable.

You can however use the following technique to go back and remove your past emotional shocks by thinking of the incident, or acknowledging when it resurfaces, allowing the emotions to surface and then doing the release steps.

Emotional shocks are related to specific events that we feel emotionally, therefore are not about our life worries or resolving situations.

Activity - Your First Release

Something in your life is causing you great discomfort. It is your focus every waking moment, and probably haunts your dreams as well. You may know what it relates to or merely have a feeling of doom, depression and deep fear or sadness.

You may be coping with general life, experiencing repeated illnesses, or have become so fearful that your daily functioning is being affected. It does not matter if you are aware of what is happening or not, you FEEL it.

So let us do a quick exercise to release this overwhelming

emotion you are feeling. Read this entire section first so you have a general idea what it involves, then come back and proceed step by step.

1. Find a comfortable chair or lie in bed and have tissues and a glass of water nearby.

2. Try this. Every time you breathe out, do it as if you are softly blowing out a candle. Very gently so you are not using excess energy. Can you do it?
   Put your finger in front of your mouth and feel the breath. Feel the air you are blowing out. It is important that you are able to do this before proceeding.

3. Now I want you to let yourself feel your overwhelming emotions. It is now safe to do so because they can no longer hurt you.
   Try not to think about the problem or event, but instead feel the emotions of it. If you start physically feeling it, ask what this relates to, ask to feel the emotion. Tell yourself that you want to feel this emotion and then decide to walk into it.

4. You are feeling an emotion come to the surface, don't stop or block it but instead allow it to keep building and become stronger. The point you want to reach is a peak of emotion. You want to feel this overwhelming emotion strongly.

5. When you do, feel it then breathe in. Imagine that breath wrapping itself around the emotion and picking it up.
   As you breathe out again imagine the emotion is carried up and out with your breath.
   Blow it out! Tell it, see it, feel it physically leaving your body each time you blow out.
   Again. Feel, breathe in, imagine your breath grabbing the emotion, then blow it out. Tell yourself these words as you do it. Tell yourself what to do.

Keep going until you feel different which will only take a few minutes.

6. You have calmed, so relax your breathing. You may feel ready for a long sleep now that this weight has been lifted, or lighter and freer than you have in a long time.

Take some nice in and out breaths, feel the air circulating as your body relaxes and becomes very comfortable.

Don't think about what happened, stay in this one moment. For now you are quiet and calm and your body feels much better.

Close your eyes and feel my hands as I place them on your shoulders. I come to share calming energy with you. Feel its warmth flowing through your body. Relax and breathe. You are surrounded by the softest baby pink air, which fills your lungs with every breath you take. This is calm love air to replace the fear air that you just removed. Feel its warm and gentle energy. Enjoy!

Difficulty Feeling the Emotion

If you are having difficulty feeling your emotions, don't stress.

The norm is to repress and burry emotions so the painful ones are avoided at all cost. Unfortunately the better people get at this, the harder it is to actually feel emotions - the happy and sad ones.

Or that you do know the hurt well, and are afraid to let it come up again? You have gone over it many, many times and it hurts, so you've built strong walls to stop yourself from feeling it, and other hurtful emotions.

Spend time with each exercise in the Feeling and Energy Chapters, watch chick flicks and let your emotions go, get outside and open to connect with the birds and wildlife. Want to feel everything; the good, the bad and the ugly and in the process discover a whole new world of experience. Then come back to this chapter and it will be easy.

Perhaps you are jumping from one issue to another and bringing up too many? Stop yourself quickly, and come back to one topic and feeling. Keep yourself focused on what you feel, not what you think about it and where that leads. You may need to practice with this skill.

Relax, and most of all, listen to you and whatever feelings you're having.

Explanation

You have experienced opening the door to your emotional storehouse. This exercise has triggered you to finally let go of some overwhelming emotions that you have been holding onto. You finally became ready to begin releasing some of the anxiety and stress from within you.

Releasing overwhelming emotions is not related to specific topics like the Greene's Release technique, but instead learning what it is to let go. It is an important step that will make full releases much easier, so take the time to build your skill.

Activity - Write About Your Experience

So, what do you think about your first release? What did it feel like, how do you feel now, what difference has it made?

Write your story of this experience and create your very own concept based on your specific experience.

Fear

Fear is one of our biggest and most unpleasant triggers. But, it is an emotion we can use to speed up our healing work by consciously deciding to say "No, I refuse to ever feel this again" each time we feel a fear, which motivates and helps us to go inward much easier to locate and heal its cause.

When you complete this chapter you will be able to:

- Stop judging and condemning yourself for feeling fearful
- Investigate and appreciate the reasons for your fears
- Decide that you can be fear-less one day
- Use your fears as important triggers to initiate healing
- Take charge of your anxiety levels

This chapter is an introduction to the concept that there could be more to, and something you can do about your fears. Knowledge is power and just understanding that there are reasons for what you feel will help you feel much better about yourself.

Many of your fears will be triggered and released as you work through this book, so you will be able to permanently remove many of them one by one. Once you have completed all of the work from this book, and become competent at the

Greene's Release technique, you will be quite able to come back and comfortably spend some time working to alleviate any remaining fears by deciding to notice them, stopping and taking action learned from the releasing chapter whenever one surfaces.

What Is Fear?

Why is everyone so scared of fear? The talk is always about 'getting past our fears', 'being the master of our fears', 'replacing them with love', doing everything we possibly can to eliminate fear from our lives. Why?

Fear is our body and mind's way of forcing us to know something is not right, something needing our attention. Fear is a wonderful trigger for our growth and future happiness.

It is a natural and very important survival instinct, the fight and flight response that reacts with surges of adrenaline during times of crisis. Without this man would not survive. We need this on hand rush of energy to give us required courage and stamina; it is a magnificent byproduct of the human condition.

What went wrong with our fear mechanism, for it seems many have heightened fear responses that kick in during times it is definitely not required? Why do some shake in terror at the mere thought of going to the dentist, or confronting another, or even being out in public? Are people becoming more fearful over the decades, or is it merely that we are more aware of what doesn't feel good generally? Or perhaps our lives are demanding more of us, forcing us to face new experiences and the unknown more frequently?

Uncontrolled fear stops us doing something by sending a clear message that it is either dangerous, we cant do it, it will be an awful experience, or the unknown, we don't belong, wont be provided for, or it will be a repeat of past experiences.

Every thought, every belief, every emotion and every action has a profound and definite impact on our physical bodies. Fears are no exception to that so cannot be discounted. How many times have we not felt fearful, or been able to force our fears into the back of our minds, yet we break out in a rash, or develop a cold or some other illness. This is discussed in detail in the later chapter Health and Well-Being.

Heightened Fear Responses

Let's take a back step and go over the fear response itself. Anxiety and fear are closely related so I include them together. A wise psychologist explained this to me once as a means of comprehending anxiety and panic attacks to create the situation of self-empowerment and control. For it is this lack of feeling in control that feeds and allows the anxiety/fear to build.

Activity - Draw The Fear Response Mechanism

By drawing a simple diagram it becomes easy to see the fear response mechanism. We each have a base anxiety/fear level so we will put a small horizontal line just above the bottom of a page. This marking is our natural resting-place for anxiety/fear levels. When we encounter a fear the level rises, depending on how strong the fear, so we will put another small horizontal line 1/3 up the page.

Now it gets interesting, because it is our reaction at this point which determines what happens to our base anxiety/fear level. If the fear is so strong as to make us undertake actions to avoid the trigger, like removing ourselves from the stimuli, escaping, our fear levels do decrease but at a slow rate, but our anxiety/fear level does not go back down to its natural resting place. So we will draw another small horizontal - between the other 2.

That is the cycle. This new level - becomes our carried forward base anxiety/fear level and everything begins from this point. If we continued this demonstration we could see how each time we encounter a strong fear and subsequently escape its stimuli by using the flight response, our generally held onto level of fear and anxiety gradually gets higher and higher. Therefore our base level and the fear we experience each time during situations becomes heightened at a much faster rate.

Natural Fear Responses

The natural process of fear responses is quite different. Again we begin with a base level of anxiety/fear, and encounter an event that creates the fear response. Yet if we do not go into the flight response, instead staying with the situation and riding it through, it will naturally peak at a very safe level, then automatically return right down to the original base level.

I must speak on this peak, for feeling the fear of stimuli is not the only consideration, we also feel the fear of the fear reaction. Our response to the fear is in itself very frightening and exaggerates the whole event. Human fear responses have a built in maximum peak level and will plateau when reached, although when we are in the midst of experiencing great fear we feel it will keep rising so want to escape. Knowing it will not go past a safe peak enables us the strength to stay and ride it through, knowing it will plateau and reduce as a natural psychological occurrence. No matter how strong the fear stimuli, the level of fear is not physically able to keep rising without end, it will peak, plateau then reduce.

Activity - Normalizing Fear Responses

We can reverse the built up anxiety/fear levels we have produced in ourselves by deliberately following the natural fear response. It is not an instant fix and will take some conscious effort and determination to gradually bring the base level of anxiety/fear back down to its proper natural resting-place. I personally found, following this process eliminated my anxiety and panic attacks within 3 weeks.

Where Do Our Fears Come From?

As I have said, feeling the fear response is a lifesaving natural response for survival. Yet many of our fears have no basis on, nor necessitate such drastic responses. What is it we are afraid of, and why? When we speak of fears, they can be anything from animals, closed spaces, social situations, or self-beliefs. They can be conscious (aware) and sub conscious (not aware), yet we will react to them just as often and strongly.

The range of fears and triggers initiating original fear beliefs are as diverse as the people experiencing them, therefore the following examples are merely that, examples hoped to prompt and encourage you thinking about your own fears and the reasons behind them. It is by no means exclusive, nor does it imply that fears may only fall under one category. 3 categories will be discussed; memories, self and ego.

Memories

The memory category covers all fears that are related to specific objects or events, we are scared of repeating past negative experiences, or we have taken on a fear belief because of a frightening concurrent experience.

Frights may come from unexpected shocks, loud noises, being lost, hearing an unknown noise, not understanding an event, being hurt, other's fears, being trapped in a situation where the child had no control (locked in a cupboard, teased, abused). There are many variations of what triggered the initial fear to such a magnitude that it was decided this object/event is to be avoided and feared. Sometimes we have taken on a fear belief because of a frightening concurrent experience. This type of fear is just as real and profound, even though the fear object may never have actually done anything to scare us.

For example; one could be scared of dogs because the scream 'don't go near the dog, it will bite you!!' was so unexpected and frightening it created a referred fear belief.

Basic fears found in this category include:

Thunderstorms, lightening, dogs, water, boats, sleep, darkness, being alone, illness, doctors, dentists, abandonment, dark, closed in places - claustrophobia, not being in control, life, panic attacks, anxiety.

We all encounter experiences ranging in intensity that we wish never happened in our lives. Dependent on the personality, perceptions and situation, individuals are sometimes so impressed by the incident a definite decision is made. This event is not to be repeated, it is to be avoided at all cost, and this event ranks a 10 out of 10 in fear ratings. Remember that associating fear to a situation is a guaranteed way for it to be automatically avoided. A new belief has been taken on so this decision is filed away in the subconscious.

The situations may involve others actions towards us such as in the case of loss of a loved one (the parent left, does not matter they died and had no choice in the matter) or teasing. Or actions of ours that created strong repercussions like not caring for an animal and it dying, or failing to be of help to someone who relied on us. Or a situation may have merely led to events we found too uncomfortable to accept. Whatever the reason, various specific events have triggered this fear belief inception.

Basic fears found in this category include:

Guilt, life, success, failures, loss of loved ones or possessions, not completing, social phobias.

Self

The self-category covers a range of issues all relating to the person we are, how we fit into this world and are accepted by society. It is far too broad to cover in real detail, but is raised to introduce the idea.

If we don't believe we are special we can become very insecure. Creating situation after situation to feed our negative belief of self. Fears of this nature are often very noticeable.

Basic fears found in this category include:

Scared of who we actually are, of being alone, invisible, unknown, unloved, unrecognized, misunderstood, ill, loss of control, facing situations or people (often the results from negative situations our fear responses have created).

People with low self-esteem create many fears, both of not being good enough and to prevent them having to test their belief of not being good enough.

For example; one may want to establish their own business which they are more than capable and skilled to do. Their lack of self-esteem may cause them to avoid the daily management activities because they cannot bring themselves to physically do them. Preventing business success, and failure being a reflection of self. Fear of all activities relating to proving themselves are strong in this category, as it is in opposition to their belief.

This section would include:

All activities required in organizing daily living, self rights, activities, business, personal skills/achievements, social activities (social phobias), success, failure, not completing.

Another self-issue is where we each fit into or belong in this living experience. If we have low self worth added fears might make it more difficult to become part of living, survival and understanding self. If one does not feel connected to family, community, the world, life, almost everything can become a fear.

Examples of this section include:

That we are not real, that this living is merely a dream, that we have no part in life, death, living, god and his place in our world, loss, personal safety, being cared and provided for.

Ego

My belief is that we are a spirit undertaking a physical experience and feelings can broadly be divided into 2 categories. Fears from our mind and ego, and love from spirit. Anything that is not based on loved is believed to be fear related.

Ego is covered in great detail within the What am I? chapter, but mentioned here because ego not only creates and holds onto our fears, but also perpetuates them. Ego self is often as a child, a scared child, fearful of being rejected and abandoned as we no longer need ego's fears.

It is this mind-based fear belonging to ego that creates a battle between it and our inner knowing (spirit), for control of our person. We often find that as we progress with our healing work, we seem to experience more fears. Some due to issues being 'stirred up' in readiness for learning, but others as a ploy for ego to keep us fear bound where it is difficult to accomplish any growth.

We can find ourselves experiencing fear for its own sake, of nothing in particular, but of everything. Like the door has been opened and all our fears are rushing out to show themselves. A cycle of fear for fears sake. When we appreciate this fully, we are then able to stay consciously aware and take appropriate measures to combat. Dispelling ego's unnecessary fear of us abandoning it for we never will.

Conscious Versus Subconscious Fears

Before continuing on, it is important to also consider the relevance of conscious versus subconscious fears. Rarely is the conscious reason you think is causing the fear, the actual base (subconscious) belief/reason for it. You may have read this chapter so far and said to yourself, no they do not apply to me, or that's silly, but the fact is fears are related to negative beliefs we have each taken on in our subconscious. Discussing the various types of fears is only to inform you, not as a basis guide for which fears to work on.

You will find that as you heal your base self-confidence beliefs, through work on your subconscious, the associated fears will reduce naturally. We may know something very well (conscious), but unless we believe it from deep within (subconscious), it means nothing to us. Therefore we may wish and want and attempt as hard as we can to eliminate our fears with words and affirmations and mind power (conscious), but unless we reach the place where those fears are stored (subconscious) success is limited and incredibly slow.

How Fears Manifest

Now let's take a look at how fears show themselves to us. This can be very obvious as in the case of fear of dogs, where the person might shake, become flushed and feel quite ill, physically and emotionally feeling as that young child who took on the original fear. Or they may be totally hidden from our conscious perceptions where we may undertake behaviors seemingly foreign and strange even to ourselves. Behaviors that build our low self-concepts because we feel as a failure or watch in horror the things we do.

Say a person has a base subconscious fear of confrontations. Such a fear is likely to be both subtly obvious and totally hidden as they go about their days. An enormous amount of our living activities can be classified as confrontations; everything involving us approaching another human being, whether for pleasure, business or what we usually comprehend confrontations to be.

For the person with this fear, life is incredibly scary. To return an item to the store, to undertake any actions involving self rights, to speak out within a group, to even telephone the gas company for an extension of payment date, reporting a problem to a landlord, every situation where this person is required to face another person.

So perhaps avoidance may become the escape; putting off ringing for a gas extension, not reporting a leaking pipe to the landlord, missing appointments. Each time something is avoided the situation becomes worse and rectifying the situation through confrontation more difficult. You can now begin to see the cycle of fear and reaction situations, how they can build on each other. Amenities being disconnected, damaged apartments, unnecessary illness, and the list is extensive.

The person with this confrontation fear may outwardly appear quite confident and happy, yet they become increasingly depressed within, continually building self concepts of dislike and reproach as they feel self as such a failure. They also face much hardship and lead unhappy lives, created by their avoidance of confrontations. Perhaps they have no concept of being scared of confrontations, no idea why they react and behave so strangely. Each time a confrontation looms they revert emotionally and physically back to the age of the fear belief inception. So if it was a 5 year old who took on this belief, their responses to the fear are based on a 5 year olds perceptions and reactions. A very sad situation for any grown man or woman.

What of a person with a social phobia fear, their lives are equally miserable. Having to force themselves to participate in social situations, actually feel as if they will survive the situation, watching their own inadequacies, blaming self, being subjected to others reactions of their anti social behavior.

Conclusion

Fears can indeed make our lives miserable. When I look at fears I simply divide behaviors into 2 groups for simplicity, then it is easy to become aware. What we are comfortable with and what are we not comfortable with, for everything in our lives. Everything we are not comfortable with I use as a signal, a trigger of another issue. Something is not right.

I have spoken much on the reasons behind fears, their affects and the sadness fears bring into our lives. This was merely to lay groundwork for your thinking and deeper understanding of this very important part of who you are. As I said in the beginning of this chapter, fear is our body and mind's way of forcing us to know something is not right, something needing our attention. Fear is a wonderful trigger for our growth and future happiness. How you might say?

We are each undertaking a magical experience, of growth and learning. So what better prompt could there be than fear to highlight issues for our work. Fear is one of those very special parts of the human condition, one that's sole purpose is for our greater good. Embrace your fears and welcome them. For they are your very special way, your determination and want to grow.

Activity - Write About Your Fears

What fears do you have? Do you know what causes them or are they just feelings you have? How often do you feel fearful? What are your goals for this topic? Write your story of fear, the current implications, and your future desires.

Life Lessons

This chapter is another step in opening your mind to contemplate how life events may be created by many things. Another piece to add to your thoughts about life, and what it is. To see that the human experience may indeed be a journey, of self discovery. That perhaps each step along the way may be a process of discovering another piece of ourselves.

When you complete this chapter you will be able to:

- Reach a deeper level of understanding about the concept of beliefs, how they apply to your experiences and life plays

Think about it. Why do we have repeat cycles in our life? Why do good or bad things happen to us? Why are some people plagued by one bad thing happening after another in their life?

Why do some people flow through life effortlessly while others constantly struggle? Why do so many of us behave in such self-harmful ways, repeatedly sabotaging the good in our lives? Why do some people live with such a love of life, while others are depressed, not wanting to be in this existence? What is it all about? Why does everything seem to be speeding up and becoming more dramatic at this time? Do we have any control? Can we really do anything about it?

We ask ourselves these questions everyday, driven by some reasoning from within that there must be more, there must be an answer. There must be some purpose to this life of dread and despair. The human condition is to continually seek out answers, to find solutions.

You will find that there IS a definite purpose behind living, there IS a reason for all the myriad of experiences people have, and there ARE answers and solutions to all the questions. There IS something we can do about it. But first we need to consider more on what it is to be human, what lies behind all these events, what part we have in creating our lives.

Learning

From the moment we are born to the moment we leave this physical existence we are learning. Cause and effect, reasoning, understanding, the list is endless. Every experience, from feeling the sun shining on our faces, eating, interacting with our peers, being well or ill, to coping with the death of a loved one. They each stimulate our senses, our minds, and our bodies. They each send our minds into overdrive to assimilate this new input. Every part of this physical existence is learning! It is that simple.

Hang on a minute I hear you say. How can feeling physical pain or unhappiness or abuse or any of the life experiences we dismay at have anything to do with learning? Is a person who sabotages their life, or is subjected to a life of despair and hardship learning? That doesn't make sense. And if that is learning I want no part of it.

I will use the young child to example this concept. Babies begin exploration very early in life. They turn their heads to see what it is they hear, they smile in recognition of a parent, they touch and feel and taste everything possible, they push themselves to the limit, stacking objects, and climbing and running as fast as they can before falling.

A baby's life is experience. Pure and simple. For the act of learning. What happens when the baby becomes mobile? They have no fears yet, so climb and touch and explore every object before them. Do we stop a child from climbing because they may fall, or do we allow them to do it under a watchful eye so they may have that experience they chose to learn from? A baby learns about feeling, warmth and hugs, sharp objects, of hurts from jammed fingers and grazed knees, to cry and laugh and love.

Dorothy L Nolte wrote a verse called 'Children learn what they live'. It speaks of how children learn base beliefs of themselves, the world around them and what part they play in it. Beliefs are the foundation of what we all perceive our lives to be, how we react to all about us, how we become as a person, confident and loving or apprehensive and fearful. Beliefs are the subconscious controllers of our every thought and act.

Children Learn What They Live

If children live with criticism, they learn to condemn.
If children live with hostility, they learn to fight.
If children live with fear, they learn to be apprehensive.
If children live with pity, they learn to feel sorry for themselves.
If children live with ridicule, they learn to be shy.
If children live with jealousy, they learn what envy is.
If children live with shame, they learn to feel guilty.
If children live with Tolerance, they learn to be Patient.
If children live with Encouragement, they learn to be Confident
If children live with Praise, they learn to Appreciate.
If children live with Approval, they learn to Be Themselves.
If children live with Acceptance, they learn to Find Love In The World.
If children live with Recognition, they learn to Have A Goal.
If children live with Sharing, they learn to be Generous.
If children live with Honesty and Fairness, they learn what Truth and Justice are.

If children live with Security, they learn to have Faith in themselves and in those around them.
If children live with Friendliness, they learn that the world is a Nice Place in which to live.
If children live with Serenity, they learn to have Peace Of Mind.

What are your children living?
Dorothy L. Nolte

From this verse we can gain a glimpse of the reasons and learning behind our attitudes and behaviors.

Activity - What Do You Believe?

Reread Dorothy Nolte's verse and think about the possible range of subconscious beliefs people have and how they really do dictate what we think and how we act.

Apply the top 7 to yourself or someone else to rationalize how these beliefs may impact on this person. For example; A child who was teased and ridiculed at school withdraws and becomes quiet, not wanting to gain attention that risks further insult. Now the adult, but still shy and quiet, this person does not speak out, stand up for themselves, or engage in social situations. This one belief has a profound impact on this person's life.

Activity - Appreciating Life Plays

Although we are often oblivious to our own plays (the situations and dramas in our lives), we can sometimes look at others and see the reasoning behind events in their lives. We can use this as a basis for the possibility we are in fact undertaking actions within our own lives that predispose us to certain situations. Think of some around you and the plays in their lives, then perhaps your own play may begin to show itself.

The person who is shy and self doubting, who misses opportunity after opportunity for success, the lonely one seeking love in all the wrong places, the one who feels inadequate, finding themselves in controlling relationships, the ones who are always short of cash although plenty comes to them. People everywhere are undertaking their own micro plays, which combine and form macro plays of our cultures and then of the world.

Pick 5 people to use as examples. Write about their life dramas in your journal. Step back and take note so you are able to appreciate each person's role and experience. The objective is to introduce the possibility that there could be more to your life experiences than you realized, not to find fault, immediate answers or to criticize.

Life Dynamics

If we take this one step further, we may now begin to realize the detailed dynamics of living. How we each are undertaking a continual process of experience and learning, how our unique belief system dictates our responses, and how those responses create further cycles of events in our lives.

Just as the baby, every part of this physical existence is experience therefore learning! It is that simple. It is up to us to choose whether to play the game of life or not.

Ever noticed how until we learn the lesson, situations repeat themselves? How these repeats appear to occur within shorter time periods and more dramatically each time? The human mind's predisposition for learning is very strong. Just as the baby is driven to explore and investigate its world, so are we driven to undertake a vast range of experiences. Each seemingly more profound than the last. The human mind knows inner growth and learning will often only occur when we are pushed to the limit, when things get so bad we scream out stop, there must be another way and search for it.

Have you ever thought of the deep learning from within after facing and surviving a difficult situation, the sense of change in self? The strength of conviction and belief in self after leaving an abusive relationship, the sense of achievement in a job well done after fighting all the odds, the sense of closeness and deep love for a dear one after the two join and face a life threatening situation as a team, the compassion and acceptance that comes from being a caregiver. Are not the perfect situations created so we may learn the exact things we need, so we may know their opposite?

A New Thought

What if we expand on Dorothy L. Nolte's concept?

If people experience Fears, they have the opportunity to learn the world is a Safe and Wondrous place.
If people experience Self-Doubt, they have the opportunity to learn Self-Value.
If people experience Hardship, they have the opportunity to learn of their Own Strength and Abilities.
If people experience Want, they have the opportunity to learn they are Always Provided For.
If people experience Loss, they have the opportunity to learn there is No Separation of spirit.
If people experience Alienation For Their Ethics, they have the opportunity to learn how Special These Ethics Are.
If people experience Self-Sabotage, they have the opportunity to learn They Are Valuable.
If people experience Aloneness, they have the opportunity to learn They Are Special.
If people experience Tragedy, they have the opportunity to learn the Love Of Friends.
If people experience Creating Life, they have the opportunity to

learn How Special And Unique Each Spirit Is.
If people experience Hard Work, they have the opportunity to learn Pride In Self.
If people experience Feeling, they have the opportunity to learn how Special Life Feels.
If people experience Each Moment In Time, they have the opportunity to learn how to Slow Down And Enjoy Life.
If people experience Negative Beliefs, they have the opportunity to learn how to Create Their Own Beliefs.
If people experience Releasing Emotions, they have the opportunity to learn how to be Calm And Happy.

Activity - I Choose

As you progress with your Greene's Releasing, you will discover the above opposites for yourself. For now, know they will be part of your future and enjoy thinking about living them.

Make a list of the opposites that you have already experienced in your journal, and describe what you learned.

Make a list of the opposites you would like to experience in the future. Why did you choose them? What is your reasoning? What do you hope to learn from each?

Activity - Write Your Thoughts of Life Lessons

The ideas that have been introduced may have seemed rather odd to you, but hopefully after doing some of the activities your mind is opening to the possibility that there may be more to life than you thought.

Write your thoughts of life lessons, what you have experienced while doing this chapter, and your hopes for how this concept may help you find some understanding of the things that have confused you about yourself and your life.

Time for Some Fun

Greene's Meditation & Greene's Dreamtime
Developed by Janet Greene in 2002

Life is a series of individual moments and experiences. The goal may be what motivates us into action, but it is the journey itself that becomes the experience. One day you will discover life IS fun. So, lighten up. Discover new ways to bring pleasure and relaxation into your hectic life. Remember to take care of you.

When you complete this chapter you will be able to:

- Reduce stress by physically relaxing yourself at will
- Go into your own meditative state
- Create your own dream movies while awake
- Allow your inner dreams and visions to surface
- Discover what makes you really feel good
- Clearly document your dream life and current life
- Appreciate where you begin & where you are headed
- Understand your part in creating your daily life
- Become clear thinking and focused on your life goals

Meditation

We have all heard of meditation, and how beneficial it is meant to be. Everyone wants time to escape our constant chatter and fear thoughts. Well, I for one could never achieve this quiet state I kept hearing about.

But, then, quite by accident I discovered another way. A magical way to fly and float freely. And it was simple.

This activity creates a way for us to spend some quiet peaceful time, a form of relaxation, and then go on and learn how to use dream time to locate then manifest our inner desires.

Activity - Greene's Meditation

Get comfortable and try this. Rather than focus on one thing and forcing your thoughts to cease, as most meditation teaches, let them flow freely. Sit or lie comfortably and allow every thought in your mind full freedom. But add one thing. Don't pay any attention to them.

I found that 'a thought' and 'thinking about thoughts' are two separate things. And that when we allow each thought full freedom without jumping in to ponder them, they have nowhere to go and cease on their own. Simple eh?

So, close your eyes, relax your body and get comfortable. Let every thought float through your mind one by one. Whenever you find yourself paying attention to them, go back to ignoring again. It is like sitting back watching all of these thoughts go by, as a 3rd person.

I found that after a couple of minutes the thoughts became more intense, trying to get my attention I assume, but when not achieved, they totally ceased after about 3 minutes. Then I enjoyed the most amazing experience. I literally felt like I was flying. It was like dreaming while awake. I'm sure experiences vary, but all I have shown this technique to have succeeded and enjoyed the process.

Play with it, try out your own variations. See if you can find a lovely place to sit and float for some quiet time. Don't stress if your first time is not successful, it will be very soon.

Spend a week developing your technique prior to moving on

with the next part, as this exercise will become your daily relaxation. Its usage will build continually, and soon you will be able to quiet and float at will, no matter where you are.

Now We Add Greene's Dreamtime

Did you know that you can create your very own movie, to feel and experience as if it is happening in your life right now? That this movie is free from all your life and mind's thoughts and fears? You can create a movie of your choice.

Activity - Create Dream Movies

Go into your relaxation mode from above, then allow yourself to dream of an event. Create your own magical movie of some experience, nothing related to your current life.

I found that as soon as I felt the intent of wishing to do this, various stories would automatically appear. I had full control and could do and be anything within them. It is like, once you totally relax and free yourself of your mind worries and thoughts, the dreams of what you would delight in doing are free to be imagined and experienced.

For me this was a stumbled upon activity, therefore at first you might like to initiate it by thinking of an adventure you would like to encounter in your dream state, prior. Once you are comfortable with this practice, I'm sure your inner dreams will come of their own accord, just as mine did.

The affect of both the relaxation technique, and movie creation was noticeable. I was less stressed, able to physically relax myself more often, smiled whenever I thought of dreaming, because each time I felt such immense pleasure and joy, which stayed with me afterwards.

By developing these techniques, we learn to physically relax and let our inner dreams and visions surface. When we experience movies of our choosing, we learn what makes us smile from the inside out. Something our lives have been lacking.

Keep working on and enjoying your relaxation and movies, use them daily and they will build your intent, because you know what feeling good is like, and want more. You will discover what you want, then have to bring that back into your physical life. You will naturally progress.

One way my movie dream time carried over was in my thoughts. Dreaming is not a way of creating wanted things, such as money. I can however, allow my imagination to find a life of its own, and invite that into my physical life.

When I received a telephone call saying some money would be deposited into my bank account, I automatically dreamed of an amount, and enjoyed that dream for nothing more than the pleasure of it. There was no mind fear relationship involved. But, when I checked my bank account, I smiled as the amount, far greater than expected, was that from my dream. I did not preplan having, nor the events of the dream. It was like imagining for fun what ifs without any relevance or thought of my physical life. That is the trick of this imagination. Enjoy it for its own sake, pleasure and fun, and how good it makes you feel. It is not an escape from your life. It is release and enrichment of your life experiences through free flowing imagination.

Activity - Discover and Document Your Dream Life

Now it's time to discover your dreams and desires for your future life. Then coming to a clear understanding of where you begin, so you know where to aim.

Find a comfortable chair, some quiet space and get a notebook. Begin dreaming of a life for yourself piece by piece, each adding onto the previous and expanding the picture. What is the life that would make you smile?

You will find that although your mind may instantly think

of elaborate situations, like winning lotto, unless they feel right to you, you're unable to feel them.

Where would you live, who would live there with you, what would it be like, what work would you undertake, your financial situation, hobbies, health, personal relationships, happiness, activities, family, self-care, how your time is spent, things you wish to do, friends/social activities, education, how you feel/your state of mind, your personal work, organization, your place in the world, how you feel about you. Include every category imaginable.

Let yourself feel and dream of this life, spend time floating in this picture, then document it clearly. Forget about all obstacles.

Spend at least a week feeling and floating in this dream life, prior to moving on to the next section.

You may adjust this dream life, but this will be your foundation for working towards its creation.

This is YOUR life we are discussing, so rather than scribble notes on loose paper, create a very special booklet. A physical documentation of your beginnings and path. Honor and be proud of it, make it special.

Activity - Clearly Document Your Current Life

Now, document each section of your current life, matching the categories. Write the story, being honest, specific and detailed regarding each circumstance. Grasp an honest picture.

For example: My dream life may include living in a comfortable and clean home, whereas my current life may include living in an often uncomfortable and messy home.

When I clarify and feel what I want, then recognize what I currently have, I give myself a focus to work towards.

Smile as you do this. For now you know where you begin, and where you will end. You have a goal, and you have purpose!

This is NOT about having to come up with solutions. This is

NOT about becoming more aware of your sadness. This is NOT about the reality diminishing the dream. This IS about clarifying a starting point, and moving forward from that.

Get out the cards from The Plan chapter, modify if necessary, and keep them with the documents you have just created.

These pieces become your work in action, your control tool to stand back, recognize, and then forward plan your own game of life using your daily events. Each section in your list represents a game component. Each a specific area for action, whereby you can then plan and take control and manipulate outcomes you desire. You will learn how to think and write your future events to come.

Remember to reread and alter this plan and set of life goals to keep them up to date with your progress after you complete each chapter and section.

For now, spend a few minutes each day holding your dream life in your hands, feel and be it. Just a few minutes every day.

Whenever you feel deflated, read your dream life vision, feel and float within them. Feel the future you will create!

The fears and obstacles you now feel preventing it, will become issues to work on, setting a clear path to create your very own future. I want this, but feel the panic at it not being possible. So I look into that panic and its reasoning, once cleared, I am one step closer to realizing my dream.

Plan For Your Future

Next, you can start formulating your specific plan to achieve your goal and dream life. There is no particular time frame to begin this process; instead, it will be something you naturally feel like doing when you are ready, because you feel a sense of personal control and ability coming back.

Leave it until that is felt, especially as your life will automatically be changing as you heal and grow. Often we pressure ourselves into having to do things before we are ready, and consequentially struggle.

Activity - Become Aware of Your Part

The basis of achieving this is becoming aware and taking control of your part in creating your life. Each day for a week, note down every event in relationship to the sections of your current life document. Watch as your actions, then the corresponding consequences build a picture of what is creating the situation, knowing that whenever we focus intent on achieving, all obstacles will be highlighted so we know where to do the work.

For example: Using a dream of having a comfortable and clean home, today I might go overboard and spend the entire day cleaning and organizing, feeling very tired at the end of the day rather than pleased with my efforts, which goes in how I feel within myself. The next few days might involve my having no desire to keep my home clean at all. I may feel depressed as it becomes messy again.

At first you may not see much correlation between events and your creating them, keep writing anyway. Very soon you will begin to see patterns and your part in each event. Then you can begin noticing hidden issues and triggers that perpetuate unwanted situations.

For example: Until consciously noticing each days events regarding my clean and comfortable dream home, I would not have become aware how my actions sabotage my realizing that dream right now. Once understood, I can change my behavior therefore the situation.

I could plan a daily schedule to keep my home in the state I wish to live in, even allocating jobs to other members of the household. I can plan each weeks schedule to include what is wanted in my home environment, then see and decide what is and is not important, and what is worry for its own sake.

Conclusion

Some of your dream life circumstances will gradually become, others can be organized to manifest right now, with some understanding and careful planning. It is possible to see and become aspects of your dream life this very minute, IF that is what you choose to do and believe you can do.

You can use your daily dream work to experience desired changes, then work with some of the easiest areas to create change now. This will help boost your confidence and enthusiasm about your progress.

As you work within each chapter, the relative issues to your dream life can then be assimilated to correspond. Although change will be gradual and often sneak up on you unexpectedly.

While undertaking chapters, familiarize yourself with the goal for each topic, have some idea of the desired outcome. Spend time floating in dreamland experiencing what it will be like. Use this to motivate you through your work. Have a focused intent for the desired outcome of each section as you work through the book. Know the future you will create, prior to creating it. Become clear, focused and correct in your thinking and actions. Watch them carefully. Plan for your best interests. Focus on creating the life and experiences you want.

If you desire to be a calm and relaxed person, feel that, undertake activities to encourage it. If you desire quality family and social time, make it so. Take an active role in creating the life you desire! Remember to spend as much time analyzing your strengths as you do perplexed by your fears and weaknesses.

You may learn how you create all your life circumstances, but then go outside, look and feel the beauty in a tree, leaf, the birdsong you hear. Know also that YOU created this as well. Wonder at the beauty you indeed create.

It does not matter if that is not understood yet, it will come soon. Know, feel and experience it in the meantime.

Releasing

You are about to learn a technique that **will** transform you and your life.

This simple technique will allow you to go inside and one by one, permanently remove and heal every single pain and heartache that has, up to this point, sabotaged your life.

Just imagine what your life will be like without these feelings. How it will feel to live the exact opposite experience of what you have up to now. Then imagine what it will be like to have the power to dream of a magical life and then make that dream come true.

A Personal Introduction to Greene's Release

Greene's Release developed by Janet Greene in 1999

I will go over the process of how beliefs are initiated, discuss secondary implications, use examples from true Greene's Releases I've talked people through, review beliefs and their implications on you and your life, then take you through the entire process.

When you complete this chapter you will be able to:

- Know what beliefs are and how they are formed
- See the impact your beliefs have had on your life
- Recognize and act on triggers
- Understand why you feel and behave as you do
- Know that you are not crazy
- Self direct the Greene's Release Process
- Complete a Greene's Release from start to finish
- Heal anything you wish to
- Undertake releases at will
- Investigate the origins of feelings, fears & situations
- Be ready and able to release whatever is triggered in the upcoming chapters and your life in general

During our lives we have all manner of experience, sometimes these experiences are strong enough as to make an impact on our deep decision making process. We decide most firmly, on believing something new. This is then stored in the subconscious to be noted and acted on during all activities. Most beliefs are taken on as young children, especially during the time when they are developing all their self-image concepts.

Because they are from a young child's perspective, they may seem odd to you now. Know this is irrelevant; they are very real within your mind.

Remember the different things that are life important to children as they grow? A broken dummy can leave a baby screaming all night long, a left behind teddy bear can destroy a 2-year-olds security, and so it progresses. The trick I found is to ignore what I 'think' of the feelings and beliefs, and know that 'feeling' this emotion is real within my mind, and that is what is important. Deep feelings like these cannot be made up.

Examples of taking on beliefs as a child might be the dog scenario. A child is running ahead of her parents in the park, when suddenly she hears screams; she jumps and becomes very scared. Then a dog knocks her down and licks her face. She screams and cries in terror.

The screaming which frightened the child was her parent's. They saw how she was running towards a dog unaware, and feared the dog attacking. So they screamed out to get her attention so she would stop. Little did they know it was their action which terrified the child, and the dog that was friendly just wanted to lick and play with her.

The affect of this terrifying experience was that the child associated the fear with the dog. And at that moment, she decided to consciously and deliberately make a firm decision in her mind that dogs were to be feared. This decision was automatically sent to her subconscious and stored as one of her beliefs. Like all of us, this child grew up living each day according to her subconscious belief system, and in this case, terrified of dogs.

This affects the child, now a grown adult, every time a dog is thought of, or seen, even if only on television. She feels the fear as strongly now, as if it was the original incident. She relives the feelings of that moment of terror, over and over, as if happening now.

The child couldn't go to friend's houses because they had a dog, so she isolated herself by missing social activities. Her friends thinking her strange, gradually drifted away, so then she became isolated at school, which led to loneliness, depression, and disliking people in general.

As an adult, life isn't any easier. She still avoids contact with dogs, and people now. Making excuses not to visit friends who own dogs, not walking or jogging because she saw a dog off lead while driving, not allowing her own children to get a puppy. People still think she is rather a strange person and more often than not avoid contact with her too, which creates even more issues.

The funny thing is, that if you ask the woman why she is so scared of dogs and now people, she couldn't tell you. Just like the person who is scared of heights, or doesn't think they deserve, or thinks they are a failure, the memory of the incident that led to the inception of her fear of dogs belief has faded, while the terrifying feelings from that event remain strong, and grow with each repeated fear experience.

Another example will sound odd, but it is a true belief that was taken on. Upon returning home very late one evening 2 young children were very tired, the older had fallen asleep. The father decided to carry the sleeping child inside rather than wake and risk the usual tantrums he constantly displayed. Yet the other child who was awake wanted some attention too, a hug from being carried, so she pretended to be asleep as well.

The mother, tired, and knowing this younger child was never difficult decided to wake her. The child kept pretending to stay asleep, wanting that hug and the attention. In the end the mother became impatient, yelled and walked inside.

At this point the little girl, around 6 years of age decided (then created the belief in her subconscious) the parents cared for the older brother and not her. She was not loved. She would have to be independent and not need help ever again. The ramifications of this carried with her well into her adult life.

Activity - Impacts of Beliefs 1

Imagine yourself in the above situation, taking on the belief that you are not loved. How might this have impacted on your life in general as you grew up?

Make a list of the possible implications, actions, and scenarios; note the secondary impacts on other areas of your life (e.g. The fear of dogs belief resulted in the child becoming socially isolated). Include relationships, friendships, how you feel about yourself, etc.

Activity - Impacts of Beliefs 2

Another example relates to a young woman I worked with, who was feeling very uncomfortable about an upcoming reunion of sorts.

While reading the following, try and put the pieces together to find the inception of the original belief, and the secondary implications/impact on the woman's life.

It was a family and friends affair from her old hometown, the celebration of a wedding. She didn't know why she was becoming more and more nervous exactly, why she was developing a cold, only that she was becoming very anxious.

The first thing I asked was why so nervous about going? She explained that she would be seeing people she had not seen in many years, in a town she had been happy to escape the unhappy memories of. If only she could see the people she wanted to and ignore the rest. Leave the past in the past.

I talked to her about how we are often led into triggers, like she is feeling now. Not so we may feel uncomfortable, but so we have the opportunity to finally release what obviously was still bothering us. To finally be clear of that past event.

When I asked about the people she did not want to see, they all revolved around an old boyfriend. She described briefly how he had cheated on her with another woman, known to her. And how that had embarrassed her no end, everyone knew everyone in this small town. She felt betrayed and made a fool of.

We discussed her romantic life since that time and the impact of this relationship became apparent. She has been unable to feel secure in any relationship since, becoming sneaky and jealous; always on the watch for their repeating what she knew would happen.

At this point this young woman began to realize how the previous relationship had indeed been carried with her, the fears. She had taken on a belief from it and used it to base all consequential relationships on. She also realized why she was feeling nervous about the trip and smiled at the opportunity this had created. To finally be rid of this man's effect on her.

We were then able to undertake the lesson in depth. Discussing the past events and allowing the emotions to surface. This young woman had several different associated lessons (anger, letting go, not feeling good enough, etc), which were done one by one at different times.

I must stress at this point, only do one topic at a time. Whatever comes to mind is what you work on. Do not let yourself get sidetracked with different issues, as this is merely your mind trying to avoid feeling pain. It will be fine, as the actual feeling you will experience is far easier than forcing yourself not to feel (the fear of feeling).

Activity - Answer to Impacts of Beliefs Exercise

If you picked out something like men can't be trusted as a belief, and having to be extra cautious and observant to protect yourself which leads to being sneaky, mistrusting, insecure, and jealous then you got it. Can you think of one of your own situations, and relate the full impact?

Please use this exercise and chapter to demonstrate the life changing impact secondary implications of beliefs can have on you and your life. They show how you became the person you are today.

Overview of the Belief and Secondary Implication Process

Conception: We experience an event so strongly that we make a conscious decision to believe something from now on.

Example: A child decides that her parents do not love her, therefore she is unlovable.

Transfer: This new belief is immediately transferred into our subconscious to be used as the basis for all thoughts, actions and reactions.

Example: The child grows up knowing from deep inside her subconscious that she is not loved because she is unlovable. This is her basis of viewing herself, all people around her, and the world.

She is always distant, cannot believe that anyone could love her, cannot see any love aimed at her, and avoids situations of love because feeling the pain of not being loved is too strong.

These are subconscious beliefs and thoughts, so in her everyday life the girl does not realize that she cannot see love aimed at her, or runs from romantic situations because she doesn't want to feel that deep pain again. She just reacts without understanding why.

Memory: The memory of the original incident fades completely from conscious memory.

Example: We have millions of thoughts and make thousands of decisions through our life. Naturally we do not remember every thought we have ever had; therefore don't remember many of the reasons behind our decisions.

Feelings: The feelings from the original incident remain as strong as that day.

Example: A person with a fear of dog's belief feels the same terror every time they see a dog, even if the dog may be across the road, on a leash, and of no threat to them. They have no idea why they feel as they do.

Implications: Because the beliefs that control our behaviors are subconscious, we respond to situations automatically without being able to control our responses or understand why we behave as we do.

Example: A person with a subconscious belief that men always cheat will act suspiciously and fearful, ask questions, be needy and generally treat all partners as if they are doing something wrong, even when they are being very loving, usually causing the relationship to end.

This woman described earlier watches herself jump from one situation of behaving badly to the next, without any ability to control or change her actions. She has no understanding of herself.

Secondary implications: We go through life experiencing the implications of this belief. As more and more areas are affected by our subconscious responses, the impact of this one belief continues to spiral to create many layers.

Example: The woman above teaches herself new beliefs and resultant behaviors. Men leave, who would love anyone who behaves like me, I am horrible, I have to distance myself from people because I am no good, love hurts, people don't want to be around or help me.

She acts distant, is lonely, dislikes herself thoroughly, literally goes crazy if a man tries to get close to her, stops caring for herself, puts on weight, marries but can't let her husband get close, cannot show emotion, etc.

One belief goes on to create many layers of actions, reactions, events and subsequent new beliefs.

The releasing process peels back these layers one by one, to understand each as we journey to reach the original belief inception that is stored in the subconscious.

It is very interesting to start with a topic, and then as you peel the layers, discover the various events that are connected, and the reasons for your actions and reactions. It can be a real wow moment to realize why you behave as you do, and understand how you became the person you are today.

A Release Example

As the 6 year old girl was I, and I still remember the incident and healing lesson as if yesterday, I will make this the example of working through a lesson from the discovery stage to finish.

The issue of feeling unloved (secondary implications of a belief) that I was looking into at the time triggered strong feelings. I felt a real pang in my heart, becoming very emotional for some unknown reason.

After peeling back some layers, I began seeing a picture of my grandparent's back yard very clearly. It was night and a car was pulling into the driveway. Allowing the 'movie' to play in its own way and speed in my mind, I became more and more distressed, feeling every emotion I did from that night. Feeling every thought that occurred in my mind as the 6-year-old child. How I wanted a hug, how it wasn't fair that 'he' got one, he was bigger than me, and always bad. I was always good and never got any attention. Didn't they love me too?

I allowed myself to tell the whole story, what happened, how I felt, what I thought. I allowed every feeling to be 'felt' through my entire being. As the story was revealed, I began to understand the secondary implications of this event, how it had affected many areas of my life, why I felt and acted as I did. Another piece of why I am the person I am had been discovered.

Then, when I had finished the 'movie' I kept allowing myself to feel, to make sure there wasn't anything I had missed. No, I had it all. It all makes sense to me now; what happened, how I reacted and took on a belief, how that belief has determined subsequent actions and reactions throughout my life. I finally understand the strange behavior I have watched myself doing without being able to change. I am ready to let it go.

The next process is the key to healing our hurts, one we forget to do when experiencing emotions.

The emotion and upset was still at its peak. As I breathed in I focused on feeling this emotion. Then with every out breath I pictured it leaving my body piece by piece and floating up to the universe. I literally cried each thing I felt and thought outwards with breathing. I let myself feel then release it totally.

This is a very conscious act and feels strange at first. As I kept blowing it out gently I began to calm little by little, then when it was all gone from me I calmed and felt very peaceful. No longer feeling as that little 6-year-old emotionally, instead the adult I am now.

The healing process involved the person I am now, being able to speak to the child, just as you would a young child before you. I reasoned in ways that a child comprehended. I explained the truth I felt about the situation now, as if it had happened to my own child and they came to me. I told her how her brother was difficult, and why they carried him, how they knew what a good girl she was. How they had absolutely no idea a cuddle and attention was so badly wanted. I then gave this child a big hug and all my love. I gave that child a new belief to replace the one released. In doing so, every impact of that previous belief dissolved because the belief itself was no longer present to create any impacts.

It is far more than releasing one particular belief then replacing it. This process removes all the fears and heartaches created by such beliefs, we instantly become a new person, and feel a great weight has been lifted from our shoulders.

I have always known that when each part of this process is finished for I feel it deeply. I feel the change as the emotional reaction to finding the correct issue is felt, the build up as I run the movie, the climax when all the feelings are being felt, the calm and peace when all has been released out of my being, and the re-insertion of a new belief. That is when you go WOW, for it is a feeling words cannot explain. Like a giant weight has been lifted, you feel instantly different and invigorated. An amazing feeling and how you can always tell if a healing lesson has been fully completed.

Epiphanies

You have lived your entire life believing that you are a failure/not good enough/not lovable etc. Twenty, thirty, or perhaps sixty years thinking this about you, condemning and treating yourself badly because of this impediment. Repeatedly living the life experience of being a person who is a failure/not good enough/not lovable.

And now, suddenly, you learn that it wasn't true, that there is nothing wrong with you after all, that they were wrong, and you feel the truth of who and what you really are from deep inside you. A very special being.

The epiphany of this experience can be mind blowing to say the least. Yet you will become accustomed to the epiphany experience as it is a natural conclusion to each release, and then again as you reach deeper levels of awareness that naturally come as more and more of 'their' beliefs are permanently removed from your mind.

If you feel overwhelmed by this experience, relax, listen to how you feel, and do whatever feels right. Let your inner self be your guide.

Activity - Doing A Release

Please read this entire chapter, Summary: Greene's Release,

Heal Your Self

and A Releasing Session before undertaking this exercise.

Now let's help you get underway. I am sure the reading so far is prompting you to feel many uncomfortable things. Good!! That just makes it easier to get into. So let yourself relax, close your eyes for a moment, be aware of what you are feeling right now. What event or issue is coming to your mind and emotions? Now is the time to allow it to flow, to let it be felt no matter what it is or how silly it feels.

What are you feeling? Nervous, anxious, upset? What is the situation you are thinking of? Let your emotions lead you. Relax knowing all will be well and feel.

Is it a recent event? If so go right through the 'movie' of that event. Feel what concerned you about it, follow all leads that come to mind. Keep asking yourself why. Why am I feeling this, what is this related to?

Ask yourself all the w questions (what, why, where, when, how) as you dig through your maze of this topic. You may start with a recent story, then be led to a similar one when you were younger, then another when you were younger still. You will find that each layer is a repeat of the initial incident when the belief was taken on. You are peeling the layers through time and secondary implications via a feeling. Listen to the stories, understand how they impacted on you.

Keep digging and digging through the layers until you 'feel' the pang. When you find the trigger to the 'real' issue you will definitely feel it loud and clear.

Then let yourself go back to it, further and further as the emotion builds. Play the old movie as exampled. Let yourself feel it all. Know it is okay and this will be the very last time you feel this. Go and sit somewhere quiet and comfortable and let it all come out. Blow it out of your being as if at a candle. Force every ounce of it out. Watch it leave your being with each breathe; see it go up to the sky. See, feel, know, and demand it leave. Keep feeling the emotion and blowing it out till you don't feel any of it anymore. Then think of the event and feel. Is there anything left? If there is let it be felt so it too can be removed from within you. Keep breathing it out till you calm and relax.

Become the calm strong self that is your inner knowing. Pretend there is a child the same age as your memory, sitting right in front of you. Feeling the same as you just have. Asking all the same questions. Thinking the same things. Feel your compassion for this child, as you would if he/she were your own. Then tell another story, another reason for what happened.

Make it simple and logical, speak your truth to this child. When you are finished you will know by feel. Enjoy that new feel, that new lightness, energy. Smile and congratulate yourself. You did it!!! You succeeded in doing your first Greene's Release Session.

Undertaking such clearing work is emotional I know, yet as you become proficient with the process each can take as little as 15 minutes to complete, and you will never feel it again. One by one you will literally feel the weight lift from your shoulders, and the sense of strength of self increase, you will feel your inner knowing and self grow and enjoy discovering this new part of you.

The purpose of learning how to find, release then replace beliefs is to clear those you have taken on from the outside, the ones which sabotage your health, happiness and love life.

This clearing work is not a one-time event, it is a tool to be used regularly, as a way of eliminating all and every feeling you choose not to keep experiencing. From being uncomfortable around people, becoming annoyed at yourself or loved ones, or hesitating making a phone call. Any and every single emotion you feel that you choose not to continue feeling can be eliminated using this process. Imagine all the worry you have daily, decreasing.

Of course it is neither possible nor practical to do this emotional work whenever emotions surface, but you can note them and make a conscious decision of when you will undertake their clearing. This will quiet them, and also allow resurfacing on demand. Become comfortable and proficient with your emotional clearing, for it is a major tool as you progress.

Activity - Write About Your Experience

How did your first release make you feel? What did you discover? After you complete a few releases, write about them to help clarify your thoughts about this process, what it means and the impact it has. Write your story of releasing and create your very own concept from your very own experiences.

Activity - Clearing

Spend at least 2 weeks doing spontaneous clearings using the 'Release Technique' chapter to guide you. Get comfortable before attempting 'Childhood Issues' which will trigger you strongly.

While childhood releases may seem emotional, they are the easiest and quickest ones to access and release. All you need do is plan specific time for your healing work, sit or lie down in a quiet space, think about your childhood, and feel. Issues will automatically come up to be felt. Focus on the first one that comes, do your healing and release.

Repeat this process during your next planned healing time, and the next and the next. Once you feel comfortable doing releases from start to finish, continue with the next chapter.

Applying Greene's Release Technique to Chapters

Read the entire chapter to get a feel for it, then go back to the beginning and begin reading again, slowly. Notice the first thing you feel, stop and release.

Continue reading until you feel the next trigger, then again stop, feel and release. Practice becoming aware and ready to feel, notice and act as you read all chapters from 'Childhood Issues' on.

Summary: Greene's Release

You have been triggered into feeling something strongly, and have decided that you would like to heal and remove it forever.

Validate all feelings, no matter how strange they may seem. Remember that the feelings children have will feel odd to adults. It is okay to feel anger, resentment, rage, hurt, anything. If you feel something it is valid so do not feel guilty for anything you feel.

Feelings tell the hidden stories. Welcome any feelings that come, allow them to envelop you, ask to hear their stories.

Be encouraging, compassionate and supportive of the part of you that shares the feelings. It may feel like a child, youngster or adult.

You may feel the three different parts of yourself during releasing sessions (A. the adult you are now - conscious mind/me, B. subconscious memories/child self, C. your real self/inner knowing). Your conscious mind directs the releasing process, so you need to speak the words following A. in your head.

Remember that the feelings you are experiencing, and the stories you are hearing are about you. Listen, understand or ask for more information, relate them to you, your life now, your past experiences, why you feel and act as you do. These feelings

Heal Your Self

and stories are your insights into you.

All you need do is decide that you want to understand this topic, and you will automatically do the above paragraph. You do not need to think of it consciously, as this will distract yourself from feeling. It is like telling yourself to unlock a file cabinet to get specific files.

1. Find a quiet space where you can be alone.

2. A. Remind yourself that you are directing this process of peeling the layers to find a subconscious belief to release.

3. A. Quiet your mind and body then think of your topic or the feeling that has been bothering you. Invite the feeling to come up and share its story.

4. A. This is the first layer, so encourage yourself to feel whatever is shared with you, listen to the story, ask for clarification or more information. Feel, listen and understand how it relates to you. Validate the feeling and story. Now follow the strongest feeling to move into the next layer.

5. A. Ask where this layer came from, for more information. Ask to go deeper into the feeling, and the second layer will appear.

6. A. Keep peeling layers until you reach the one where you feel a very strong pang of emotion, you will know when you reach it. This is the base one.

Remember to pay attention to what you feel and keep pulling all the stories together, then something will click and you'll know exactly how this topic has affected many aspects of you and your life. Another piece of yourself has been discovered. When you are finished move onto the next step.

7. A. Return your full focus to the pang feeling, encourage and let it build again.

Feel the emotion, breathe in, picture this breathe going down to physically encircle and grab the emotion, pulling it up, then blowing it out of your mouth softly (like at a candle). See, feel, know it is leaving your being forever. Make it leave!

A. Talk yourself through it; feel, breathe, grab the emotion, then blow it out. Repeat until you feel different in a couple of minutes.

8. A. Go back and check for any remnants. Think of the topic, then feel and listen. If you feel anything repeat the grabbing and blowing out step, then check again for remnants. Keep going until there is nothing left to feel or grab. You will feel different, perhaps calm or blank.

9. Open and allow yourself to become the calm self that is your inner knowing. Pretend there is a child the same age as your memory in front of you. Feeling the same as you just have. Asking the same questions. Thinking the same things. Feel your compassion for this child, as you would if he/she were your own.

Then tell another story, another reason for what happened. Make it simple and logical; speak your truth to this child. You will automatically know what to say. When you are finished you will know by feel.

10. At the moment when the old negative belief has been completely removed from your being, and the new opposite belief is being told to the child, you will feel an all inspiring epiphany which will alter how you view yourself for ever. Each release is the same, with some epiphanies being stronger and more life changing than others.

11. Initially you may feel blank, relaxed, ready for a nap, or invigorated. Enjoy your new feel, new lightness, energy. Smile and congratulate yourself.

A Greene's Release Session

The following is a transcript from a client's first release session using Greene's Release. Names are altered to ensure confidentiality, yet I have witnessed this exact same theme countless times. Sometimes there is a new belief to instill after the release, other times merely feeling love for your inner child is sufficient. You will always know what to do or say automatically.

Janet: Why shouldn't they like her? Be her and feel her as you.

Shirley: Mother told ME I was useless, lazy, she wished I'd never been born, and was always criticizing me. She taught me that I was good for nothing and that no man would ever want me. After all... she didn't. She's supposed to love me dammit

Janet: lots of words...what do they feel like?

Shirley: There's nothing I can do to make her love me... no matter how I tried and tried and tried... it never worked.

Janet: How does it feel to know your mother didn't want you?

Shirley: I feel pain... deep pain... like I'm having an emotional tantrum... like I'm going to explode and I don't know how to deal with it.

Janet: feel it!!!!!!!...let it keep growing...

Shirley: I hate her! Oh my God... right now I hate her!! How could she do this to me??? My hands are shaking, I'm bawling my eyes out... like that child.

Janet: Then feel that hate...let it grow...let it peak in intensity then tell me when it does.

Shirley: It's so intense right now Janet. What do you want me to do... explode???

Shirley: I can't. I'm back there... I'm afraid of this space.

Janet: As you breathe in feel the emotion...then blow out as if at a candle...see/feel/know that emotion leave with the breathe...watch it go out of your being...keep breathing in then blowing out, till its all gone.

Shirley: I feel bawled out. My eyes hurt, my head hurts... I always felt this way after... then I'd go into my shell.

Janet: Breathe into the emotion and feel it...pick it up and blow it out...little by little...see it leave your being

Janet: Keep the intensity of the emotion...breathe in and FEEL it...It is a conscious act you do with this breathing...tell yourself what your doing...know it!!

Shirley: This may take a while.

Janet: No it wont!!...focus on feeling then blowing it out...that is your only thought

Shirley: still breathing

Janet: are you blowing it out??...feeling it leave you??

Shirley: Yes, the breath out feels very different than I'm accustomed to

Janet: Make sure you breathe into feeling the emotion...then pick it up and get that sucker out of you...you want it OUT!!!

Shirley: okay, am continuing

Shirley: It's like I can see darkness leaving with my breath... it's warm and murky. I feel lighter, but tired, drained.

Janet: Think of her not wanting you...what do you feel??

Shirley: Oh my gosh... I never knew I felt such incredible anger towards my mom! I could never get there, to that space before... I knew it was there, but I could never access it!

Shirley: Her not wanting me... there's an empty feeling. Not sure how to take that feeling.

Janet: Finish releasing then I'll explain how it works....you must feel what is left and remove it too.

Shirley: I feel empty, devoid feeling, drained.

Janet: Ok...do you still feel anger towards your mother??

Shirley: Not at all... nothing, indifferent

Janet: Good...now lets see if something else comes up on its own...or you are finished for now...don't try to find something else, if its meant to it'll tell you

Shirley: Janet I don't know if I'm able to do this again, now. That was incredibly painful. Am I wimping out?

Janet: Still just feeling indifferent?? Do not worry...you'll be fine in a minute....

Shirley: Okay, I'll chill and just feel... think I do feel something... sorrow. I'm feeling sorry for myself now

Janet: Good!!!!...feel the injustice...and sadness for that little girl...she did nothing wrong...feel for HER!! Feel that sadness...let it be felt fully...let it grow and climax, and be released like the anger

Shirley: I want to hug that little girl... me!

Janet: That is the healing...but first let her find and feel and show you her deep sadness, so you can help her release it...ok

Janet: Let her tell you for the first time ever...how she hurts...

Shirley: She's so forlorn... so lost and sad... she's crying for herself and all the mean things mother has done and said to her. She's feeling empty with nowhere to turn, no one to turn to

Janet: Not SHE!!!!!...feel it as YOU!!!!....

Shirley: She's all scrunched up, rocking. She feels like a non entity. She's numb, afraid, has a boulder in her gut

Shirley: I'm tired of crying, tired of crying out on deaf ears... no one cares... no one cares!... a bit of anger creeping up

Janet: Keep feeling the hurt...let it build and peak and tell you its story...feel it as you not a 3rd person

Heal Your Self

Shirley: Maybe if I go away all the hurt will go away too. Maybe I can hurt them back by hurting myself. Yeah, like they'll care. I'll just hurt myself because I deserve the punishment for being useless... tears again.

Janet: Let yourself finish this tantrum...feel sorry for yourself, feel angry...feel whatever it is...acknowledge it for the first time

Janet: You do not feel as the little girl now do you??

Shirley: I deserve nothing, no one... life is bs. I'm an empty shell no one will miss. My body feel numb... I don't care about anything...

Shirley: Now, as a 39 year old? NO! I'm not going to commit suicide, if that's what you're asking straight out

Janet: Is this feeling still as that child, or someone else??...the tantrum I mean

Janet: I know your not...it is fine...keep feeling!!!...when you know the full story of this emotion and it peaks, release with breathing like you did before

Shirley: I'm too numb to have a tantrum... no energy left to physically act out. I'm feeling too sorry for myself... pity poor me... no one else will.

Janet: Yes!!!...feel that self pity...acknowledge it has a good reason for being there...it is alright to be felt...

Shirley: Okay, ready to breath and feel

Janet: Good...you'll grab this one and remove it quickly...go for it

Shirley: It's almost gone!

Janet: Great...then tell me what you feel after you check to see if any of it is left

Shirley: Hey, guess what? I'm feeling energized!
Instead of feeling drained, like after the first exercise, I feel like I have physical energy... mental energy... I feel like crying out of happiness... really!
   I feel a sense of freedom, as sense of accomplishment for even "going there"... a sense that something has changed within.
   I used myself as the third person as a means of avoidance... avoiding Being those emotions... a cop out. Immediately when I started with "ME" the emotions were much more intense.

Janet: Not a cop out...you have avoided for survival...

Shirley: I feel rejuvenated, and a sense of freedom... I can't really explain... it's a feeling... nothing intellectual.

Janet: Yep...the lightness after release is awesome!!
You will find everything this topic affected re your behavior and thoughts will be changed automatically....

Shirley: Janet I so appreciate you doing this with me... taking time out for a virtual stranger (so to speak), giving of yourself and time... I love your heart!

Shirley: That little girl, is asleep :-)

Janet: You'll still cuddle her (you) tonight and dream happy dreams

Shirley: You betcha I will

What am I?

If you let yourself feel and listen you can open to recognize the three different parts of you. So put aside your preconceived ideas and feel your way through the following exercises to discover your own answers.

When you complete this chapter you will be able to:

- Stop judging yourself
- Understand the actions and interactions between the different parts of you
- Care for your emotional child self 'ego'
- Know how to become the director of your life

Inner Self / Spirit Self

We were each born with the freedom to be and express ourselves fully. When we were hungry we screamed for food, when we were tired we slept, when we were sad we cried, when we were happy we laughed, when they hugged us we delighted in the warmth of love and playtime was a time for joyous laughter.

Activity - Remember The Freedom To Be You

Many of us have forgotten about the complete freedom babies are born with, so spend some time observing young babies. You could visit friends or relatives, visit the toy store or supermarket. Notice how they express themselves without restriction, their interactions with their caregivers, and interest in the environment. Become fully aware of the freedom babies have to be themselves, without doubts, second guessing, fears, or even when their parents tell them to stop.

Activity - Your Inner Self/ Spirit

Can you remember a time when you felt total peace and the freedom to be yourself? Can you remember the feeling of an inner knowing that everything will be alright?

Did you feel a sense of love and peace while doing some of the activities in the Feeling, Energy or Meditation chapters?

Inner self is the essence of each one of us that is based on pure love and peace, just like the baby, so whenever you feel these sensations or listening to dreams, you are experiencing your inner or spirit self. There are no fears, no doubts, no worries. Only love.

Find some memory or experience that you can recreate to experience your inner self. Float around in this state of mind, notice how you feel, what thoughts come to mind, enjoy the experience and ponder what it will be like to spend more time in this state, then write about it.

Activity - Draw

Now that you have a sense of your inner self draw a small circle in the middle of a blank piece of paper to represent this magical part of you.

Life Rules

By the time we reached one or two, we were well adapt at learning the rules of life that our parents taught us. "Good girls sit quietly in the shopping cart", "Children are seen and not heard", "Do what I say you can do, not what you want to do", "You can't have everything you want."

These rules or inner beliefs as they came to be, restricted our ability to be, think and act spontaneously.

Activity - Formation of Beliefs

Imagine the initial rules or beliefs young children are taught, perhaps you taught them to your own children. Make a list of at least 10.

Activity - Draw

Very lightly, just to show the outline shape, draw a second circle about an inch out from the first.

Now, using your list of 10 early childhood beliefs, draw small dashes along this circle line to represent each new belief.

Activity - Your Childhood Beliefs

Using the releases you have already undertaken, make a list of the beliefs you were taught as a young child.

For example, not being good enough, can't do anything right, think before you act, be quiet. Include as many as you can, so you will appreciate this part fully.

Now add some of your childhood fears to the list, if you aren't sure of them yet, imagine ones that children could have. Fear of dogs, being left alone, someone dying, getting into trouble, being yelled at, not doing things right the first time.

When your list is complete, stop and think about each one, and how it served to restrict your actions and freedom to do and be whatever came naturally. For example, I couldn't run around the house singing loudly because daddy said I had a horrible voice which gave him a headache, so I stopped singing all together.

Or I wanted to run outside and play but I was scared because mummy wouldn't come outside with me.

Write your thoughts and observations so you form a good understanding of how your childhood fears and beliefs restricted you.

Activity - Draw

Now, using your list of childhood beliefs and fears, add a dash to represent each one on the largest circle.

The dashes are beginning to join together and form a solid line very quickly aren't they?

When you are finished take a good look at this solid outer circle, and become aware of how it represents all of the fears, emotions and beliefs you were told when a child, and how it is effectively forming a veil around your true inner self that you love to be.

For you to live as your inner self, that part of you has to get past this veil of fears and beliefs without being stopped or having the original love feeling distorted. Hard to do. Are you beginning to see how your inner self got buried?

Your Subconscious Mind/Ego

The outer circle you have drawn and filled in with dashes to represent your beliefs is your subconscious mind or ego/child self. This is where every single emotion, fear and belief is stored.

Ego feels like a child, and the part you are getting to know very well during your releasing as it tells the stories of fear and pain that you are listening to. Ego self feels very different to the calm, loving inner self part doesn't it?

Your Conscious Mind/Me

Can you feel another part of you that is actively living your daily life, the conscious awareness part of you that has to deal with events as they happen? We work, organize, plan, and act consciously. It feels very different to the fear and worry ego part, or the calm, loving inner self part doesn't it?

Conscious mind is the part that experiences life, it is the adult you are now while ego is the frightened child you were then. If you need clarification, make a list of the things you do consciously each day. Look at the list and see how its components make you feel very different to ego child and inner self.

Activity - Draw

Draw a third circle about an inch outside the ego one to represent your conscious mind self. The space outside the circle represents the world and life, therefore this outer circle of your conscious mind experiences everything directly, while the two inner circles only experience the world via their impact on the conscious mind.

How It Works

As the 'experiencer', conscious mind experiences life through the emotions, fears and beliefs of ego, or the calm, loving knowing of inner self. Hence the two states of mind, love and fear.

Listen to your thoughts; are they about ego's fears and beliefs, or inner self's dreams of special life events to experience?

When you feel and listen, you can easily discover which of your inner circles is controlling your current thoughts, feelings and experiences.

Activity - What Part Is Influencing Your Day?

Even though your current life is still mostly influenced by your ego emotions and fears, rather than your free flowing inner self, try this out just for the experience.

Each day for the next week, become aware of your feelings and thoughts (especially notice what the thoughts are about). Feel, listen and recognize where they are coming from. Do some activities to help you open to your inner self (meditate, relax, play with animals, something fun). Watch yourself jump from ego's fear state to inner self's love state and notice the difference. Build your awareness and understanding.

Taking Control

Until now, we felt helpless to control the events in our life because ego creates them without our conscious input. This is probably the reason we decided to blame and condemn the ego part of us.

But, now that we understand the roles of each component, we can use our conscious mind to effectively direct our life in whichever way we desire.

It is conscious mind that directs the release process from start to finish, then after each one, one of the dashes you initially placed on your ego circle is permanently removed, opening a gap for inner self to flow through. The more you release, the more gaps you create. Initially you won't feel this, but as you continue to use Greene's Release the balance will shift and one day you will awake feeling like 'your self', because your inner self is flowing through freely.

If you experience an event or emotion that you never wish to again, use your conscious mind control to direct the releasing process and permanently remove ego's belief that created it.

If you want to allow your true inner self to come forth again, like it did when you were a baby, direct ego through the releases to open the gaps for inner self to flow through freely.

It really is totally up to you to decide what you want, then make it happen.

Activity - Decide

Before moving to the next chapter, write a review about the three parts of you, how you see their impact on your life experience, and the potential you (conscious mind) have in directing your own life.

Think about what you want from life, what direction you would like it to head in, feel the power you do have to decide what is created within it.

Decide what you want for you!

Activity - Write About The 3 Parts Of You

After each release you do during the next month, review and write about the different parts of yourself that you felt during the process. Get to know you.

For example; I felt like a young child when I was feeling and listening to the story about not being loved, he/she was very scared, so I hugged him/her in my mind until it settled. I felt a strong desire to care for this part of me once I understood him/her.

When I was talking myself through the instructions to do the healing and releasing I felt like I was listening to and feeling a separate person who had the emotion, then I felt calm and very mature as I told the new story that came from somewhere else automatically.

Develop the story of the three parts of you as you experience the interactions. Form your own concept from your very own experiences.

My Thoughts

Once we are competent at feeling and releasing, it becomes clear that ego is the subconscious part where our beliefs and fears are held, then demonstrated in all our conscious thoughts and actions. Like a frightened child reacting constantly without restriction.

I have heard people speak of ego as unwanted; a part of ourselves to be scorned and hidden for it demonstrates our bad side. Ego is no such thing my friend. Ego is your child self, ego is that wondrous part of you who willingly took on all your fears and hurts as they occurred, packed them away so you wouldn't constantly feel them, then set about organizing your life in a way to prevent further hurts by avoiding those same situations. Ego cares deeply for you. Ego's only purpose is to help you.

Yet ego's disposition is such that it operates from a child's perspective and knowledge, therefore not appropriate to be in control of adult thoughts and actions. Although, what a magnificent mechanism ego is to prompt and trigger growth from learning. In order to escape the childish behaviors we are forced to look to their cause, locate the stockpile of fears and beliefs we have taken on from the outside world.

The self creates situations in order to experience and take on fearful beliefs, stockpiles them to be used whenever similar situations reoccur, creates new nightmare situations to push for the discovery of this stockpile as the only means of escape, all so we have the opportunity to experience living in a way to promote self discovery and growth.

As you progress with your lesson work, this frightened child will become well known to you, he/she will sit on your lap often as you share comfort, love, compassion and new beliefs. You will begin to see ego as a separate identity, one to be protected and nurtured. You will learn true compassion for this child and marvel at the strength of character.

Whenever I find myself feeling fearful, or reacting strongly to lesson work I am undertaking, or feeling as though I am blocking access to specific areas, I call ego and listen to her, allow her to feel and express, then release all that worries her.

Ego is fearful of being neglected and abandoned again, that is why she has put up a good fight for control over spirit influence. Remember the two states of being, love and fear. As we clear our fear beliefs we begin spending time in a calm and knowing state, this builds until we reach a point of spending more time feeling calm than feeling fearful. It is indeed a very pleasant point to reach, until ego becomes fearful and kicks in for control, attempting to sabotage our work progress. When this happens, spend time listening and comforting ego, let him/her feel, express and release.

While ego is the child part of me, 'me' is the adult one living this life and connecting ego and spirit. It is 'me' who works with ego in helping her grow up and feel loved. This I commenced doing in meditation, I would picture my ego child and call her to me, talk to her, reassure her, keep her comforted and close to me, all the while encouraging her to grow up, that the world was safe. The process of ego growing up and becoming an adult is in line with clearing childhood emotional beliefs, gradually over time.

I cannot remember a time when I did not feel as an observer of my life, standing outside yet being responsible for it. I cannot remember a time when I did not cringe with disgust and hate being me. It was truly awful being this person with all these reactions and emotions, so very many of them. It was like I was literally shown constantly all the awful parts of me, the things I did. I had to be part of it without being able to play any part, I had no input at all.

During my lessons of self-love, these were among the feelings that arose. It was very difficult to comprehend where such a strong self-dislike originated. I knew that in general humans dislike being human, and other humans. This is demonstrated by our dislike of our, and others actions, and how many do not like the living experience at all. We humans are incredibly cruel to ourselves.

Think of all the activities you undertake that are not in your best interest and you will see what I mean. We smoke, drink, eat poorly, don't exercise or keep our physical beings healthy. We push ourselves to the limit without thought for our own well-being. It is in every facet of our lives, this self-punishment. Being a general viewpoint I was curious why.

One area I found was from my 'me' part. I listened to my deep sense of hatred for all that I was, and allowed the anger and frustration to tell their stories. What I heard surprised me greatly. This 'me' part carried the hurt and despair and a sense of complete loss of control over oneself, that ego went about doing whatever whenever, yet 'me' was dragged along unable to interfere at all. Then felt the anger at being held accountable for ego's actions. The sense of lack of control over ones own being was profound, a very strong emotion. I came to realize that my 'me' part also had some form of ego, unknown to me previously, and how this part initiated and controlled all the self punishment I was undertaking. I had realized this self-punishment could not be ego's issue as ego felt deep hurt from experiencing it.

As with all emotions that surface I allowed unconditional validation of 'me's' viewpoint and hurt, I allowed 'me' to feel and express all that had been held onto, then I released it fully with breathing. 'Me' no longer felt the anger and want of reprisal against ego, the validation, acknowledgement and recognition of its suffering was sufficient.

Heal Your Self

I then felt compassion for my ego self, not only had it taken on all the hurts from my fears and beliefs, but then was punished for reacting to them. I felt ego had been done a great disservice. No judgment of either 'me' or ego was undertaken, merely becoming aware of their feelings and allowing them to express and work through them. A genuine love and want to be kind was felt for ego, I wanted, for the first time in my life to be nice and kind and loving to myself. Even now as I write this chapter, the sense of love for self grows as it is discussed and felt. I have done nothing wrong, I do not deserve punishment, and I am a special person and deserve to be treated as such.

It is a process to eliminate no longer wanted habits, although instantly I notice and act on my wants and needs. I no longer ignore what is good for me. The chapter on difficult lives speaks of this self-abuse issue also.

The third part is spirit, inner knowing or whatever name feels comfortable for you. Many people assume being spiritual involves religion, guides, gurus, or other beings outside us. To me, I am an independent life force, that essence of myself I call my spirit, it is this spirit sense of who I am that is calm and knowing and provides initiation and ideas and original thoughts. Therefore to me, living a spiritual life is undertaking a journey of self discovery into ones spirit self, our true self.

When I feel my spirit I smile, the energy is warm and comforting, and it is good to feel me. When I listen to my intuition or messages from spirit, the activities I then undertake make me smile from the inside out. When I work with people, my knowing and words flow without thought, just as when I write, I feel my spirit self.

Think of a time when you were undertaking an activity that you enjoyed thoroughly, something you feel you need to do, how right it feels. Like the nurse who returns to her professional love, or the man who picks up his musical instrument and begins playing after a long absence, or beginning your writing again, some activity you feel you are meant to do, it flows, it is easy, you smile and feel alive when doing it.

Now think of times when you were too busy to undertake any activities that pleased you, how listless and lifeless you became, something was missing.

To feel our spirit is to feel our life force, that drive and passion and happiness from within, the calm and knowing that all will be well, peace. Spirit is indeed a very special part of us. Yet it will not interfere with our path, our problems and struggles, it sits on the sideline waiting for times when our fears settle and it can freely come to us. Spirit has no fears, no dislike, and no problems. Spirit merely is, an experience in motion.

The man who smiles and has faith, in the face of adversity, the woman who, although her world is falling apart around her, remains peaceful and calm, the young child who is driven to pursue an odd pass-time, stating this is his future, all display spirit energies at work.

Can you find one thing each day to make you smile from the inside out?

Why is it that during recent world events, amidst all the panic and fears, some people remained calm and clear headed, not fearful for their lives at all? Having a strong sense of spirit self is calming, strengthens us and we know all is well, no matter what is appearing around us.

So now, we see the three parts of us, ego, me and spirit, yet being three individual parts of a whole is to feel disjointed. I found it a natural process to recognize and come to learn of my three parts as I undertook my personal work, then as I came to know each well, I began to see a point whereby the three could be merged as one.

Me is the adult person I am now, the organizer, ego is my beliefs and motivator to undertake actions, and spirit is the ideas person. As I allow my ego self to heal and grow up in line with the adult me, I am able to explain its role to ego. Until now it has been responsible for all thinking, comprehending, figuring out and their resultant actions, that is why ego is constantly fearful. It cannot see a way out of situations, cannot grasp faith and belief that all will be well unless it is seen physically before it, ego is a very physical aspect of ourselves.

During the writing of the Self-importance chapter, I accidentally stumbled upon more information of the spirit, me, ego triad. It seems that while the three remain separate, only one is in control at a time and the others are unaware of its actions. While I had undertaken conscious work in creating communication between me and ego, it had not occurred to me that apart from these specific times, there is no direct communication between the two. Neither knows what the other is thinking or doing. An understanding and resolution was found so 'me' and ego learned how to become as one and work together with love and compassion.

Activity - Develop Your Own Understanding

The 'My Thoughts' section was included so you can come back and use it as a chapter to work on once you reach the point of developing more understanding of yourself.

When you are ready to create a deeper understanding of you, read this entire chapter again, then create your own concept of the components that make you, their roles, their personalities, and how they work together.

Review and re-strengthen if necessary the ability and use of your conscious mind to direct your life events.

Pulling The Pieces Together

You have learned so many new things and I am sure seen many changes in yourself and your life already. This section is to regroup, revise and pull everything together so you are ready, willing and able to apply all that you have learned both in the upcoming life topic sections and your everyday life.

Use the contents here as your redirect to pull yourself back to the basics when things get too stressful, undirected, or you are ready to refocus.

Stumbling Blocks

Self beliefs are the reason for all your doubts. You are not accustomed to believing in yourself and your abilities, therefore don't realize that you don't need other people to tell you every answer because they are, and have always been within you.

All you need to do is focus on becoming a competent director of the release process and then everything else will automatically happen. This is your role and the most important skill to teach yourself in order to self direct your future life.

When you complete this chapter you will be able to:

- Bring yourself back to the basics when you get stuck
- Feel in control of all that you do in your healing work
- Learn how to believe in and trust your own inner knowing

Scared To Feel

Sometimes the triggers and emotions will seem so strong that you fear letting yourself feel them completely. If you remain calm and focused on your role as director, you will soon discover that the ones that seem to be the most emotional are the quickest and easiest ones to complete. So decide to do it, reassuring yourself that it will be over with very soon, and then you can feel much better.

Extreme Topics

Perhaps the issue and experience of the child is so horrific that you can't think of anything that could make it alright, so you hesitate doing the release at all.

Use your conscious mind to patiently control the situation, comfort yourself by remembering to trust the process and your inner knowing. Imagine how wonderful it will be to never feel this pain again, so do whatever you need to in order to help this person (you) let it go.

The 'How do I know the new belief?' section below suggests methods for dealing with these topics.

I Can't Get To It

You feel something stirring, but feel as if you are not able to get to it. Again this is a common thought people have and one that can sabotage your work and confidence.

You are in charge, so you decide what you want to do. Is it an issue you are determined to finish with? Then do it by following the procedure. As soon as you stop thinking and let yourself feel, it will pop up.

Thinking Too Much

Thinking about issues that are triggered is another way to sabotage yourself. The thinking and answers you hear are coming from ego's fears, and not your rational mind.

Haven't you spent enough time thinking and worrying about the fears in your life? That is all this thinking is. Wasting

Heal Your Self

time thinking about the baggage in your ego mind. You couldn't have these thoughts if the belief had been released, so decide if you want to live your life like this or release it permanently.

Old theory was to use affirmations to control your thoughts, but now you know where they come from, so instead of masking them behind affirmations, you can remove their cause, permanently.

Whenever you notice yourself debating topics back and forth, or wanting answers prior to the release, stop, come back to your conscious determination and do the procedure.

It's really interesting to notice how quiet your mind gets as the fears and beliefs are cleared. There is no baggage to think about. Then you start to automatically think about wondrous things you could do with your life. Much nicer things to think about than fears.

Staying In The Drama

When you find yourself overwhelmed with the emotions of a topic, and can't think straight, your thoughts are not rational enough to direct a release.

Come back to the basics and look at the role you are playing in this experience, and decide if you wish to remain in the emotions or end the play. By making yourself step outside to look at the situation like a third person, or saying the 5 times table back and forth to kick in your logic mind, you will ground and be able to do the release.

The topic of dramas and roles we play is addressed in detail within the 'Experience' chapter.

Forgetting To Do It

Every single time a client tells me that they have a problem with an issue, I ask "what does it feel like?" and they instantly become un-stuck.

Whenever you feel stuck, stop, feel and listen. You are stuck because you forgot to feel and go from there.

Negative Self Talk

Whenever we attempt to do anything, ego is kind enough to share all of its fears and doubts of what can go wrong (Doesn't believe it can work, too difficult, fear of change, don't need to change anything, etc.) Previously, we accepted this advice, but now we know it is fear based and we do not have to let it impact on our life.

So you can do one of two things. One, feel and listen to ego's story and decide to remove its cause permanently by doing a quick release. Or secondly, if it is a topic that is way outside your current one, listen, thank ego's input, and write its fears down on a list of topics to address in the future. Then you can ignore ego's input and decide for yourself.

Sabotage

Change is scary, letting your deepest fears come up is scary, all that you are doing for yourself can be viewed as very scary to an already nervous ego self.

Therefore it will not come as any surprise that your fearful child self might throw out some obstacles to sabotage your healing work (no time, lack of concentration needed to do releasing, can't find the pang, feeling physically ill instead of feeling the emotions).

Become aware of what is happening, then step back as your calm conscious self and decide what to do. Remember that the more you ignore ego's cries, the louder he or she will scream them out. So resolve the situation then it doesn't have to happen again.

Feel, listen and understand the fears or concerns so you can decide whether you need to do a release or merely provide comfort and care while ego gets use to the situation. Sometimes when ego screams loudly about new insights, sidetracking your thoughts with a different activity for a few days will give ego a chance to get use to the change, therefore alleviate it completely.

Frustration

We have lived with situations for decades, yet as soon as we decide to resolve it we want instant answers. Then if they don't appear as if by magic we decide that it is pointless and give up.

Come back to your conscious mind, think clearly without fear about the topic and decide its importance to you!

Then you can make a game plan to include the knowing and guidance of your inner self, or how to make time everyday to focus on this issue so it will get resolved piece by piece.

For example, say money is the topic and you desperately need it, but nothing is materializing. Come back to the basics, escape the drama of the situation and take a fresh look at the entire topic. Regroup and plan how you will complete it. Remember that if you focus each day on wanting this one finished to increase your determination, events will happen to trigger that happening. Notice everything and release whatever comes up. Perhaps making time every night to stop and think about the issue, feel and listen to what comes up, and do the release. Then becoming more aware of situations that present themselves each day.

I Don't Know What To Do

People want someone to tell them what to do. They want guidance and advice because they have not yet discovered how to believe in themselves.

You don't need me to tell you what to do. You have learned how to release, you are learning something new about you every day, so isn't it time that you started to listen to the intelligence that is inside you?

Activity - Discover You

This activity will teach you how to stop needing the outside world to 'tell you', so you can begin to open the door to your own inner knowing. For one entire week, consciously stop and notice each time you think about needing an answer to something (what to do, what is the right thing, how to decide etc.), stop the automatic thoughts of looking for someone out there to provide it, and ask yourself for this answer, then feel and listen. Doing this may seem strange at first, but once you start to automatically ask yourself for answers, they will come automatically without you having to think of the need for them.

Discover how, by asking yourself for answers, you are acknowledging your own ability and what that feels like. Learn how to trust in you, and how to believe in you. Learn to follow your gut instincts and let the all knowing confidence and love of your inner self become part of your life. Open the door to your inner self.

How Do I Know The New Belief?

You will experience a gradual range of release types and new beliefs as you take this journey. It is not uncommon for people to want the answers prior to being able to do a release. Kind of like reinforcing to themselves that if they do this scary thing everything will be alright. These thoughts are ego fears and nothing more. You are quite able to comfort ego so they settle.

1. Initially, the new belief is automatically known by your conscious mind, as discussed in the Greene's Release chapters.

2. As you progress you will feel like you need to know more about the issue prior to being able to undertake the release. That's fine because I have included exercises to assist your formation of new concepts and understanding, ready for you to use with these releases.

Don't worry about not having the answer for a new belief prior, because the new understanding you developed will automatically allow the new belief to come as soon as the release is finished.

3. Gradually, your new beliefs will start to come from your inner self's knowing. They will be profound.

4. Sometimes the issue and experience of the child is so horrific that you can't think of anything that could make it alright, so you hesitate doing the release at all.

Extreme abuse or the death of a parent are a good examples. If you follow the process and do whatever you naturally feel led to do, your answers will come and it *will* be okay.

I personally felt my child being held by a cloud of love and carried off into the sky after this release. She found the most profound peace imaginable.

After the release, one of my clients had a conversation with their deceased mother, who had all of the perfect answers for them. Their epiphany was beyond anything they had ever experienced.

5. At some point you will reach the stage of needing to 'let go of something' rather than release it. This can feel overwhelming because in ego's mind, if you let go of your strong need for some condition then it means you can never have it.

Letting go of the expectation that everyone who loves you will act in one specific way, and if they don't then they don't truly love you can feel extreme. But as you decide to let it go and feel the despair of never having love again, and sink further and further into that, once you reach the point of giving it up fully, you will come out of the fog (feeling a sense of emptiness rather that the high of a release). It will assimilate so you feel balanced again within a day or to, then you'll be able to see the love that people shower you with every day.

Whatever the situation, know that the more you listen to you, the easier and speedier the process will be. I think that perhaps that is the point of all of this. Putting yourself in your own hands and feeling safe and trusting of that.

Every single one of your new beliefs will feel good. It is impossible to have a true self belief that does not feel wonderful.

Everything that does not feel good is foreign. Focus on becoming fully aware of the things that do not feel good, and know that they are the ones to be removed from your being because they are foreign and not yours.

A New View of Life

Are you happy with your life and where it is heading? Are you always in catch up mode from one life drama to the next? Are you living the life you want? Are you feeling good about yourself and your abilities?

What if there was a way to view life and all that it encompasses differently? To change the game tactics?

When you complete this chapter you will be able to:

- Appreciate the bigger picture of yourself, your life and the control you can have in dictating its direction
- Make a decision of what steps to take next
- Feel confident and motivated to create the life you desire

Living as a human being brings with it some amazing mechanisms of forced self-learning. It is indeed a journey of self-discovery. One in which we take on beliefs of ourselves, the world around us and how we fit into it; then perpetuate repeat situations to validate those beliefs, finally reaching a point of being forced to question them, as the only means of escape from the situations they create. To teach what to believe about self for oneself.

Let me clarify. A person believes they are a failure; this

experience is perpetuated in various repeat situations throughout their life. No matter what successes are achieved, the belief of failure is prominent, inevitably resulting in successes floundering. Life becomes more extreme until a crisis point is reached; now other people are also affected so this person must find some solution. They finally look into self and face their beliefs and fears of failure, a release is achieved, and a way is found to come to know self is no failure, self is a wonderful human being. This person finds from deep within a new sense, feeling and belief of self. This person is changed forever.

Each belief creates a drama, or play, to enable full experience of the belief. This is required so we will be pushed to look beyond the obvious, to question. Then eventually reach the goal of self-learning. We believe we are poor so may experience all manner of financial nightmares. We believe we are unloved or unlovable, and dismay at how that is mirrored back to us repeatedly. We believe we will never have sufficient, so are forced to watch in horror as everything we accumulate vanishes before our eyes.

Every experience is so we have the future opportunity to know and live its opposite!

You are indeed living what you believe. So if you don't like what you are living, change what you believe about you and your life. It is a simple concept, yet determination, perseverance, and work are required.

Life may be viewed as a series of plays then; each with the purpose of forced inner learning, each where we are to teach ourselves some personal value of self. So, what if once we realize this, we turn it around so instead of being dragged through life without any sense of input or control, we are able to stand back and remove ourselves from the emotions of living the plays, to dictate our own rules of this game?

What if we then realize all those around us are living this same experience, of beliefs for personal learning? We can stand in a crowded room and feel the enormity of this realization, for it is truly awesome. We are surrounded in a world of people, all undertaking the exact same journey as ourselves, each with their own beliefs and dramas and plays, each feeling in no more control of this game than we do.

What if we look at all the implications of this play? The parts we play in perpetuating it. Beliefs, the living experience, life purpose, dreams and how to achieve them, lessons, releasing and healing emotions, reasons for hurtful situations, feeling, fears, loss/lack/failure, perceptions, free will, we choose how we feel, energy, ego, money, love, relationships, work, difficult lives, health and vitality, strength and belief in self, triumph of spirit as we undertake this work, imagination, creativity, ideals and putting it all together.

We can indeed come to know and feel the sense of a journey of finding true self. To be fully aware and in control of this living experience; planning, evaluating and enjoying knowing each step is one closer to our goal and dreams. We can find value and purpose and a hope in living and of our future.

The emotions we experience during the plays are but one small part of ourselves. Yet we allow them to rule our quality of life. Isn't it time we search out and demand more for ourselves? Don't we deserve that? Isn't it time we become more constructive and purposeful with this life experience?

Activity - What Do You Think?

What do you think of the ideas presented in this chapter?

Write your thoughts about each one and form your own conclusions, which I am sure will be modified as you work through this book.

Living Consciously
How to apply what you have learned

This chapter is to cement your understanding of the tools and techniques that you have learned so you may not only apply them while you work through the upcoming chapters, but also in your everyday life.

- Feeling
- Triggers
- Releasing
- Energy
- Fear
- The 3 parts of You
- Life Goals
- Meditation and Dream Life
- Intuitive Reading
- Journal Writing
- Awareness and Knowledge
- Research, Understand, Forming own Conclusions/Concepts

You have learned and used all of the tools above, now one by one, go through the list and reinforce your understanding by writing about each in detail.

Using Feeling as an example. It is one thing to learn how to make specific time to feel and enjoy the sensations of feeling as you did in the feeling chapter, but another entirely to have to describe what feeling is, its benefits, how it can be used, how you avoided it previously and now apply it.

What about the way feeling is used to discover topics to be released, hidden issues, fears and your inner dreams? Create your own unique understanding of feeling as a concept.

This may seem silly, but try just one and watch your understanding and knowledge blossom, and imagine how much easier it will now be to incorporate this topic into your healing work and daily life.

The ability to apply the information contained in the upcoming chapters which teach you how to make the life altering changes you desire, is dependant on the application of the tools and techniques learned thus far. They are critical to your journey, so make it as easy as you can for yourself by making sure that you have a complete understanding of each.

Working Through This Book

Chapters introduce new ideas and are meant to trigger you feeling your related issues. You may feel strong emotions, hurts, fears or sadness, from any of the three parts of you, whatever you feel is perfect for you. Each chapter is for you to go right into your own experience of the particular topic addressed. Feel it, live it, become it, and heal it.

Read the entire chapter without doing or thinking about anything, then come back to the beginning and use your intuitive reading skills to read each sentence purposefully, think how it applies to you, feel and listen to what emotions are triggered.

If there is an exercise that applies to this trigger do it and finish with the topic before continuing to read.

If there is not a related exercise, let yourself feel the trigger, listen to the stories revealed, form an understanding of the topic, the implications on you and your life, keep feeling and listening until you reach the pang, then release and listen for the new story and/or knowing that flows through.

Use the exercises provided to discover hidden issues, form new understanding, do releases and create new beliefs. Remember to also use your own ability to investigate the topic discussed. Want to learn all about this issue, from your own perspective, for yourself.

When you finish each chapter write the story of this topic in your life, the past, what you discovered and the new understanding you have formed of it.

When you finish each section write the story of all that you learned and how it is relative to you and your life. What it means, the possibilities, how it has changed your perceptions and improved your daily life.

Unexpected Life Challenges

Because you have embarked on a journey of wanting to heal your fears and beliefs, they will begin to stir and show themselves automatically in your everyday life.

But as we all know, when something unexpected happens in our lives, we automatically focus on it at the expense of everything else.

REMEMBER that the reason you are working with this book is to heal and eliminate the impact of your past experiences and beliefs on your current life, and to take charge and consciously create the future life of your choice.

When unexpected life challenges occur remember to pull yourself back to the tools you are learning in this book, and do the work to finish with whatever is creating the challenge.

Create a mindset of welcoming everything that surfaces, whether related to a topic you are working on in this book, or during your everyday life, because it is one more thing that you can permanently remove forever!

Resolving Unexpected Life Challenges

1. Know that every single unpleasant emotion, event or circumstance comes from a belief or stored past memory.
   Disagreements with family, employment or money difficulties, health problems etc. are all topics that can be resolved by using the tools and techniques in this book.

2. Stop and notice what is happening, become aware.

3. Come back to the basics of feeling and using Greene's Release for EVERYTHING that comes up!

4. Whether it is a topic you are working on in this book, or a totally separate issue, use the same process.

5. If you feel overwhelmed, let yourself feel that and release it as its own topic. Do whatever you need to step out of the emotional drama so you can take the necessary steps to resolve the issue permanently, rather than stay in the play which does nothing to end it.

Living Life Consciously

Conscious living is about coming out of the fog and help-less-ness view of life to be completely aware that you are in control of what you want, where you are headed, and what you have to do to get there.

You know how you are feeling at all times, are able to stop and recognize events and feelings that do not feel good, make firm decisions to clear obstacles and refuse to accept repeats, get on with doing the healing work without effort or fuss and enjoy happy and fulfilling experiences each day. Here are some examples.

Awareness: Notice how you feel and recognize the activities that make you smile from the inside out and those that make you uncomfortable.

Action: Taking charge and do something to permanently heal any discomfort, obstacles, or emotions that surface.

Experience: Live in the 'now' so you experience everything fully, then if you don't like it, do the work to prevent it ever happening again.

Planning To Live Consciously

This involves using all the tools at your disposal to deliberately plan and create a life that is filled with everything that you dream of doing. Plan time for relaxing and meditating, reading and healing, pondering and floating in energy, when to work and when to play, time to care for you, how you will incorporate each new insight into your daily life, specific times to review and modify your dream life, goals and activity cards. Here are some examples.

Daily: Relaxation and you time, activity card, reviewing the day and releasing or healing anything that is left unfinished, writing. Falling asleep as you float away in meditation or your dream life.

Weekly: Special feeling and/or relaxation activity, plan reading and healing work time, reviewing the week's activities, learning and achievements, planning special events or things to focus your attention on during the next week, attainable goals to reach.

Monthly: Review and modify your dream life and goals, write a summary of your achievements, plan what is to come next, things to do during the next month, how you will spend time enjoying life.

I Feel Something But Am Unsure What It Relates To?

Whenever you feel anything uncomfortable all you have to do is feel, listen, and go within to discover the topic so you may resolve it. Just as you do with releasing.

Becoming aware and interested in what is happening in your life will help you see clearly.

Sometimes when a new concept comes up on its own, you need to have formed your own understanding prior to being able to go in and release or let go. Just be aware and curious about what it means, then you will automatically find your answers. See below 'How do I learn about a new topic/concept?'

Listen to what you feel and trust your gut instinct of what feels right to do. You will find that all of the answers you seek can only come from within you!

I Don't Know Anything About This Topic, Should I Ask Someone or Look For A Book To Read About It?

No, you don't need anyone else to tell you what to believe any more! This book gives you the tools and techniques to become a strong and independent person who knows how to go inside, find your own answers and form your own beliefs on any topic.

How Can I Learn About A New Topic/Concept Then?

Investigate! Want to know all about it! Forming your own understanding and beliefs of a new concept is rather like a school research project, with an added twist. With an open and interested mind you gather available information from various sources like your own thoughts and experiences, the dictionary, friends, and books.

But, unlike the usual process where after deciding that they want to know about a topic, people then open themselves up to **listen** and **believe** everything that other people say about it, hence forming a new belief of happiness **based on other people's beliefs**, we gather information with the intention of wanting to make our own decisions of what to conclude about the concept.

When you read, and listen, and remember, without the automatic assumption that whoever said it must be correct, you are free to review, ponder and decide to believe whatever feels good to you, without guilt or doubt that you are allowed to do this.

Just because someone said that "you are not allowed to feel happy" does not mean it is written in stone. It is their opinion and you are free to say okay, that is your belief but I can choose to live my life with my own belief "I am free to live a happy life".

We are creating new beliefs, new understanding and new lives because we are choosing what to believe for ourselves. You can always tell when you have found your answer because it makes you smile. If it doesn't, then you aren't finished yet.

We grew up taking on other people's beliefs blindly, and look where it got us, into a painful mess. Therefore your goal is to investigate and come up with your own unique concept and belief of topics, just like you did with the 'Smile' exercise in 'The Plan'.

If you are still unsure about how to develop your own views on a topic note it down, and as you read some of the chapters become more aware of the process I used to investigate each. Many chapters are written as pondering sessions, and in the process of doing so I found my answers and understanding. The concept of Happiness in 'To Change or Not to Change' is a good example of the process.

When you feel ready, go back to your notes on the topic of interest and try it for yourself and see what comes up.

It is very cool and so much fun to create your very own concepts of life.

Activity - Conclusion

Spend a week thinking about this chapter, and all that you have experienced and learned thus far, then come to a conclusion and write about your life and what you want before moving onto the next section.

Review your dream life, goals, and your current situations and make a list, then divide it into 'things I wish to change' and 'things I have to change'.

This conclusion you make automatically becomes your decision and your new belief of what you can have, therefore will have in your life.

Now, plan how you will implement the tools so you begin to live your Life Consciously.

I wish you the very best you can dream for yourself!

Healing Childhood Issues

The first stage of healing work is to clear childhood issues which mostly come up by themselves as soon as you start thinking about your childhood.

You may find yourself beginning at the earliest part of your life and progressing through, or heading straight to the major issues. Whatever comes up on its own is the perfect way for childhood releasing. Know and have faith in this.

Most people have just a few major issues which they are fully aware of, therefore those become the first to surface. All that is needed is to sit quietly and think on the topic, and listen, feel, and follow the lead. Telling yourself that once you do this, you will never feel it again!

As these are completed a definite change is felt. Then people begin listening and following everyday triggers as they surface, surprised to find more hidden and forgotten childhood issues.

Remember to plan specific times to do your healing work. When things surface outside those times, take note and tell them you will undertake this topic at the planned time. This will quiet them.

There is no rush to complete the work, each clearing/healing you do will change you as a person and help you feel better.

You may do one clearing a day, or week. Know that everything you do is your choice, so do what you feel led to,

Heal Your Self

what feels right to do. Whatever you do will be just fine.

Read through each chapter in its entirely, then come back to the beginning and go through it slowly, stopping to do the work for each emotion that is triggered. Take your time and work with them one by one.

Healing can be rather deep and emotional; if we become too focused within it the other parts of our lives may be affected. Please be careful not to become overwhelmed, and if you should, stop work for a while and relax. When you are ready to continue you will know.

As each belief is cleared your outlook will improve and you will gain an understanding of why you are who you are.

When you can sit and read a chapter, thinking carefully about its content and the goals listed, yet feel nothing, then you are ready to move onto the next.

For those inquisitive people who do read all the chapters immediately, then find themselves feeling the pang of too many triggers, stop, go into a quiet space and remind yourself that you have been living with these issues for a long time, so there is nothing new. Tell yourself that you now know how to resolve any issue you choose to, and will one by one when the time is right. This will quiet them down, so you can come back to the beginning, and do one chapter at a time.

Note

Unless the behavior rules your parents taught you, social norms, control and abuse issues surface on their own, leave them for when you work on the Abuse/Inhibitions chapter. This will prevent you becoming too overloaded with triggers.

Reasons/Beliefs/ Working with Fears

As I have said, the reasons behind all the hurt and sadness we experience in our lives is purely for experience, learning and growth, but as I have myself, I am sure you are questioning the validity of the ends justifying the means. This chapter provides a new perspective for you.

When you complete this chapter you will be able to:

- Appreciate the bigger picture of life experiences and issues
- Form new concepts of the ends justifying the means
- Release the sadness for your inner child

Beginning lessons do bring painful memories and feelings, but they are the quickest lessons to heal. You will be much stronger, experienced in helping yourself through this work, and far more knowledgeable about the workings of events prior to commencing deeper lessons, the ones you now fear facing.

When the time is right and you are ready, a natural progression will occur between the types of lessons. You will find the initial lessons that come up will relate to all manner of situation, some, you will visit several times. Each time from a different perspective, a different angle of the topic. Just because you find a topic that you have already done work on does not mean you were unsuccessful in clearing it properly.

For an example let's look at the young woman who was attending a wedding (from Greene's Release), initially she felt the issue of embarrassment at facing people who knew what happened. First we worked through that issue, which resulted in her then feeling comfortable about attending the wedding, then she thought about the event again and listened for related issues, which were then released one by one. Rejection, being lied to, deceived etc. Each a very different emotion and release although from the same issue or event.

I call them simple or quickest lessons for a specific reason. Beginning lessons tend to be those you already have the new belief understood, ready and waiting to replace the old one, you automatically know the new belief to tell the child as you watch the movie being played. They are emotionally hard, I know, but the plus side is that once you allow yourself to really feel, the rest will fall into place and you will never feel it again.

Let's think then on some of the ends justifying the means. They are just as painful, felt very deeply and effect many aspects of who we become and how we live our lives. When we think on them we may feel regret or sadness or even anger at that happening to a young child. We may feel depressed at the thought of more hurtful experiences coming into our lives, and to think of reliving those most painful times, scary and unwanted.

Let me assure you, and you can prove this to yourself easily, until old hurts are healed they keep surfacing time after time after time. Think about that for yourself. Think on how many times the same issue keeps popping up in your life. That is the way of it.

Feeling this sadness, you may ask, why? What purpose can justify all this pain? To answer this clearly and provide information for your own thought, I would like to briefly speak of what I believe is the purpose of life. As I said earlier in relation to expanding Dorothy L Nolte's piece 'Children learn what they live', there are many concepts of knowledge we only do learn through experience. Experience is indeed our teacher. For how could we learn compassion if people around us were not in need of it? How would we be forced to come to our own conclusions that we are not 'too fat', 'too thin', dumb, unable, and all the rest, unless we are led into situations where we have to find out for ourselves? What better way to realize and learn from the deepest core of our being how special love is, than to experience it in its entirety, then loose it. What about learning to believe in our own abilities and strengths and belonging?

We do indeed learn many, many self beliefs from our environment as we grow up, yet the more profound ones, the deeper spiritual ones only come from experiences where we are able to teach ourselves these things. As you felt after your first release.

Would you rather not have the opportunity of learning about self-love, compassion, tolerance, forgiveness, and acceptance? We are each individual, independent beings, who as you have hopefully begun to realize are responsible for all our thoughts, feelings and beliefs through our perceptions. So how would it be possible that something or someone outside us is able to teach us these deep beliefs, simply by their actions and our non-involvement? Are we watchers of living or participants?

Perhaps a couple of true stories may help cement my intended meaning. This first story is of an adopted child. The personal issues of adoption are profound; self worth, value, being wanted, being loved, belonging, just to name a few. This story involves the issue of abandonment of one mother, feeling unwanted by the new mother and sadness at the whole situation having to happen.

Whether you believe in yourself being a spirit, reincarnation, life after death, anything of a spiritual nature does not matter. Remember that everything only relates to what you feel. So if it seems silly but it feels right, so what. If it is something that allows you to feel and therefore find peace about a situation, a replacement positive belief, use it. You will know and not be able to use anything that doesn't 'feel' right, or match

Heal Your Self

your inner knowing.

This is a story a lady was told when she was attempting to find rationale to explain to her hurt child about adoption. She could see no explanation that made sense so would work. This story changed her whole perception and allowed her to create a way of not only accepting what happened, but only to feel love for it and everyone involved. She found peace.

When a child is adopted may people are involved, the birth mother, the adoptive mother and the child herself. Many say, and I believe, that we lead many lives and that we decide and plan what we wish to learn in this life before it is begun. For us to set up what is needed, the other participants must be organized. These participants agree to act in ways they would never wish, to do things that hurt and harm others, but agree because they are asked to do so by the person affected.

Back to the story. With this particular woman's adoption, her birth mother agreed to give up a sacred part of herself, one that grew within her for 9 months, and the love naturally shared between mother and child. The adoptive mother agreed to give up her ability to bring life into the world, to feel growth within her, to reproduce part of herself, and to raise another person's child with none of her own characteristics or looks or likes. The gift these two women gave this child is amazing to think on in this light. What love must have been involved for another soul. What self-sacrifice and self-hurt accepted merely to fulfill another's wanted experience.

And the child. She herself set up horrendous hurt and harm. To feel the rejection and want of a mother she could never have, to herself reject the one who took her home and raised her, because she was not the right one, to join in the set up herself and retreat from all who loved her because she didn't want this event. What strong personal learning this woman chose within this life.

I truly salute all three women! Courage, strength, and the purest unconditional love!

After hearing this story the woman wept, personally feeling

the love of this event. How could she ever feel regret or blame for these two women, or to not be loved so deeply? How could she not know what a very special being she is?

That is the point of all this. That is the magic of living, and personally, I would live each and every painful experience over again, just for knowing how special the learning I have felt from each has been. I have come to this conclusion slowly as I progressed through my lessons and growing, so don't be alarmed or unsure if you do not feel it now. Instead please feel my strength of conviction in the hope and knowing I speak of, for I couldn't unless it was believed deeply.

Can it hurt to try and see if there is another way? What have you to loose? Pain, hardship, repeats? If any of what I have said feels right, or makes sense, or seems logical, take that as my goal and find your own thoughts on all I speak of.

Another story involves my own daughter. One of the hardest decisions I have ever faced was to leave her, my grandson and my parents behind in Australia, when my son and I moved to America. A mother does not abandon her child. But, we all decided this was what had to happen, there was no choice, so we just had to deal as best we could.

It was incredibly hard, I ached for her and felt incredible guilt constantly. Every time we spoke to each other I cried, and for the rest of that day, every time I thought of her or mentioned her to friends, my heart ached. I knew she felt the same, yet we never spoke of it. This went on for more than a year.

Something changed when she became pregnant. Our contact increased from exceptionally rare icq messages back and forth to regular telephone calls, 3 times weekly online contact, my grandson began using icq as well. He delighted in racing me with messages. I was told he was very animate and vocal as he typed his odd number and letter messages, he could not read or write yet. I enjoyed this time with him immensely, he began feeling and knowing me again, we re-found our relationship that was very special prior to my leaving when he was a mere 2 years old. He now calls me 'my nan' again, as he use to.

Over the months my daughter came back to asking all the questions she use to, the little things about recipes and child rearing, the usual discussions between mother and daughter. But she was different, a new strength and belief in self was immerging, my baby was growing up. She would tell me of her relationship with her son, the crazy conversations they had, their activities and her parenting strategies. Conversations with my daughter made me smile again, we were finally re-building our relationship. I literally watched my daughter mature before my very eyes, it was wonderful to experience. A most outstanding young woman and incredibly devoted, intuitive and good mother. I am more proud of her than words can convey, and always tell her so.

The point of this story I hope has become clear. Yes it was tragic that a mother and daughter were separated, half a world away, but, because of that separation the child has been given her wings. To fly and experience and find herself, for herself. Often difficult when parents and children are together.

My daughter is now self-sufficient, determined, strong, has a strong belief developing in self, and best of all, she is happy. Another aspect of this is we are all learning from first hand experience that physical separation is not real. We are connected and no matter where we are, that will remain. As she finds, I am coincidentally always online when she wants to speak to me, I always have the answers to what she seeks, I feel her whenever she thinks of me, and she feels me. We are together in love and spirit, and feel as close as if we lived around the corner from each other. This lesson of love and separation is a deep one to experience.

The Fear chapter discussed various categories and implications of our fears. I have found that fear itself is more a topic to flow with, rather than become impatient to eliminate quickly. You will find, as you proceed through the chapters, very few do not contain something related to fear. We do fear our life situations, so naturally we experience fear. As I progressed along my journey, discovering then releasing each belief and its associated fear, I very soon found a calmness, a peacefulness creeping into my person and life. I am sure you will do so also. All I can suggest is that rather than put aside your feelings of fear, face them head on with intent. Make the decision that you no longer wish to feel this, and decide to remove the cause of each fear. Your triggers to do so will then come forth and be recognized.

Activity - Sadness

If you think about it, we do go through many sad experiences and it is very hard to think of children suffering.

You may be feeling this quite strongly, good. That means you are beginning to feel compassion for your child self, rather than the usual condemnation. Allow yourself to feel **sadness** for this child, and his/her experiences. Focus on sadness as your topic, **not** the things that happened to him/her, just the sadness. Listen and feel, let it come up and tell the story, so you are able to release this pain and tell the new story, for which I will give you a hint. Just as you would hold and share comfort with your own child, do it with your inner child. Tell her all that he/she has wanted to hear, that you will be there for him/her. Help, and be by his/her side. That you love him/her.

Activity - Write About Your Experience

This chapter has introduced many new ideas and concepts, so spend some time clearing your thoughts and relating it to you so it makes sense. Grasping an understanding will greatly help you work through the childhood issues in the next chapter.

Write your thoughts and beginning understanding of each topic that has been presented. You may wish to relate as many as you can to you and write about them.

Do your Greene's Release for any that you feel strongly.

The Hurt Child

This chapter requires very little explanation as we all remember our childhood events clearly. It does not matter whether your childhood was happy and loving, full of neglect and abuse, or non-eventful. They were each filled with hurts and fears, sadness and regrets.

When you complete this chapter you will be able to:

- Know what to expect of healing work
- Direct your child self through releasing sessions
- Comfort your child self
- Clear childhood issues

To be a child is to evaluate and take on countless beliefs of who we are and our place in the world. From a child's perception. That last sentence is the key, because each age came with natural perceptions that encouraged us to find fear in the world, and test for comfort, love and protection from our caregivers.

A baby may feel abandoned if mother leaves them for a short time, a toddler distraught if told no, a preschooler unprotected if its fears are not reassured, even when the parent knows there is nothing to fear, a youngster unloved if that proof of care and love is not instantly forthcoming.

If this is not a belief you have about your parents that's fine. Being the primary caregivers, parents facilitate a vast range of situations for children to experience. Neglect, abuse, criticism, disapproval, lack of love and compassion to name a few. There are many events children experience so we can learn and become its opposite. It is nice to carry the thought that the exact opposite is the result you will find.

When you finish clearing your family issues, understanding, forgiveness, reasons, etc it will become clear naturally, so there is no need to focus on them now.

I am yet to find a person, with whom the first major direction of releasing work is not about their parents and family. We begin our work at the beginning of this life. You may be like me and remember the first moments of your life onwards, or only have vague glimpses of episodes. Its okay, because your subconscious knows all that is required. Your role is merely to facilitate access.

Up until this point in our lives, we have avoided rerunning those childhood movies; we do not wish to feel the pain again. We know the stories well and have pushed them back out of view, in an attempt to forget. Or you may have spent much time pondering the sadness of your childhood and feel you have already healed it.

Until we replay the movies in a way so as to become part of them, from the emotional perspective of that child, honor and listen to their stories openly even if they don't make sense or seem silly, take charge and do the releasing with breathing, feel our mature selves come back into being, then hold, comfort and love that child, telling them a new explanation for the event, each and every hurt is still held within our subconscious and affects every aspect of us and our lives.

You may have used other methods along your journey. A clear way to know if they have been released and healed fully is to feel. If you can think of a painful situation and feel nothing at all but peace, then it is healed. Yet, if it is already finished with, it wouldn't come to mind as a painful experience because there wouldn't be any emotional pain left. Basically, all you need do is relax, feel and let it flow. Decide to do this clearing work and it will be so.

As each feeling comes up, most often after being triggered by something in your current life or while reading this book, keep asking the why questions, keep following that lead and path to the source of the feeling, and allow yourself to feel everything, no matter what it is. Knowing as soon as you do, you can make it disappear forever!

Current Events

Here are some examples of how current events lead back to childhood issues.

A lady volunteered at a local festival, yet found it to be a most disturbing event. She felt that the stall was not an honorable one as it was in opposition to her ethics. She fulfilled her duty as promised and felt quite ill by the end of the day. When we discussed this, it very quickly became apparent that ethics and her family's judgment of hers was the issue. She followed this lead back through the layers to her childhood and discovered an experience where she was not accepted for who she was and what she believed. She was not loved for herself.

A man met and fell in love, only to be shunned when the lady became fearful. He felt physically ill in his stomach and chest for some unknown reason. When we followed this lead we found a childhood belief about abandonment and lost love. This current situation was a direct repeat.

Another man experienced constant anger and rage, for no particular reason it appeared. Allowing then following the feelings led him to discover that the cause was unresolved rage at a parent who did not believing in him. He realized they were wrong, and felt great freedom after arriving at that conclusion.

Then there are the obvious issues like the death of a parent, physical inability to care for a child, abuse or failure to protect. With all, the emotions and beliefs are carried strongly.

Activity - Listen For Your Triggers

Do you feel anything after reading this chapter so far? Are any of your current life experiences coming to mind? Whatever pops up, whether it relates to your childhood or adult life its fine. It has surfaced for a reason, so let yourself feel, follow the lead and do your Greene's Release.

Activity - Heal What I Believe Of Myself

Did you know that everything you think about yourself is a direct result of what someone else told or led you to believe?

Make a list of everything you think about yourself. From I'm no good, not good enough, can't do anything right, dumb, too fat, too thin, not worth anything, not lovable, all of them. Can you imagine the impact on a person who believes these?

Write the opposites next to each one and know that there is nothing wrong with you! It is all what they told you to believe, nothing to do with what you did or who you are!

Keep using this list as your trigger until you can read it and feel nothing. Remember to find your own special new belief to tell the child after healing each.

Activity - Heal Childhood Issues

Make a list of all of the childhood memories you can think of, then use this list as a trigger for your releasing sessions until you can read the list and feel nothing. Take time with this one.

Abuse/Inhibitions

Many of us have had the experience of being controlled, whether as children or adults. We can begin to notice how often we still hear their voices in our head, telling us the right way to do things, telling us we are always wrong, always reminding us that they know best and we know nothing. What awful words and beliefs to constantly hear!

When you complete this chapter you will be able to:

- Recognize control and abuse issues
- Release and heal your control and abuse issues
- Reevaluate your own controlling behaviors
- Undertake relationship abuse healing

Trips to the Laundromat always leave me in awe of how particular and neat Americans are with their laundry. Each fold and crease has to be in a certain place, which then when stacked creates the perfect pile. The opposite of my own casual way. It is amazing to watch, especially as I have never even thought of clothes and towels being folded in this manner. And the sheets, well. They are so perfect they would slide straight back into the plastic pocket originally purchased in.

The other day, I was exchanging pleasantries with a lady,

then as I became yet again intrigued by this phenomenon of meticulous handling of laundry, I asked "are American's really taught or trained how to fold laundry? It seems everyone is so proficient at it".

We both laughed then she began telling me of her particular 'training' from her mother. I don't understand how, but it seems that some American children spend considerable time participating in laundry duties. Being taught the parents specific methods, and severely reprimanded if not precise.

She showed me how everything had to be folded in from the outside edge, so no rough edges could be seen, and how if you did it with a certain measurement, when folded again, they sat as flat as can be.

This lady then went on to tell me the correct handling she was taught about each item. I commented how she casually folded some items and she described them as rags, so they didn't matter. But, how her mother would be absolutely horrified if she knew these so called rags were washed with the good items. Four ragged face cloths could not be washed with the good face cloths. Interesting.

It seems the care of laundry goes further than the folding. Specific bleaches and cleaners are used, and after folding so perfectly, once home again even sheets are unfolded, ironed, then refolded perfectly again.

All I could do was laugh when I tried to fold my washing neatly, unable to give it the necessary focus and intent to do so.

At one point I asked this lady if she enjoyed laundry. She didn't, but said she 'had' to do it this way, her mother's way.

That is the comment that got me thinking.

That woman, without any realization, undertakes this regular activity while still being controlled by her mother's desires and expectations. Another's way has become hers, not by choice or comparing then deciding it is preferred, but because that is the way it 'has' to be done.

Each item she folds is against her own desire to do and be her innate self. When we think about it, this concept is rather like that inner voice we hear, telling us what and how to do and behave, about everything.

It seems like a little watchdog sits on our shoulders ready to tell us that every thought and desire we have is not appropriate and why, then going on to how it should be done. The right way, the socially accepted way, the way that will not embarrass or disgrace our families.

The implications of this concept are enormous to say the least. How I dress, appear, groom, behave during all situations, even when standing in a line at the store, when I should and should not speak, the correct thing to say, the list is endless.

I found myself feeling several different overlapping perceptions as to how these inhibitions arose. Parental Behaviors, Social Norms, Control, Relationship Abuse, Childhood Abuse, Physical Abuse, 'Our Way' and Social Norms.

Parental Behaviors

Think about the things you do with and for your children. Do you discipline them because you wish them to be responsible? Do you tell them world fears so they are protected? Do you teach them all the beliefs you were taught? A parent is always doing the very best they possibly can. But a child views the world from an entirely different perspective. You viewed the world from an very different perspective when growing up!

Activity - Parental Behaviors

How do you discipline your children? Are you strict or easy? What are your reasons for each type of discipline?

What fears have you scared your children with to make them behave? Try and think of the odd things you have told them. Find at least 1, and then clarify your reasoning for the use of this tactic.

Think about your reasons for this behavior. Perhaps what began as a desire to keep your children under control and safe when they were little, didn't adjust as they grew up?

Do you want to treat your children like this? If not, formulate your own concept on this whole issue and decide for yourself, thereby instilling a new belief.

Now you have created your own perspectives so you will be able to help share new stories and beliefs on this topic with your child after you finish your releasing.

This method of seeing both sides is great for creating your own new viewpoint and perspectives generally. And necessary when the stories to share with your child after releasing don't automatically come.

But always remember that whatever you or the child feels IS valid! There are NO exceptions.

Sit and feel all the ways your parents disciplined, and then scared you. Let each come up, be felt, listened to, released and replaced with a new belief.

Our Way

We all teach our children 'our' way of doing things, thinking how it is beneficial. Do we realize how that can easily become control? Have we ever looked into how controlling we need to be with people in our lives? And why it is so important to be in control? A very interesting one to allow ourselves to feel and explore.

Activity - Recognize 'Our' Way

What do you do and make other people do 'your' way? Folding clothes, stacking dishes, cleaning, etc.

Watch yourself for a week, and note down each thing you think or comment on. Notice other people's reactions.

Now, step back and look at the list. Does it really matter which way the towels are folded, or the clothes put away?

How do you feel about controlling another person like this, which demeans 'their' way because it is not 'your' way?

Lastly, think about your reasons for this behavior. Perhaps what began as a desire to teach new activities forgot to stop once they were learned. Do you want to control another person? If not, formulate your own concept on this whole issue and decide for yourself, thereby instilling a new belief.

Again, now you have created your own perspective so you will be able to help share new stories and beliefs on this topic with your inner child after releasing.

Sit and feel all the ways your parents controlled how you did things. Let things come up, be felt, listened to, released and replaced with a new belief.

Social Norms

Some parents teach their children 'the right way' out of the pure desire for their children to have a life that is easier than their own. Having pre-knowledge of certain expectations can only help, or so it is thought.

We each take on the beliefs taught to us as children, so is it any wonder a parent who was taught 'children are seen and not heard' would pass it along to the next generation.

My parents taught me many such beliefs, luckily none were overly controlling or fear based. I was taught the right way to be and behave in this world. To speak only when spoken to, to not speak my mind, to not make waves.

I have seen many other beliefs in American's. How the table must be set, how one must appear before going out in public, how others must not know family business. I am speaking of all the societal rules you were taught while growing up.

Abuse / Inhibitions

Activity - Understanding Social Norms

Make a list of all the social norms you were taught growing up. Which ones have you passed on to your children? Why?

Now is the time to ponder each norm, the reasons why people wanted to teach them to children, the benefits, and restrictions. This is a great exercise to do with friends. Come to your own conclusions and understanding of social norms, and the people who use them.

You should come up with an appreciation for why your parents did certain things.

Activity - Changing Social Norms

Make a list of all the social norms you can think of, including those taught when you were growing up. Be as detailed as you can, ask friends to make suggestions.

Now go through each, one by one, and select those you do not wish to keep. For example; do you want to have to follow certain rituals like dressing a certain way before going out, just because it is what you are suppose to do?

One by one, rerun the movie and find the story and the belief, release then teach yourself a brand new belief that suits you. Feel the delight as you create each one.

Control - Relationship Abuse

I began thinking about the level of control and domination that might be required before one person's method of doing simple tasks like washing and folding clothes became another person's automatic way of life.

This woman had triggered my remembering the feeling when another person wished to control and decide who and what I should be.

Heal Your Self

My x husband was just like her mother with laundry. He would inspect to see if I hung it correctly on the clothes line, then re-hang. He would come home from work and inspect the linen closets, checking that the folding was correct, then pull it all out to be redone. Always with a look of disapproval, always with the snide comments about how this is not good enough and that I must learn to do it correctly.

I still remember how this annoyed me so, and how I would deliberately not do it his way. I was furious that another person would treat me so. What is the big deal about how clothes and linen must be treated? Who cares?

I fought very hard against his controlling efforts. Needless to say, when a person is so very particular that their wishes are followed to the letter about a simple item such as clothing, this is but one aspect of their controlling ways. My husband would fix the shower curtain each day, straighten the bathroom towels, rearrange dishes that I put away; he would virtually adjust everything I touched so it was perfect again. His perfect. Then make sure I knew how it must be.

At the time I felt like a failure, because his control was very subtle. I felt that everything I did was wrong, and did try hard to improve. I had no idea of how controlling this man was. The issue of control is to deem my way as better than yours, and force you by whatever means seem appropriate, whether domination, coercion or trickery, into doing it my way.

Being controlled has been a big issue to me, one which I have worked hard to rid myself of. I am finding myself becoming rather angry while remembering this experience. If everything I did was so wrong in his eyes, how could he have loved me, and why wish to marry me? I would think it would be the opposite, dislike of a person's mannerisms.

Perhaps that's the key to the controlling personality. They seek out those who they feel stronger than, search out weaknesses to make use of. Just as parents do with children.

The more I allowed myself to feel this one, the angrier I got. I was furious at how I had always been told that I was wrong and useless. So I allowed myself to feel it all and listen to the stories, then released and create my own new beliefs. I was me, and refused to have another person's control or wishes in my head. My head was mine and mine alone! It was time to stand up for myself and demand my self as my self.

When my anger at being controlled peaked, I felt a strong sensation to scream out 'I was right and they were wrong'. I remembered and felt all the times they told me I wasn't good enough, I would never succeed in life, I was a failure, I was of no value. I was furious because I know who and what I am. I know I am a good person, I am happy being who I am, I love the feeling of being myself. I was right and they were wrong! I had no idea. I also realized why they did it, and how it was nothing to do with me, only them. As I remembered and felt each incident with each controlling person in my life, then released, I gradually calmed my anger.

Childhood Abuse

A friend sent his experience and feelings to me unexpectedly, so I could know first hand this perspective and belief.

A child growing up in a home where everything they say and do is criticized and demeaned hurts deeply. For it to be reinforced in a child that the person they naturally are is not good enough, is to tell a child they are worthless, they do not deserve or are loved. The hurt and then overwhelming pain that comes after taking on these beliefs often makes a child want to run and hide. Sometimes that is exactly what happens.

I was sent the experience of a young boy; they seem to take on hurts and sadness very differently from girls. I felt such strong sadness and hurt, from not being loved, evidenced by this treatment that's repeated over and over. It was about not being good enough as a person themselves, total condemnation for every aspect of them.

This hurt and sadness is magnified because with regret, the child shut themselves down. They decided to stop being who they are. I felt a very strong chest/heart block physically in my body. An even deeper sadness than experiencing this abuse is felt by spirit shutting down its knowing and being self. The child closed down his natural personality, in an attempt to stop the abuse and because he didn't feel good enough to be himself.

The abuser's beliefs then became the boy's inner voice, continually telling him how to be and act. I felt it as total mind control. Then it felt like in an attempt to stop reliving hearing the voice continually, he then shuts down more, so this even can't be felt and experienced. The child's sadness kept spiraling deeper into the psyche.

The child grows up while continually shutting down his real self, so much so that he is no longer able to feel or be who he wishes to. He becomes totally apathetic to life and circumstances.

The child is filled with anger and resentment, which increases with each repeat episode. How dare they treat me like this? How dare they do this to a child? I did nothing wrong. They were supposed to love me, not hate me. I hate them and everyone who does not prove they love me.

Of course events are repeated and the now adult finds himself reliving the same abuse. Never being good enough, never being accepted for who he is. Because this is a base self issue, it must continue until faced, events become extreme and out of control.

The now man, is forced to face his greatest fear, as the only means of escaping his unreal nightmare he finds himself in.

We all have hurts and beliefs, just like the above one. They may be about different topics and emotions, but they are felt and held onto as hurts. They then become the person's reality and life experience.

We wonder why our lives become so out of control. The answer is simple. As the only means to get us to finally stop and listen to what is inside us, our dear sweet ego keeps the roller coaster going. With pure love. Because ego knows this is the only way to reach that so desired goal. To know the opposite of this experience from within. That we are special, deserve, belong, loved, are love itself. Ego indeed gives us a very special gift. When you finally reach breaking point, you will scream help, let me off this nightmare. I can't do this any longer. And then you will begin your journey of healing.

Physical Abuse

Then I felt an understanding of physical abuse on children. I doubt there is a person alive who has not lashed out at something during their lives. Whether yelling at a cat, or hitting a wall, blaming a child, or even hitting them in rage.

To treat another person in this manner is not about them, it is us. It is our pent up frustration and sense that there is no escape. So now we have the new belief to tell and calm our inner child with, after we do our releasing.

Activity - Healing Physical Abuse

The child who is physically abused aches. Now is the time to go back and revisit your physical abuse movies.

Place yourself in a safe and comfortable environment; make sure you are secure before you begin. Now remember and feel the terror, disbelief, anger, physical and emotional pain. Find the memory that surfaces first and follow it. Listen to whatever comes up, validate that child's experience, believe and listen intently to them. They may not have ever shared this with an adult before.

Keep letting them tell you the horror story, when it is fully revealed talk them through releasing with breathing, you are that child's caregiver at this moment. Be there for them as their support and strength.

As imagined, there may be several different aspects to this topic. Do them one by one, they may even become a mass clearing and follow closely after each other. It may take several sessions to find and heal them all. That doesn't matter because after each, the child will calm and feel a little better, and feel the love you shower them in. The child will heal piece by piece. You will heal piece by piece.

It is interesting that after I have released the anger of feeling controlled, I now feel the love shared by each belief they tried to teach us. They wanted the best for us, they wanted us to fit in easily, not be an outcast as they were, they didn't want us to have to do it as hard as they did. They gave each and every rule with pure love and the best intentions for us.

Now is the time to notice how they in effect become your inhibitions. That inner voice you hear, telling you what and how to behave, that the ideas you come up with are useless.

It is your time to become 'you', to think and feel for yourself, without anyone else telling you how to be. Enjoy discovering yourself!

Conclusion

You have achieved a life changing accomplishment, congratulations! Look back at the person you were prior to beginning this book, then see the person you are today, and be amazed at how much you have grown.

There are two signs to watch for that signal a completion of this stage of your journey. That you no longer hear 'their' voices telling you what is wrong with you, or have stopped thinking about 'them' and what they did to you, and find yourself instead noticing things with other people you come into contact with at work or in the community. And you can read this entire section on childhood issues, and think about your family but don't feel anything at all. Just remember, take your time, listen to yourself, and believe in yourself.

The Outside World

Our interactions with other people appear to go through cycles. One day people seem to be extra pleasant and the next they are walking all over us, making us feel rejected and not appreciated. Sometimes we feel so annoyed with people in general that we distance ourselves completely.

We live in a world filled with people, many who can do nothing else but fight with each other. Learning how to get along with each other makes life much more pleasant.

Have you ever noticed how two people can see the same event and come away with opposing conclusions?

That is because we each wear a set of perceptual glasses, with which to view the world.

Our beliefs create perceptions, which then dictate how we perceive, judge, accept and act towards ourselves, and all those we come into contact with.

Each person really does see a different world relative to their beliefs. One person sees a half full glass while another sees a half empty one. One hears a beautiful bird song while another hears an annoying screech. One sees people being kind and helpful while another only sees those who are out to get for themselves.

Our perceptions can either make life pleasant or difficult, but we can modify them to create a more balanced view of the world. It is a very freeing experience to remove all the hurts and reactions we experience during our everyday interactions.

Reading the following chapters could easily become just that, reading without doing the work. Before commencing, ask yourself what is your intent with this work? How often do you get upset with interactions? Do you have problems relating with the outside world? How often do you say 'it is their fault I feel like this'?

What you do is your choice entirely. If a concept sounds interesting, even if you disagree with it, prove it to yourself either way. Take the challenge of bringing each and every section into your world to test them out. Have your own experiences then come to your own conclusions.

What goals would you like to reach from this section? What outside world effects would you like to eliminate? Perhaps always feeling judged, uncomfortable around people, not understanding why your parents treated you like a failure?

Enjoy creating your new view of yourself and the world you live in.

Perception & Free Will

This chapter exposes all of the myths so you can create your own new perceptions from which to view yourself and the world.

When you complete this chapter you will be able to:

- Feel more comfortable in the world
- Stop reacting to other people's behavior
- Stop judging, condemning or controlling
- Feel more comfortable in your own skin
- Like and accept the person you are

How People Relate To Us

Our beliefs create perceptions, which then dictate how we perceive, judge, accept and act towards ourselves, and all those we come into contact with. It is as though we put on a set of perceptual glasses, with which to view the world. Let's take a look at how people's behavior relates to us.

Many of us go through life believing people do things 'to' us, everyone is out to get us. We often gauge our self worth and emotions by our perception of how others react to us. Everything is from outside, continually aimed at and controlling our lives. We do not have control. But, we miss an almighty piece of understanding when we hold this belief.

Every single thing only comes from within! There is nothing outside of us!

But that doesn't make sense, I know they love to push my buttons, he did this or she did that. It is all the people around me making me not feel good or fail at something, they prevent my success or happiness we say.

Think on this carefully then. We are in the grocery store and we see a good friend, we know they see us but bow their head and walk in the opposite direction. What would we think? That they don't want to talk to us, they don't like us, we worry because we may have done something to offend them. We search for answers of what we have done wrong, automatically assuming it is our responsibility, our fault they do not wish to talk to us. This is a very confusing situation.

We truly do take everyone's behavior as relative to US, when in fact every behavior is only related to them.

Their behavior relates to them just as our behavior relates to us. How can that be?

Activity - Comparisons

Bring this back to yourself. Think of several situations where you have not wanted to be sociable, perhaps avoided people, even canceling social invitations. Times when your worry and preoccupation about issues has resulted in your being moody, unpleasant, or snappy with loved ones. Now list each one in your journal; noting the basics of each event, what was on your mind, how you were feeling, what you were worrying about and the eventual outcome. Become fully aware of why you avoid social interactions sometimes.

Were any of these events related to anyone outside you? No. They all related to how you felt about you, and how you reacted because of these feelings.

Now we can come back to our friend in the grocery store and think on more appropriate suggestions for their behavior, realistic ones. They felt unwell or unsure of themselves, were not feeling up to speaking to anyone, perhaps they still haven't the money to repay us the debt. For some unknown reason, this person felt completely unable to make contact with another person, what a sad realization that people feel this way.

Do you feel different about the person and the situation now? Can you feel compassion for them, rather than thinking what is wrong with yourself?

We each act according to our beliefs and perceptions of the world, so of course it makes sense that everyone else does that too.

Why is it we feel the right to act how WE feel, yet at the same time do not allow others that same right. We assume their actions are related to their perceptions of us. We literally make everything about us!

It does not make sense to do that, and frankly, seems selfish to do so.

Activity - Concept Observations

Spend a day doing this exercise. Whenever people act in ways you normally assume are in direct relation to you, stop and think. Ask yourself these questions again, put yourself in their situation.

But most importantly, remember they may be in real discomfort and need a compassionate friend. Their behavior is absolutely nothing to do with us!

Write down all you observe yourself thinking and feeling in response to their behaviors, your perceptions. Think of some possible reasons for their behavior.

Now pick 5 different situations and rationalize each out from beginning to end, coming up with your own reasoning of the entire event.

Read this entire How People relate to us excerpt again with your new found knowledge and understanding.

Allow yourself to become even more aware, and think about then decide how you wish to react to these situations in the future.

Beliefs Controlling Perceptions

Taking this a step further, let's look at how our individual beliefs create mindsets that we view all experiences from.

It is like we already know the answers and reasons why things happen, before they actually do. We assume that what we think of us is the same thing everyone thinks of us.

If you find yourself continually upset by situations, this section will completely change your attitude and experience of life.

Activity - Observation

I want you to become fully aware of how much this topic does affect your daily happiness.

Carry a notepad with you for 2 days, and write down every single situation that leaves you feeling hurt, uncomfortable, or unhappy. Note the event details, how you felt, how you reacted and the conclusions you automatically drew.

For example: I get up each morning alone, and get ready for a 12hr work day while my wife sleeps, I don't get a "good morning", "goodbye", "have a great day", anything. She doesn't care about me, that I work hard all day, etc. If she's not going to say good morning to me, then I'm not going to say goodnight to her.

Write them all down, no matter how insignificant or typical, from your family interactions in the morning, those while you go about your day, at the store, at work, driving, and then at home again of an evening.

When you have finished, sit down quietly and go over your list. Is it larger than you thought it would be?

Spend some time thinking about each incident, how you felt, the automatic assumptions you drew, and especially how this incident went on to affect your behaviors in other situations.

Notice the feelings you had from each. For example: How many times each day do you feel used and resentful, or sad and alone.

Now imagine the freedom you would feel if none of these incidents ever happened. Imagine how much sadness, stress and resentment you would be free of. And how much happier you would feel.

Can you see how working through this section will completely change your attitude and experience of life?

Situations

Here are some examples of situations where our conclusions can either form a new decision therefore initiating our taking on a new belief without realizing, or are examples of the impacts of beliefs that we already have.

Unwanted

She didn't want to go out with me tonight because she didn't want me, when in fact it might just be she was feeling upset at herself, or undeserving of your attention.

Why do I want to create the new belief that she doesn't want me? Is it something I want to live? Does it make me feel good? Is my assumption that she doesn't want me due to a belief I already have? Do I want to keep feeling this way?

If I have a belief that I am unwanted, I am going to perceive that in all behavior from others, no matter how much they try to prove to me I am wanted. If I feel unloved the same applies.

Can you see how easily we can make ourselves feel really bad?

Activity - Relate This To Me

Think of a situation where you assumed that people didn't care, didn't love, and didn't want? It could be as simple as a friend not calling when you were unwell or canceling a movie date.

Find at least one situation, let yourself feel and find the real issue, then do a releasing and develop your understanding of how perception affects everything you think and feel, and how they can harm you.

If you have more than one topic that automatically comes up great, work through them one by one, in your own time.

Before you move on, make sure you fully understand how you have formed and used perceptions in your life.

Perceptions Make Us Blind

Two people can go to the grocery store and have opposite experiences. How is this so?

The person who believes that people are rude and unhelpful for example, will automatically react to every situation as if people are being rude and unhelpful, because that is what they expect. They grumble when they can't find an item because they will have to ask for help, which they know will be unsatisfactory. They don't even notice the kindness and help given them.

The person who believes that people are generally kind and helpful will walk around with a smile, open and encouraging to all situations of kindness and help. They aren't hesitant or afraid to ask for help because they know it will be provided. They project a pleasant attitude to all.

One person sees the clerk who can't find an item as lazy and rude, while the other sees how hard they are trying to provide help. One person is actually blind to kindness while the other is blind to rudeness.

The man from the observation activity above, who concluded that his wife didn't care because he got up alone, shows us another good example of blindness.

This man awoke to clothes carefully selected, pressed and hung, a table neatly set with breakfast bowl filled with cereal and plate on top, napkin, glass and utensils, a delicious lunch in the refrigerator, and the coffee machine all set up ready to just turn on. He was totally blind to the care his wife took to make sure his every need was met. He forgets that it is his decision to be extra quiet and shower in the spare bathroom so he doesn't wake his wife at 3am, when she has to get up for work at 6am.

He never says thank you, so his wife feels unappreciated, fueling her perceptions and beliefs.

When someone holds a belief, it is virtually impossible for them to see the opposite of their belief. It doesn't matter how much attention or love one person can give another, if that person holds a belief that they are unloved.

Just imagine the impact this has on our personal relationships!

Activity - Relate This To Me

What have your perceptions made you blind to? Think of the things you want in your life that you currently do not have. For example: being appreciated, cared for, loved, respected, and valued. What if each thing you feel painfully aware of, that you don't have, is prevented, because of your belief that it is impossible to have?

You can't experience being appreciated because you believe you are not appreciated. You can't experience being cared for because you believe that no one can care for you. You can't experience being loved because you believe that no one can love you, or that you are unlovable.

Do you see what I am getting at? Write a list of the things you would like to experience, then one by one make the time to stop, think about this topic, feel your hurt at not having it, then follow the feeling to the source and do your releasing. Enjoy the special new beliefs you replace the old ones with.

Take your time to find everything you want for yourself and create it by releasing and changing the belief about it.

Perceptions Of The World

How do you view the world? How would you like to view the world? It is your choice entirely.

If I believe the world is a scary place, everything I view in my world will reflect that. My perceptual glasses will create the situation whereby I am blind to all else, perpetuating my belief because I cannot see anything else.

People who see the world as scary, focus intently on what is wrong with the world. To the point where they cannot walk out their back door and see how it is indeed safe and beautiful. This is very sad, and must make them feel very sad inside.

If I believe the world is a friendly and caring place that is what I will see all around me. I will overlook the harshness and fears, and focus on that happy aspect in all people. I will see the good in all, and then due to my reactions and perpetuated beliefs, this view of the world will be what I fill my life with.

Activity - Choose Your Own View Of The World

Do you like the world you see with your perceptual glasses?

If not, take a look at your beliefs by way of watching, becoming aware of your thoughts and feelings, find your story, then trace where it originated, and create a new story and belief for yourself.

Activity - Using Perceptions To Change Our Life

When we feel uncomfortable about a situation, we can use this as a trigger to change a belief that makes us unhappy into one that makes us smile.

Keep raising your awareness that you have full control of your world, how you perceive it, therefore experience it.

Remember: No-one does anything TO us. It is all our beliefs and how they create our perceptions and assumptions of what situations mean.

Activity - Stop Drawing Conclusions

Spend an entire week working on this one, as it is important! Every time you draw a conclusion, you harm yourself.

You do not know what other people are thinking, or the reasons for their actions, so your conclusions are not based on fact. Therefore all conclusions are false!

How do your conclusions make you feel? Angry, resentful, sad, unloved, hurt. Why would you want to make yourself feel this way?

Come to your own understanding of conclusions, form your own concept and ideas of them, then make your decision whether to continue to allow false conclusions to make you feel bad.

Spend a week with your new found determination to stop making conclusions. Become alert and aware when you make each. Stop yourself and have a discussion in your mind, tell yourself that you no longer need to conclude anything from any situation, because you just don't know why it happened.

Mirror Work

What about when other people's actions annoy and anger us? Well this too is only about us.

Why do you think we even notice other people's actions? Why do they annoy us so very much? What someone else does has nothing to do with us. And why are they so frequent?

It seems we go through cycles of topics. For example we may have repeated experiences of noticing and being annoyed by 'loud' people, who keep butting into conversations which they don't know anything about. Everywhere we go, we are surrounded by 'loud' people. This is what I call mirror work.

We humans tend to surround ourselves with people and situations that push us to recognize our hidden dislikes of self. Whatever we find unpleasant in another is exactly what we find unpleasant in ourselves. Sometimes it's very hard to notice, but if you take the assumption that it is all reflective, you have your topic automatically.

Here is an example concerning 2 ladies. Each had a specific dislike for each other, thinking the other offensive and outspoken. Whenever they came into contact through mutual friends the air was very tense, often resulting in a debate of wills and opinions.

One could never say anything without the other disagreeing. They were indeed perfect mirrors of each other. One lady decided she did not like the situation and became consciously aware, horrified to realize she indeed had the same behaviors so disliked in the other person. After working on these issues she no longer had a need for the mirroring, so coincidentally her contact with the other lady virtually disappeared.

Activity - Clean The Mirrors

Make other people's behaviors that annoy you your focus topic for a week. Notice and write down your thoughts about their behaviors, what and why they annoy you.

Can you see those behaviors in yourself? It can be very humbling to realize behaviors you really do find most unpleasant in another are actually ones you have yourself. This use to make me cringe constantly, but I learned to think of it positively, for if they weren't kind enough to show me this action, I would never have noticed and been able to make the decision that if I didn't like it, to change it in myself.

Next time you have someone pushing you to hurry up, or being loud and demanding, or not speaking up for themselves, stop and think. Think on how this is merely a wonderful opportunity for a reflection of self.

When you find reflections, sit and think on them. Pick a person or situation to ponder deeply, listen to what you feel, become aware of your behavior, feel it deeply, discover why you act like this, the ramifications, how it makes you feel.

Go into it to see if there is a belief to be cleared, or merely a decision of how you would like to behave in the future. Do what feels right and you will know when it is finished, and the situation will never be repeated. If it does, then you haven't finished with it.

Reflections

Have you ever been really hurt and upset by another's actions towards you? Why I wonder?

When we hold certain beliefs in and of ourselves, all our behaviors are affected. So the undeserving person acts unworthy, the unloved person acts unlovable etc. We radiate to the world what we think of ourselves and act as if they will treat us this way. Of course they comply. These reflections create prompts and triggers for our learning and growth.

Some examples would be others pushing in front of lines at the store, employers treating us less favorably, friends taking advantage of us, family and husbands bossing us around.

Activity - What Do You Think Of Yourself?

We all have a list of things we know about us, our faults and flaws, the things we don't like about ourselves.

Imagine how your life would be if you didn't have these traits. Well now you can fix some of your flaws, permanently.

If you instantly know some of your faults, write them down to be worked on one at a time. Go into each, feel your sadness at thinking this of yourself, go back and find the incident when you first decided to think this, when it became your belief, and heal it once and for all.

For example: Jenny's mother constantly told her that she was hopeless. Jenny grew up knowing that she couldn't do anything right, that there was something wrong with her.

As an adult Jenny constantly questioned herself, worried because she just knew she would do it wrong, and that became the usual result. Life was very difficult. People were always trying to control and push Jenny around because she always acted so helpless.

One day Jenny decided to look into this issue, so she let herself feel the self condemnation and sadness, and followed the feeling back to when her mother reprimanded her constantly as a child. Not only did Jenny release the belief that she was a failure, but also learned that she did nothing to deserve her mother's comments, and most importantly she came to the realization that there was nothing wrong with her.

Jenny then began a whole new life where she naturally acted confident and self assured. People responded to this new found confidence by respecting her more and even asking for her advice.

We play the role of each belief we have of us! You can choose what to believe of yourself, therefore how you act and the people around you react!

The following exercise will help you find the beliefs that aren't so obvious.

For one day, as you notice every person's behavior and reaction towards you, begin to think if that is reflecting what you really think of yourself. Begin to wonder what you do think of yourself and how you radiate that to the world in your behaviors and attitudes. Write your list and add as much insight as you can gain from this exercise.

An easy way to find your topic is to notice how you feel when others treat you this way. Feel and listen for the topic. If for example, you hear that people always tell you what to do, wonder why you believe that you need other people to tell you what to do. What is wrong with you that you aren't capable of making your own decisions? Feel, listen and heal the belief creating this experience, so it has no need to be repeated.

Free Will

Free will is such an incredibly important thing. Not only that we allow others to have it completely, but also that we claim it for ourselves. Free will is a basic acceptance that it is ok to be us, we are worthwhile and lovable people, whatever path we are on and actions we take are fine. Everything is as it should be, and we are on our path of learning through experience. Allowing and accepting another's free will is very liberating. I allow me to be me and I allow you to be you.

We each are on individual paths, I believe chosen prior to birth. We selected simple or difficult lives depending on the amount of growth we aspired to. Living is learning through experience. Remember, all experience is just that, an individual event in it's own right, therefore not comparable with other experiences. All experience is neutral, an event to have so we may learn and grow from it.

If you are having difficulties with this concept go through the Feelings chapter again before continuing on.

Taking it further, it makes sense that it really does not matter whether we live here or there, chose a job we like or hate, it is our choice completely. The free will to do what comes to mind, and then experience the outcome of that.

Life is about experience, which naturally causes growth. The type of experience is not important, because that is only relative to what we chose at that time. All experience is valuable

People often think their beliefs or path is better than another's, they know what you need and may belittle your actions or beliefs. Who is to say what is correct, who is to know ones path is better than another's? We each are on magical journeys, we each are equal. A leaf or bee is just as important as you and me; we are not better or worse than anything or anyone. We are a collection of humans and animals and earth, all undertaking a living experience.

I always had a real problem with mothering, wanting to fix things for others, of wanting to spare them the hurt I could see coming. But that is in fact my deciding that I know more and am better than another, that what I think is more important than what they think. I felt compelled to tell them what they must do and became angry if they do not do as I had said.

Telling others what to do is just that. Without realizing, deciding my own beliefs and viewpoints are better than another's. Sounds awful doesn't it?

But what if person is doing something obviously harmful, don't we have the responsibility to speak up?

I do honestly believe all anyone can do is offer information to another, and then, preferably only when asked for. Then it is the person's free will to take what feels right to them and discard the rest. It is our role to be a support when needed, but to accept their choices unconditionally as theirs alone, and not interfere nor hold any judgment of their decisions.

What of smoking? A partner and you may agree smoking is

bad for their health, and want it to stop. But is it one person's place to demand the other do so, as if he/she has no right to any say? No-one knows what is going on in another person's mind, so they cannot judge. How does he know that she doesn't continually attempt to stop, and that she has come to realize that just like her chocolate addiction, which ceased on its own, smoking will also when the time is right.

What if the person who is taking drugs, is indeed creating the opportunity to learn a most valuable lesson about self worth that they wanted to experience this life? What if it was their choice for growth and learning?

Who made our fear for their safety more important than their free will?

Who are we to prevent their original choice and their growth? Who is to say the experience of drug abuse is any less important to that person than our desire to be happy in our work? Each person's experience is only relative to them and their plans, we cannot know them so should not judge and decide we must take control. Just as we would not prevent a young child from experiencing climbing just because they might fall, it is their wanted and needed experience for growth.

What of the teenager who undertakes perceived dangerous behaviors? His/her parents may be constantly worried, even hiding the car keys when they know he/she is going out, or paying fines and organizing bills so he/she doesn't get into more trouble. Are they being a help or a hindrance? How will this young person learn about consequences if he or she is denied the opportunity for learning that this behavior creates?

This is a difficult topic to adequately cover as an example, but all I will say is that we parents often without realizing, become codependent with our children, leading to a continuation of destructive behaviors.

I see tough love as the answer and what I gave my own daughter when she was on drugs. I would not give money, nor allow drugs or her in our home when she was high. I would take her potatoes and oranges (she loved mashed potatoes) rather than good food that would be eaten by her druggy friends.

Yet, I told her every single time we spoke. I love you dearly, even though I do not like this behavior (separating the two), I am and always will be here for you. She knew that when she was in trouble, she could call me any hour of the day or night, and did so. Many times I went to collect my daughter from unsafe situations after she telephoned. I am very proud to say she has now been drug free for more than 8 years and is the wonderful mother of 2 adorable healthy children.

A book that I recommend to everyone is 'Help! I've got a teenager (Australia) renamed Coping with difficult teenagers' (America) by Robert T and Jean Bayard. This book is what I used to literally save my and my daughters sanity.

It speaks of handing back responsibility to them, of lightening up and not being so stressed at their behaviors, of playing tricks rather than getting angry, of bringing the fun back into parenting, of developing your own ways to resolve the issues bothering you.

When we judge another's behavior we take away their free will. It is in fact saying to that person "you are less a person than me, you have no right to your own decisions, I know better than you." None of us has the right to think we are better than another person.

When we interfere and take control, we prevent them from having the experience and growth that comes from it, creating the need for repeats. Then we say, we did everything for them, we helped and they threw it back in our faces. They didn't listen and now are in trouble again. Of course they are, THEY need their own experience, not OURS.

We all teach our children 'our' way of doing things, thinking how this is a beneficial thing for them to learn. Do parents realize how that can easily become control? Have we ever looked into how controlling we need to be with people in our lives?

And why it is so important to be in control?

A very interesting one to allow ourselves to feel and explore.

Activity - Let Go Of The Need To Control

Let's take this topic one step at a time.

What do you do and make other people do 'your' way? Folding clothes, stacking dishes, cleaning, etc.

Watch yourself for a week, and note down each thing you think or comment on. Notice their reactions.

Now, step back and look at the list. Does it really matter which way the towels are folded, or the clothes put away? How do you feel about controlling another person like this, meaning demeaning 'their' way because it is not 'your' way?

Lastly, think about your reasons for this behavior. Perhaps what began as a desire to teach new activities forgot to stop once they were learned. Do you want to control another person? If not, formulate your own concept on this whole issue and decide for yourself, thereby instilling a new belief. Give your child a gift! Let them become a responsible person!

By saying that you are giving them the responsibility for themselves because you know they can do it, they will take on the new belief that they are a responsible person and can do anything. Hence living and being that belief.

Activity - Next Step

Do this one when you feel ready to let go of your need to control other people's lives.

Spend at least a day thinking about 5 people in your life. What are their actions and paths you are concerned with, what actions you normally undertake, are they productive or codependent, how are your thoughts and actions undermining respect and acceptance of that person. Write it all down for each person, come up with a story about each, and grasp the real picture.

Come to your own conclusion about each person and situation. How would you like it to be? Feel and listen to see what comes up, this topic often relates to your fears, which can be eliminated by locating the belief and undertaking the healing process.

When you are finished, take some special time to hand them back their free will, give them that gift in your mind. Smile as they go on their individual journey.

You will find as you release this need to judge their choices and then take control, you become freer to support and love. Anything is possible with those ingredients.

Our Treatment Of Other People

What of our responsibility in how we treat other people. Are we kind and considerate, or are our behaviors based on our personal issues?

Just because I am feeling unsure of myself, does that give me the right to treat another rudely or negatively? No. What of how we treat our loved ones, allowing all our fears and moods to hang out, regardless of the impact on them.

What of our children? Do we get impatient and angry at something then yell at them? Is it in anyway related to their action or our mood? The child has done nothing wrong, but will believe it is their fault.

Children will take all actions we display towards them personally, just as we have been doing. We can cause severe harm to their feeling loved and valued and worthy, simply because we forgot to keep reactions to our emotions to ourselves.

Activity - Stop Reacting

Spend a day consciously watching and examining how you treat those around you. Write down 5 situations you interacted with others today.

What was the incident, how was your temperament and behavior and the other persons, what did you bring into the situation from your own personal feelings?

Write down each situation fully, notice it from all sides and honestly remember your behavior and what you now feel about that.

You will begin to notice how, whenever you are annoyed, impatient or critical of others, it is yourself you are really angry with.

Make sure that you find your feelings that are responsible for each incident.

How you perceive and treat the outside is how you perceive and treat yourself. The mirrors work both ways.

For each situation, find the real reason for your behavior. Own and take responsibility for it. Feel and listen to the story, do your own inner work to heal what is bothering you.

Make decisions on how you wish to behave with other people. It is your choice!

Activity - Relationships

Your behavior dictates your relationships!

Take the time to think about the people who are important to you. Spouse, children, siblings, parents, friends. Write a story describing the ideal relationship you want to have with each person.

Now, write the current relationship story, and then compare the two.

If your relationships are important, spend the time with this book to become the person you wish to be in your relationships, and make your ideal become true.

Notice how the topic in each chapter impacts on your relationships. Do the work. The outcome is your choice and under your control entirely.

Our Treatment Of Ourselves

Have you ever sat down and really noticed how hard you are on you? Have you ever listened to all the nasty things you say to and about you all day long?

We would be horrified if another person spoke to us like this and surely would not to someone else.

Activity - Awareness

Be consciously aware for just one day. Listen to all your self-talk. Make a list of all the things you have said to yourself, and at the end of the day read it. I am sure you will have your mouth open in horror.

Seriously, we humans are far more judgmental, condemning and unkind to ourselves than any one outside ourselves could ever be. We literally spend our days in constant mind chatter, how we do every single thing wrong, are not good enough, anything and everything negative about ourselves we seem to notice and magnify.

Activity - Organize The List

Leave the list for a day or two, then sit down and go through it logically. Do you really have all these things wrong with you? Surely not. Do you think these are faults in others with the same behaviors? You can divide the list into the main issues each negative self talk relates to. Is it that what you do is never good enough, make mistakes that are fine for other people to do, don't complete what you intend, sabotage your success?

See how many you can notice. Now you have an understanding of the sadness you must feel inside at being treated like this.

Activity - Self Judgment

Have you ever spent time noticing how you control and judge your own thoughts and actions? How you are like a judge and jury, watching and condemning everything about yourself. We restrict all spontaneity with this constant mind talk, we belittle all the ideas and positive thoughts constantly. The restriction and inner sadness this creates is profound.

Spend a couple of days listening to your self judgment, notice the process from the initial idea, the excitement at it, the judgment and condemnation making it appear worthless, then the sense of defeat we feel. Notice how you do in fact restrict your freedom of thought and act.

Activity - Let Go

Now, spend a couple of days forcing yourself to let go of this act, allow yourself spontaneity and fun, allow yourself to do whatever comes to mind as it comes to mind, allow yourself freedom to make mistakes or undertake actions which do not seem worthwhile.

What I do is take a back seat. It is like being a third person and watching all the things I do as if they are another person. Sure I cringe sometimes and hide with embarrassment, but those are the very events I am grateful for. They are the ones that build character for self, the ones I can examine and make good decisions as to the why's and what's of, then I can decide to keep or remove them and do the learning. I find it is the embarrassing actions I see myself undertaking that are the very beliefs I want to seek out and heal.

Every action is for a purpose, every event for a specific reason. For learning and growth. Yet, how can we achieve this when we restrict ourselves from the experience?

So allow yourself to be, perhaps at first you may notice how impulsive you are, cringe at what you do, that's fine. These events will be noticeable, so afterwards review them, make a firm decision if it is a desired action or one you wish to alter, then spend time pondering the action, why it happened, what you think about it, what it means, what you would prefer to have done. Allow yourself to act spontaneously, then review and learn from each action.

You will notice it is not only the disliked actions you now become aware of, but this freedom allows the enjoyable ones to surface, the child freedom part of you. Enjoy watching yourself become happy and open in your actions, like a child again. Smile at them all, for they are fun.

When we allow freedom for ourselves we see lovely surprises each day. We get to become aware of all the sweet and likeable characteristics of ourselves, the things we never see because we've been too busy watching out for the negatives. We allow us to be us, and we can sit back in delight watching the wonderful parts come to life. This conscious activity has always given me such pleasure and laughter.

So, how about you learn to be kind to yourself eh? I know you are special. Everyone around you knows you are special. How about you find that out for you? Have that experience from deep inside of 'feeling' special. Spend a whole week consciously allowing you to be you, no matter what happens. Is it really that bad? Make a list of all the happy surprises you found out about you, all the good things the world has always been aware of, yet you were blind to. Enjoy being you!

Conclusion

We now have some idea how our perceptions play such a major role in our daily lives. All perceptions in one way or another, relate to our self concepts, so there may be many overlapping behaviors resulting from each negative self belief. Keep reminding yourself, nothing is outside us, it all comes from within. We can no longer blame others for making us feel good or bad. It is time to release that pattern of blame. Let it go completely and you will feel much freer.

When we do self perception work, one of the major factors in success is self awareness. Consciously becoming aware of our self talk and behaviors. This can easily lead us to become overly preoccupied with too many issues, so we must be careful to focus only on one thing at a time. If a second issue surfaces, note and tell it you will attend to it when finished this one.

Piece by piece you can shed your layers taken on from the outside world, enjoying the new found self knowing and beliefs that become part of you. This work WILL change you drastically, your thoughts, your view of the world, those around you, and especially yourself. Enjoy discovering you!

Lack, Loss, Failure

What are lack, loss and failure? In reality what do these terms mean? Are they relative to overall existence or only us? Are they real terms or terms invented by our mind? This chapter explores the meaning of all three.

When you complete this chapter you will be able to:

- Know that you have plenty
- Let go of the pain from a loss
- Stop restricting yourself
- Feel like a success

Lack

Look around you at the world. Can you see all the food in each supermarket, convenience store, garage, currently being transported, grown or manufactured, filling household cupboards and refrigerators? Can you see the enormity of it all? Can you see how much food our world currently has and is producing every single day via manufacture and growth?

Look around you at the world. Can you see all the money in circulation? Piled in banks, vaults, cash registers, wallets, and piggy banks. Watch and be amazed at the constant flow as it is handed from one person to another 24hrs a day. Think of the zillions moving around the world every second. And what happens if it becomes dirty or damaged, why they literally destroy and replace it with more. How much new money is being produced each day around the world I wonder? And how much more changes hands via technology, without the need to ever be translated into actual notes?

Look around you at the world. See all the smiling faces as lovers, families, parents and their children, people and their animals, or the animal kingdom itself share love with each other. Think of your family, friends or any that you care for and feel. That is love energy. There is no lack in the world. Reality does not know the meaning of lack. Then why do many of us feel such a sense of lack, no matter how much we do currently have? A person can have $10,000 in their bank account yet still feel a deep sense of lack if it is less than their desired or wanted amount. What is the basis of our sense of lack, for it surely has no relationship to what we do and do not have?

Activity - One Dollar

To test this further, change all your money into $1 notes, cram them in your purse and feel how uncomfortable it becomes managing that quantity of notes. Yet, even if you fill your purse with 100 crisp new $1 notes you will probably still feel lack if the phone bill is $105. Stop and listen to yourself! You have $100 in your hand, which cannot be considered lack! Ask yourself why do you continue to do so? Some might say I do not have $100 to fill my purse, I lack that much. Then think carefully, when next you receive money do this exercise. It may be that your pay check of $300 is short of paying the $400 pile of bills.

The more you fight what I am saying, the more I urge you to try this exercise. Whatever money comes into your household, whether as direct deposit, check or cash. Transform that amount into $1 notes and put it in your purse, then seriously listen to your thinking. Do you lack? If indeed you still sense a strong lack that makes you fearful, you have proven my point to yourself. Your sense of lack has absolutely no connection to money coming in and out of your life. It is not money you lack.

Activity - Belief Of Lack

Have you noticed how large amounts of money do flow to you, but it is never enough for your 'needs' and is quickly gone? The belief in lack creates a situation whereby no matter how much comes to you, even $100,000, your sense that no amount will ever be sufficient dictates the outcome. That is why people who win lotto find it all squandered within a year or so. No amount is every sufficient in their minds.

Subject poverty is another example of an incredibly strong sense of lack. For no matter what the person attempts, their desperate need of the basics for survival is continually threatened.

While there can be several beliefs related to this issue, this chapter relates to our being connected to the abundance of the universe, the law of flow.

The issue is not the subject of your lack, but rather the belief of lack itself. If you are not clear on feeling, releasing with breathing and replacing beliefs reread the Greene's Release chapters prior to continuing.

Can you bring yourself to feel the emotions behind the sense of lack, that there will never be enough, that perhaps something serious or even life threatening will happen because of it? That the hurt of the lack broke your heart, perhaps felt as a young child craving the love of a parent? Flow with whatever arises, feel it, keep thinking of it deeply and feeling the sense of not having. As money is a major focus of lack I will use this as an example, but love, food, housing, work, any other topic is equally as valid.

To trigger yourself into this lesson, think of your debts, how they accumulate faster than you can keep track of them, how you always have to juggle one bill to pay another, the most important at the time, think of the money coming into you, compare that amount to what you need to pay. Feel the constant worry you have about money. Try and feel the strongest sense of not having sufficient money, of those times when you urgently need it and feel the pressure mounting. Feel the despair and panic. Feel the lack! Now stay with this feeling, let it be free to grow and be felt. Let it tell the story, and watch it unfold. It does not matter if a clear story of an event is not being shown to you, or if what you feel does not relate with any conscious memories, it feels strange or unreal. If you feel it strongly then allow it to continue, as this feeling is coming from within you, and creates much heartache in your life.

When the emotion of the feeling peaks and you feel it physically, do your breathing technique to release it from your being, force every ounce of it out of you. Keep going until you calm, and then tell yourself the new story, the new belief that automatically comes.

Sometimes this type of fear merely needs a release and no replacement belief is necessary, but, I am sure you are very capable and as soon as the fear belief is released you know what to replace it with. Perhaps like a dream, a picture of love and riches and food and all the experiences of living are seen flowing to you as if to a magnet. Feel yourself smile and open to receiving them. Feel their energy deeply. Relax and enjoy.

Activity - Acceptance

I would like to talk you through an opening and accepting experience to cement your work. Reread the 3 paragraphs on food, money and love in the world, thinking and picturing each clearly in your mind. There should be no sense of buts or maybes of lack any more. If there is you have more lack fears to clear before proceeding. Repeat the above process then continue.

Develop a picture in your mind that feels right and makes sense to you. See and feel the enormity of the world's food, money, love, and everything else. Feel the constant motion of it all and how it flows and connects us all. See and feel yourself smile at the wonder of how bountiful the world and universe are. Become one with it and find yourself floating amongst it.

Keep building the emotion until you feel it as strongly as the fear you just released. You may see food floating through the air, or children playing with money as they do snow or leaves, you may see smiling faces on all the people as they send items to you. Let your imagination go wild, have fun with it, and most importantly, feel it! Enjoy your new sense of wonderment at the energy flow of bounty in the world, which you are now a part of and forever linked to.

The final step to this is action. Once we feel the flow with the universe in all things, then we must demonstrate some personal action to access them. Whatever you wish for, think on what you can do to demonstrate your act of faith, knowing that your action will begin the flow process. For example, if it is money then what could you do? Listen to your thoughts and feelings, if you feel any doubts what so ever, notice and listen to them. Are they related to self doubt or what exactly? Find and heal them.

Loss

What happens if I drop a pen? Where does it go? Does it vanish from existence? What happens to the leaf that falls from the tree? Does it also vanish from existence? What happens when I say goodbye to a friend and board the plane? Do I disappear forever? What happens when a loved one dies? Are all the memories of them erased? Do they vanish from my heart?

The pen, the leaf, the person, and the loved one move. That is all. They each simply change their location. Are any of them lost from the world or are they merely moved to a new position?

The sense of loss you feel is for yourself, not the item or person. You feel a sadness that something has been taken away from you. You loose something, perhaps that you cared deeply about.

Activity - Feel The Loss

Let yourself feel a particular loss that bothers you, feel the emotion and sadness of the loss. Experience it, and listen to the story the emotion tells you. It will be very different to what you had thought the sadness referred to.

In the case of a lost loved one, you may feel a sense of being alone, abandoned, unwanted. With the loss of an item, you might feel you didn't deserve or couldn't keep it. Listen to your own particular story that creates this feeling of loss deep within you. As the emotion peaks, follow your clearing exercises. Flow with feeling then releasing this emotion. It is not yours so you no longer require it, let it free.

If you are not confident in releasing this emotion and replacing it with a new belief, reread the associated release chapters. You can tell yourself that you will work on this issue, but not at this very moment, and tuck it away. Remember that your feelings of loss are distorted. It is not the loss of the item but what that represents to you. There is no universal loss, nothing vanishes from being. It merely moves and changes. There is nothing 'to' loose.

Failure

What is failure exactly? The world book dictionary describes it as 'the fact of being unable to do or become what is wanted, expected or attempted'. An example is given of 'the picnic was a failure because it rained'.

So let us look at some examples. A child does not make it to the bathroom before wetting his/her pants. Is that really a failure, or could the experience serve to teach the child what happens when he/she does not head for the bathroom quickly?

A teenager drinks and is involved in a car accident. Is that his/her parent's failure, demonstrating a lack of good parenting skills, or the individual experiencing real cause and effect situations as an adult?

After a long hard work week, upon receiving his/her pay check, a worker discovers it is not sufficient to pay for the current living expenses. How is that worker a failure? Did he/she not put in the 40hrs hard labor? Did he/she physically do something wrong by doing that?

Is it actually failure, or our judgment of specific criteria we comprehend as failure, in our own eyes? How many wonderful things do we achieve, yet don't notice because they did not match that criteria? Does one thing override all else we achieve?

What about the nurse, who is kind and caring beyond expectation? Who shares great love and compassion with each and every patient, filling them with hope and future.

We all know those people, the ones who radiate the positive and make us smile from within. What if that same nurse, because she is not able to facilitate complete healing, or convince a doctor not to discharge a patient, or remove all their suffering, sees herself as a failure? Doesn't she know what a great service she provides to all she comes into contact with? In her eyes she is a failure, while to the rest of the world she is an angel of mercy!

Activity - I Am Not A Failure

As you go about your days, listen to and note your self talk about failure. Build a picture of your failure beliefs towards other people and yourself. Both relate to your beliefs of you.

Create your own concept of failure, understand it, know

how it works, the implications of believing this about oneself. Think about and see it differently.

When you are ready, address the list items one at a time. Follow the feeling and do your healing.

Enjoy allowing yourself to be you, without restriction. Enjoy watching and being part of the vast range of experiences you encounter. How can you fail when there is nothing to fail? It is all but one gigantic experience.

Them

Being independent, self ruling and only having to answer to ourselves are things we wish for. To be our own boss in life. Yet, as we work through our issues and the outside forces that come into place, we find it is not their coming to us, but our constantly thinking about them, prior to all activities.

When you complete this chapter you will be able to:

- Stand confidently on your own
- Not need other people to take care of you
- Stop feeling alone and uncared for
- Feel self confident

These thoughts are automatic and subtle, going completely unnoticed. We stop and think of something required of us prior to acting, because of what another will expect, wish for, or need. It is like everything we do is after first considering what others will think of it.

I'd better organize dinner or some other item for the kids on my way home from work. He/she will be wondering where I am so I had better tell them what I am doing. I'll show and prove them wrong. Do any of these thoughts sound familiar?

It's like we base everything that we do on how we believe

others will care about it. There is always someone who is noticing and does care what we do. That we have to prove ourselves to them, whoever they are.

If we are successful, they will be proud. If we fail, we let them down. If we are annoyed, it's to get them back, or prove a point. It is always about 'them'.

Guess what? Every thought we have like this has no relationship to anyone else. They don't care about the things we think they do. You can easily prove this to yourself by noticing how often you go out of your way because you think another is expecting you to, then experience the disappointment when they fail to acknowledge or even notice our consideration of them.

How could they be aware or notice? They did not ask or expect it, or know what goes on in our minds. They have no awareness at all of our own beliefs of others expectations of us.

We are the ones who made the decision about these expectations. We can't base our lives on made up beliefs of how and what we are suppose to do. We can't do things because we think others wish us to. We can't base our actions on that.

All this behavior facilitates disappointment, and feelings of being taken for granted and not cared for. We undertake an action believing 'they' wish it, then when we conform to their supposed wishes and they are oblivious to them, we feel ignored and rejected. Perhaps, by holding on to the belief that someone else in this world is always aware, always noticing and caring what and how we are doing, we prevent the feeling of being alone and uncared for.

How many of us do things to get our parents, relatives or friends back? Going against their beliefs, taking a different path to them, doing something we know they will disapprove of. Letting them know how badly we feel and are doing. And what is our purpose and thinking at the time? I'll show them, ill get them back for not caring about me, they made this happen because they didn't care about me, its their fault.

Perhaps we spend our time playing the game of attempting to get everyone to prove they care about us, taking on the poor me role like the abandoned child without a soul to care.

This is not about anyone or anything outside us. It is not about whether people do actually care for and about us or not. It is about our belief alone.

If we let go of the wish for others to be aware and considerate of us and all we do, we can feel very alone. If they do not take on this role there is no-one else to. No-one will care what happens to us.

When we stop having to show the world our sadness and problems, we are left to ourselves. All is quiet.

Activity - The Plays

Can you notice some of your plays? The things you do to get attention?

We can sit and think of our life, and feel the strong desire to connect with another human being and share our situation, to feel their comfort and assurance. We can feel our want for another to care about us. Of course they must care about us. We need constant validation of that fact. I don't want to face the possibility of it not being so.

So let's get down to some work. Some situation created this need. Allow yourself to find and feel your want to connect for validation. Feel your needing others to prove they do care. Find your reasons for being dependant on others guardianship over you.

Example of a true story: I feel as a child, let down by the world and its people. I feel others acted without any consideration of me and I suffered greatly. I was left alone to fend for myself, no-one cared what happened to me. I feel betrayed. I feel the want to make them see what resulted from their apathy, the consequences to me. Look what happened to me! I want them to know the guilt from their actions, to take responsibility.

They didn't abide by their responsibility to me and there

were serious repercussions because of that. I didn't have food so went hungry. Are they now going to supply food to me? I didn't have the love and care of a parent. Are they now going to be that person for me? I didn't get my right of passage of a safe and nurturing childhood.

I missed learning that the world was safe. I missed having someone to teach me this. I missed having someone to want me to succeed, and venture out into the world to explore its wonder, and to be there ready and waiting as my comfort zone to come home to. I missed having a safe place to feel loved and secure within. I missed having someone there to believe in me, to teach me that I was okay, to love me as a person in my own right. I missed having someone to support me in all I do and desire to do.

I missed having someone there who cared about me, who freely and openly showed that, just like I remember it being possible. I didn't want it to end. I wanted to grow up living that wonderful life. It was taken from me and no-one cared, even the one who left. Or he wouldn't have done so.

I feel resentment, but at the same time guilty for feeling this. He was responsible for me, and he let me down. He left me when I needed him most of all. He abandoned me.

Isn't there anyone who wishes to take responsibility for this child, to make sure she is loved and cared and provided for? Isn't there anyone out there who does care?

Am I really totally alone in this great big world? To fend for myself entirely alone? That is not how it is suppose to be. That is not the way of people. That is not how I wish to experience living, alone and uncared for.

It is clear now, how feeling as the child who was abandoned, the one who searched, wanting an adult to want and care for her, who chooses her to be the one, now brings those feelings and desires into behaviors which are aimed at locating someone who will fill this role today. They do not match.

It is almost as though this child has located and connected with all parties, then gone about sabotaging her life just so they are forced to recognize their part in creating this, and to take on her welfare now as their responsibility. That this child is still waiting.

What is your story of needing care?

You may find that the story you are being told seems very odd, and does not match the history of your life. If you feel this story then its basis is irrelevant, therefore allow whatever comes to come, and validate all that you feel. No matter how strange it may seem.

This topic is also covered in the next chapter Difficult Lives, but raised from a different perspective.

Difficult Lives

Some people's lives are very difficult. They find themselves plagued by drama after drama, whether it is financial, physical, or those very odd situations that seem to happen just to them. The people who in one week loose their job, suffer the flu, have leaking pipes, a car breakdown, countless one in a million situations. Or those who no matter how hard they try, cannot secure employment, become healthy, make ends meet, or have any flow or peace in their lives. Some refer to themselves as being jinxed.

When you complete this chapter you will be able to:

- Confidently take control of your life
- Know that you are valuable
- Make a plan to start creating an easier life

When people have lives like this, they naturally become pessimistic, always expecting and waiting for the worst to come, 'the other penny to drop'. It can become a life of playing catch up from one drama to the next. It is very easy to give up hope and expectation of improvement, and feel like they are being dragged through life by their hair, fighting and screaming all the way. Lack of control in ones own destiny can be demoralizing.

As I have previously stated, our life 'plays' are created and kept for specific reasons, and only when we no longer require them for learning will they alter. So basically if we do not like the situation, we have the choice to do something about it. Do the work.

Activity - What Are Your Opposites?

Let's look at some of the possible reasons for this kind of lifestyle. What can be the desired learning outcome from difficult lives? The exact opposite of the experience.

To feel lack of control prompts our learning that we have control in all aspects of our life as the means to escape it. Knowing that we are valuable, that we deserve good things, that the world is a safe place, that the attention we seek can only come from within, that we can do something successful, all the self-doubt issues and many more.

Write down every situation you have had in the last month. Put them into similar groupings. Now beside each, write the opposite, and smile because you know this is what you are going to create for you.

Activity - Needs

What and how could a person gain from living this nightmare? Attention, help, being noticed, others feeling sorry for them, all the empathy and compassion in the world is aimed at people with difficult lives. We stand back and silently give thanks for not being in their shoes. We also find them very draining to be around.

For each of your listed situations, what was the outcome, what did someone do to help you or what was it you wanted someone to do for you?

Activity - Understanding Dynamics

What of the energy dynamics involved? We each create our energy plays as children, dependant on our family dynamics. Have you noticed how some people seem to always need to belittle others, are always dominating, and how being around them makes you feel undermined and less sure of yourself?

Or the ones who make you feel guilty or sorry for them constantly, and how draining that becomes? Or those who are distant, making you feel like it is hard work to know them at all? Or those who are directly aggressive, demanding your attention with threats or actions of violence?

Control dramas range from passive to overly aggressive. All seek to acquire energy and control of situations and people. They involve aggressor, intimidator, poor me, and aloof plays. Which drama(s) do you live by? Until we consciously recognize this belief and act on it, we remain within these control plays, always feeling the need to pull energy/control from other people around us, always manipulating for the attention to make us feel better. This has only been a brief summary of control dramas, which are discussed in far more detail within other literature, including 'The Celestine Prophecy - Clearing the Past' by James Redfield. It is very interesting reading.

Do not get me wrong, people would be crazy if they consciously created nightmare situations merely to get attention. Quite the contrary, they cry and pray to the universe for release from this nightmare constantly. These situations are more like they are being pulled from one situation of needing rescuing after another, without any conscious desire for either the attention or situation. What is the dynamic you play in your life dramas?

Activity - Care

The want of another person to care for us can create many

nightmare abuse and controlling situations in our lives; all because we may have a deep sense that no-one cares about us. It may stem from abandonment or abuse issues, lack of love and support while growing up, our needs not having been met. Only you can search out your reasoning by allowing the feeling of aloneness and needing another to care for you to surface and tell their stories, so you may heal.

This topic is also covered in the previous chapter Them, but raised from a different perspective.

Activity - Self Punishment

Why do we punish ourselves so? What caused this extreme dislike of self? Why don't you deserve a good life? What did you do so wrong? These are the questions to ask and feel for your answers. Why do you hate and blame yourself, far more than any other person could or would possibly do?

Sometimes the answers that come when we ask these questions can be quite startling and emotional. They might be because we don't feel we deserve to live, that we were responsible for creating hardship in another's life, that we are evil, that we are a horrible person who does silly things, that we hurt the people around us and even ourselves, we may feel the loss of personal control as we see ourselves undertaking ridiculous actions, and have been forced to stand back and watch like a third person, cringing in horror. Again, the list is as individual as the people pondering it.

This topic is also covered in Perceptions & Free Will, but raised from a different perspective.

Activity - Claiming Power

Do you believe you have the power to take control of your life and future? This may seem a simple question, but please think long and hard on what you feel about it. If I told you, to this minute take control of your life and you can make it any dream or wish you like, what would be your reaction? Would you believe it or not? If not, why not? Search out your feelings.

What if you come up with the thought 'I can't do it'? What does that mean exactly? That you cant do what, live your life, create a good life for yourself, take control, do the actions necessary to create this so called life, what? Then I have a surprise for you. You are already creating everything in your life! The poverty, dis-ease, unhappiness, and failure. All of it! If you are already creating your reality, what is the difference in focusing on a different reality? None! The only difference is in changing your thoughts and methods. Changing from one who feels apathy and lack of control to one who wants the challenge and excitement of manifesting all their hearts desires.

Why do you feel that you are not capable or strong enough to be worthy of being in control of your own life? It is yours, no one else's, so why hand over your power to others?

Whether that be family, spouse, friends or others. Perhaps you feel spirits/universe/gods are a higher power and only they determine what we may and may not have in our lives. Perhaps to even contemplate bringing this control back to you will cause them to abandon or be outraged at you? You are already doing and being everything you wished for, everything you planned to ensure specific learning. If you no longer wish to remain in this situation, DO SOMETHING ABOUT IT! It is completely in your control. Find your issues, feel and listen for the stories, release and heal so you can claim control of your life!

Activity - Notice Your Actions

Life does not have to be difficult, we can each create change for ourselves. Spend a day watching your self-talk and actions. How you set up future situations that will be difficult, from the mundane to extreme.

When it is raining, why do you automatically look for a parking space far away from the store, telling yourself there wont be one closer, when heading for the line up, why is it that you always give way to everyone around you, making yourself last in the line, at dinner time do you not dish everyone else's meals before your own, as if you are eating the scraps, and waiting till all are settled and their needs met prior to your eating your now cold meal.

What of how you plan food shopping items for all the other people in your family, yet very few if any specific items for you, why is it that when you invite friends over, it always ends up that your house is a disaster area the day prior and you spend half the night cleaning, do you plan for your future needs when out shopping, like cigarettes, and other personal items, why do you keep using the empty shampoo bottle instead of purchasing another one, why do you allow people to leave their dirty dishes still stacked with food instead of scraping and rinsing them.

Why is it that your always running late so have to race to work and arrive tired because of all the chores you have attended to previously, or when you get some time off work, you decide something major needs doing around the house, therefore having no rest at all, why do you drive yourself so incredibly hard, even to the point of exhaustion without a thought of your own needs, what of not paying bills on time, when the money was in the bank, so now you have to race to get it paid or face disconnection.

The list is endless but I trust it has made you think of some of the things you do all day long, everyday to deliberately make your life hard. Much harder than it need be.

Spend just one day writing down every single action you undertake, the small incidental ones. Then watch each consequence as it occurs. You will be shocked at the extent you go to in order to create your own difficult life. Every single difficult thing you face during this day has been created, find its source and begin to understand. Then perhaps you can begin being kinder to yourself.

Fathers, Mothers & Siblings

This chapter is for you to read, and when the time is right, to apply to yourself and the companions who travel with you. I trust you gain the same sense of peace that I did.

It is a topic to ponder, quietly, over time.

When you complete this chapter you will be able to:

- Understand your family dynamics
- Find peace with your family
- Appreciate what your family has given you

There have been three fathers I remember from my living experiences, yet I have never come to terms with and understood the role being a father played in my life and person. Not until today, when I was triggered into discovering a new perspective by a book coincidentally obtained and read.

Being a person who prefers to search out my own reasoning, I do not seek and wish to learn from other's words. Yet, this book touched a part of me that has been buried until now. It became the trigger into my thinking of my own experiences, opening my eyes to a greater understanding of a person I have always felt disconnected from, and finding new understanding about the special role of fathers.

Being Australian, I held no preconceived ideas or political views of the subjects, therefore was able to experience the contents fully, without bias. I ask that you view its reference in the same manner.

The book Angels don't die by Patti Davis speaks openly and honestly of a relationship between a famous father and his daughter, and of her now looking back at the gifts given her. It speaks of a spiritual and knowing man who shares his faith and love simply with his child, in a way that encourages all parents to share their faith with children. It is a special book, which I highly recommend using as a trigger to opening your own hidden memories and beliefs with your father, and mother. This book touched my heart as this man spoke and shared deep spiritual concepts with such ease and humbleness; he lived his beliefs which also match my base ones.

I grew up not thinking much about my father this life, he worked long hours and whenever I did see him it mostly involved condemnation. So I kept my distance from this man I knew little of, feeling he was disappointed in my entire being. Nothing I could do would please him.

Recently, I remembered and re-experienced a different relationship with another father. It was incredibly special. A love affair I cherish. This man freely and openly demonstrated every ounce of his love for me, in a way that I thrived at experiencing. Then it ended unexpectedly and I was left alone.

And then there is my natural father this life, the one who was so horrified at the news of my conception that he left my mother and was never seen or heard from again.

I have three fathers, none of which I understand the dynamics or reasoning behind this form of relationship. While reading Patti Davis's book, I began to wonder at my relationship with my current father John. She spoke of being given so many gifts which she did not know of until much later. I wondered what gifts my father had given me? What his goals and dreams for me were? Things I had never even contemplated.

I began to go back over our relationship, the times that

stand out in my mind and his behavior towards me, from my own perspective as a parent. Perhaps because we are not blood relatives I did not think I took on anything from him, yet I quickly found out I was mistaken.

My father is an outspoken man as this example clearly demonstrates. Only now am I coming to some understanding behind his behavior. My mother collected me from the hospital after having my gall bladder removed the day prior, I was still dressed in my nightwear and feeling tired and faint from the trip home and climb up the steep stairs to their home. All I wanted to do was crawl into bed and go back to sleep, now that my children had been satisfied that I was alright.

He met us at the top of the stairs, waving a magazine article he insisted I read. His words can still be heard. "Look at this, read and listen to it, smoking cigarettes will kill you." I was horrified and disappointed at his apparent lack of caring for my well-being after the surgery. I felt the only thing on his mind was to condemn me, to point out my failings and the disappointment I am to him.

Other memories consist of similar incidents, all the times he was too quick to judge, condemn and point out my constant failings as a daughter, mother and human being. I have no memory of ever being told I did well, or of him being proud of me, or loving me, only the negative references.

I suppose my mother and father could be considered together in this exercise, as they always stood together, each mirroring the others opinions and thoughts about me. I would listen to her telling me what a failure I am on the telephone and hear him in the background adding his agreement and further words. It has always been like the two of them are in complete unison of a combined belief of my lack of value and ability as a human being. It has always made me feel sad.

Ms Davis's book spoke of a parent's desire to share knowledge with his offspring, in order to give a sound foundation for their development. How parents have this innate wish to share what they have learned from their own experiences, to help their children. So I began thinking about the purpose, if any behind my parent's behavior.

I pictured myself doing the same magazine article scenario with my daughter, and the why's of my reasoning. Then it clicked. Of course I would be concerned about one of my own children undertaking an activity I thought harmful to their well-being. Of course I would speak out whenever the opportunity arose. Of course I wouldn't care what they thought of me because my goal was to somehow reach them, to prevent their pain and sorrow down the road.

Of course I couldn't stand by quietly and do nothing in the same position. And then another penny clicked because that statement describes my parents to a tea. Every time I undertook any activity they believed might cause me harm or hurt they screamed out warnings from the roof top. They did everything possible to make me see what might lie ahead.

Their behavior that I grew to dread mirrored who I am now, and proud to be so. I am the one who speaks out and acts when others stand by silently. I rescue animals out of sweltering cars. I stop and help someone in need. I am the one who tells the woman her blouse button is undone, or the ups man that he has a large black grease mark on his face. I do these things because I would want another to do the same for me.

My parents gave me an incredible gift, I had no idea. By coincidence, being outspoken and forthright is an issue I have been thinking of lately, as one I wish to curb. Now I understand its reasoning from both perspectives, I no longer have the need to act it out.

It is a need and way we show our caring for another. Although we often take it as criticism when it is aimed at us, it is given with love because the giver wishes to save another person they care about having to experience hurts. If my parents had not cared, they would have kept quiet. The fact of their continual and even combined determination to get me to listen to them is in direct proportion to the love behind it. My parents did and do love me very much. Another thing I never knew.

I had wanted to experience the kind of parent and child relationship that I had with another father, again in this life. I wanted the physical love experience and nothing else. When that was not forthcoming I decided it was because they didn't love me. I had no concept that love can and is expressed and received according to each person's perceptions and beliefs.

My parents tried their hardest to share their love in a way that was appropriate for them to do so, and I wished for it to be in a way appropriate for me. Because they did not match, we each felt distance and sadness at not connecting with the other. We didn't understand each other.

What role did my father consciously take on as a father? Was it to demonstrate love and affection, teach what he believed valuable life skills, be the one to stand guard for all obstacles on my path? What was going through his mind when he first thought about his parenting role?

Tonight I believe I have gained some insight into this man's wishes for his daughter. He wanted to protect her from the hazards of life, to highlight them all so she would grow up knowing, strong and independent, with the full ability to care for herself. A wonderful gift for any father to wish for a daughter. Independence and strength in a world that viewed women as the lesser sex.

Remember that there is a reason behind all the events and dramas in our life, a reason behind everyone's actions. My current life is one of strength and self power. That is my learning. That is my purpose. That is what I write of.

My father agreed to journey along beside me in this life, to honor my wishes and do all he could in order to facilitate them. My father is an honorable man. What has my father hoped to teach me of the male sex? I know what beliefs I took on. That they were distant, hostile, uncaring, that I was never good enough. This is another issue I have not spent time pondering. What I think of and believe about the male sex.

Again, it must be stressed that whatever we each take on as beliefs is because we wish to learn the opposite, and has no relevance in other's actions. Therefore the beliefs I took on were not because of my father, instead those I chose to experience and grow from this life.

Continuing from my previous deductions of my father's motives, I can assume what he wished me to learn of men. He grew up in a time when women cared for the children, and men for the material needs of the family. Also when parents rarely demonstrated affection towards others openly. Strict gender roles were prevalent when he was growing up.

He showed me that men were hard working, and have a desire to care financially for their families. He never raised his voice or hand to my mother, showing his respect for her. My mother worked along side him always in their business, and was herself the ideas person, while he the action one. He believed and valued her input and considered her an equal.

It is interesting to note how his actions mirror my own expectations and beliefs of how I should be treated by men and society in general, even to the not knowing about open affection.

I can clearly see how much of my strength characteristics, which others are often surprised at, are a direct reflection of what my father taught me. And what I desired to learn and experience this life. Even to the point of having the will to fight for what I believe in, to make it so I fit into this world as an equal and will accept nothing less. I have indeed taken on many traits considered only to be appropriate to the male of the species.

Perhaps it is that the different people in our lives teach us aspects rather than the whole picture. I can see how my father taught me to be strong, to strive for whatever I desired and to be outspoken, overlooking the emotional aspects. Which are the exact things my father from a different time freely taught me.

Recent work has involved my blending all I have remembered and learned, to come up with a complete picture of myself, and life. Perhaps it is for each event and person we have contact with, to bring one piece of the experience to us, and us to then pull them all together.

If my now father had been the loving and kind one, he could not have taught me strength and will as he did, which I would have been lacking without. Perhaps each person in our many lives brings what they know best into our teaching. The one who is able to love freely brings that, and another who is forthright and outspoken that. Each with a different personality trait to expose us to.

Taking that further, we can think of all the people in our lives and see the individual aspects each has exposed us to. We can see how they each combined to complete the range of possibilities.

One who was loving, another uncaring, another kind, another forthright and condemning, another pushy, another who stood back, one who wanted to learn from us, another to teach, another to need, another to distance, another another another. All the aspects are there. The human race is indeed comprised of every single personality aspect, coming into our lives so we can experience them all. I feel each person's specialty and it being brought into my life especially so I can know of it first hand.

The freedom from feeling this perception makes me smile from the inside out. All the hurts and guilt and unknown reasons answered and released. I now understand why and how we come together, how we are connected, what spirits are. And now I am ready to pull it all together and know the meaning of living. I smile so much my face hurts. I feel light and full of energy. I feel their energy touching me, all of them. I am happy because I no longer feel rejected, abandoned, unloved and all the rest of those unhappy feelings. I feel peace.

Activity - What Is Your Story

Discover and write the story of your family relationships. Come to your own realizations and understanding just like I did. Find your own peace.

The Inside World - Us

We have cleared many of our painful childhood beliefs and discovered much about how we have allowed the outside world to control how we feel so now is the time to look within, at what comprises us. Claim our control and ability to do and become whatever we desire.

We do choose everything, including how we feel, what we think, what we dream of, how we behave, all of it.

Think about what you desire, what peace of mind you would like to create by doing this section, Focus your intent. Who is the person you would like to be? What current aspects would you like to alter?

Go through your dream life, your creating cards. Feel what is now becoming possible. Feel the new you ready to come forward and be known.

The following chapters will take you through a process of looking at, then creating the you it feels right to be.

We Choose How We Feel

Are you feeling happy or sad today, anxious or calm, motivated or passive? Do you know why you are feeling this way? Do you realize you have a choice in how you feel and that you CAN create happiness in your life!!

When you complete this chapter you will be able to:

- Become aware of how you feel and why
- Decide which activities to keep and which to stop
- Enjoy the 'Now' moments
- Take control of how you choose to feel every day

Activity - Try It For Yourself

Stop and notice exactly 'how' you are feeling 'generally' today? You may find you are feeling stressed, worried, unsure, a range of emotions. Ask yourself why you are feeling this, what does it relate to? Perhaps it is from an event earlier in the day, fears you may be thinking of, the future etc.

Take 10 minutes to write down your feelings, and what they relate to. Notice how events affect how you feel generally.

Now, step back from thinking about things that do not relate to this one particular moment in time, become consciously aware of how your body and mind thinks and feels only in this 'now' space, while you are sitting reading this book.

Take 10 minutes to notice and write down your feelings, both physically and mentally while you sit quietly reading this book. Compare the two. Does how you are feeling generally, agree with how you are feeling in this one moment in time? I very much doubt it does.

The Now Moment

Confused? Let me explain. Remember the chapter on Feeling, this is a carry on from that. To remain in the 'now' moment means we are only thinking and feeling what we are experiencing right now. But, when our mind keeps us thinking of other issues, we take on the feelings from them. The more we focus on something the more strength and power we give it and the more we feel it right now instead of what we are actually doing.

Say a person has major financial problems. They think and worry about this constantly. It affects their every action, from the basic need to purchase food, to being afraid to answer the phone or open mail (fear of facing bills and the landlord). This person may become so focused on their lack of money that they become depressed and feel hopeless. Does that help their situation any? No.

The effect of this pre-occupation with a money fear destroys any chance of experiencing the 'now', so the person may seem distant when out socially, miss a beautiful sunset right in front of their eyes, or not realize when someone is trying to love them. This is the person who leaves us flat and drained after spending time with them; they are sad, lifeless and not good company. The behavior might be mistakenly taken as their personality. I have used an extreme situation to highlight the power our focus of attention and thought has in determining our outlook, perceptions, moods and feelings. When we realize that we have full control and a choice, we are better able to make them wisely.

Activity - Become A Now Person

This may seem like a very simple observation, but the impact it has on your life is extreme. Think about how you would like to feel each day, enjoying the individual moments or distant and unable to take your attention away from issues.

Yes, you have issues to resolve, but you are doing just that, and you can have it both ways you know. Enjoy your moments AND fix your problems. So take a few days or a week to finish this one totally. Open your awareness throughout each day, notice, decide what you prefer to spend your time thinking about, and take action. Then go over your days activities each night. Summarize the activity, how you felt, what you did, or choose to do in the future. Use this exercise to become fully aware of how what you choose to think about controls your feelings, moods, activities, and experiences. Form your own understanding and concept of 'Living in the Now' for yourself. You will find it may be very different from anything you have read about. Know that is Perfect because it is Yours!

Activities

What about our choice of activity and people to associate with? How do they make us feel? A person who is fearful of world situations may continually watch the news, read newspaper articles, talk about it with friends, relatives and associates. This person fills their life and feelings with the horrors of war. Yet, what happens if they look outside their very own door? Is there a war, or children happily playing? Is there drama and fear, or neighbors peacefully mowing their lawns?

How does this person's perception of fear and war relate to

their own physical life circumstances? It does not. The topic of war could be replaced with world hunger, abuse, earth events, crime, the list is endless. Why would a person choose to create a life focused on such events, at the expense of experiencing their own situation? During recent world events many people were fearful, their minds constantly reliving events seen on television. Some held onto the fear, which then began to affect their sleep, well-being and lifestyle.

A very interesting situation occurred. When a person who was feeling this fear and worry turned off their television, stopped reading newspapers, and began discussed other topics, their fear left. All by itself. The act of continually bombarding their mind with fear created the fear response, yet once the actions ceased, the response shut down on its own. They in fact, perpetuated their own fear experiences.

So, what we do with our time effects how we feel. What about watching horror movies, reading murder and criminal novels etc. Is it any wonder we feel anxious about our place in the world as a result? What about those we associate with? Have you noticed that being around some people makes you feel alive, inspired, optimistic about your life and future? While being around other people leaves you feeling sad and depressed, world fear and dread heightened? What part do you play in perpetuating this?

Who says that just because someone wrote it, you must read an article depicting the horrors of the world, and are responsible for feeling sad and guilty about them? What point and purpose is there in taking on the world's woes? Does it change the world? Does it help one single person? Or does it merely serve to make you feel depressed?

Activity - Become Aware & Selective

Become aware and notice how you feel when interacting with people. Do they serve to uplift and motivate, or depress and demean? If the second is the case, why be around them?

Do the same with your regular activities. What makes you feel good, and what doesn't? Does shaking with fear after watching a horror movie make you feel good? If it doesn't then why do it? Why do people think that they are bad or selfish if they don't want to spend time doing unpleasant activities, or surrounded by people they do not enjoy being with, or that there is no alternative because if they walk away they will be alone?

Hey, if you wish to engage in pleasant activities and conversations, mightn't other people feel the same? Perhaps even being like you, hesitant to break the habit. Just like the previous activity, take the time become aware, investigate and form your own understanding then decisions of what you prefer about activities.

Spend a week noticing how you feel, and then match it with what you are doing to stimulate this feeling. Write down the feelings of each day, then after matching, form your own opinions about which activities and people make you feel good, and which don't.

Then make the decision of whether you wish to feel good, hence only doing activities and spending time with people who make you feel good, or you are happy to keep feeling unhappy. But if you choose the second then you have no right to feel or complain about how bad you feel. How you feel really is your choice.

Feelings And Physical Well Being

Did you realize your thoughts become your feelings, emotionally AND physically? If you are feeling stressed and/or unwell, look carefully to the thoughts you are focusing on.

If you choose to spend your time watching horror and fear, how can you expect not to have those emotions as part of your life? If you spend your time racing from one activity to the next, how can you expect your body not to be as rigid and hyperactive as your mind? If you spend your time sleeping and wallowing in depressive thoughts, how can you expect both your body and mind to feel any life? If you undertake no activities that make your heart sing with happiness (activity loves of your life), how can you expect to feel anything but sadness?

Each of us deserves to feel happy, to live each day fully and experience all the wonders around us. Now we've realized what we are actually doing to ourselves lets think about how to create happier times for us!

Activity - Emotions And Feelings

How does your body feel? Stressed and tired or relaxed and comfortable? How about your mind, is it racing so much that you have difficulty sleeping? Take the time to feel your emotions and physical body, notice what your chosen actions are doing to you, write about it, evaluate and form your own conclusions, then decide what is right for you.

Activity - The Perfect Life For You

Do this exercise. Get very comfortable then close your eyes. Think of the dream life you wrote of, watch as a picture of all the things you would like in your life appears. Your living situation, the type of home, location, environment, family and friends around you, work or education, all the things you would like to do, the fun things.

Keep expanding on this picture, and watch it come to life before your eyes. Enjoy it! Welcome it! Spend some time experiencing the feelings of this picture, everything is pleasant and alright. Enjoy creating this lovely picture of you and your life. Add to or update your dream life booklet. Keep what you have written for you, in some special place. It is very special and can become your gift to yourself. Read this every morning when you first wake up. This is your goal and your future!!

Activity - Time To Feel Happiness

Now, go back and redo the feeling chapter, step by step. The purpose of this is to bring some happiness into your life, some respite from the depressive thoughts and feelings. Even if you can only spend a small amount of time each day doing feeling work, do it. It will keep getting easier. You will feel some life come back into your being, some energy. Enjoy!!

When you have spent a week doing the feeling chapter and are experiencing some quality 'now' time each day, you'll find that your thinking is much clearer, and you're not feeling so hopeless and depressed. This will make you able to step back from your depressive issues and look at them clearer. Then focus on the specific issues.

Balance

Balance is a good topic for thought. How often do we become so entrenched in one specific area that we neglect all others? Is it wise or healthy to spend all our time worrying about the future, or working hard, or me even writing this book, without time for all the other things in our living experience?

Activity - Balance Your Life

What are the components of a healthy and happy balanced life? Food, rest, exercise, hard work, play and time for self.

Spend some time thinking of all 5 topics, and list what you now do in each. Now I want you to think of 5 new activities to include. Remember to use your new knowledge from the feelings chapter Develop a happier balanced life on paper. For example,

Heal Your Self

with the food topic you may have noticed you skip meals, rush through others, do not take the time to sit and enjoy healthy food and times with your loved ones. Think of all the things in each group that you would enjoy including. The time for self category may be empty, but now you include a relaxing bath once a week, time for reading and sitting in the sun, perhaps taking up some of those hobbies you have forgotten for a while.

Compiling this list is not to overwhelm with the thought of how will I find the time for these activities. It is merely about you becoming aware of how unbalanced your life currently is, so you can see that there is no wonder you become tired and listless.

Activity - Time Management

If time is a big issue try this. Make a list of all the ways you overfill your precious time, then look at it carefully and rationally. Is it really that you need to spend 2 hours each night after a long days work doing more work, as housework? Perhaps you are making work for yourself? Think carefully on each activity and give it importance to your well-being, scrap the harmful ones and replace with some new ones. You can create this list and undertake one small amount of time for new activities and gradually increase that. There is no pressure or thought of you turning your life upside down.

Here a few other simple tricks to ease the pressure you place on yourself. The first is a great idea developed by Kathy Waddill (The Organizing Sourcebook), called a require/desire grid. Divide a blank page into 4 sections, name them 'have to', 'don't have to', 'want to', 'don't want to'. Now all you do is place each task you set yourself into the appropriate box, then scrap all from the don't have or want to boxes. Simple. Other tricks include creating check lists, for grocery shopping all that you need do is to check the items, the same can be done for important and non-important tasks. Go over and write all about your time and management of that time in detail. Grasp a clear picture, noticing how each item makes you feel. You could read them and put a tick for good feeling and cross for not good feeling, then organize ways to change or remove the crossed items completely from your life.

Step back and look at how you stress yourself out with all you decide you 'must' do. When viewed on paper they don't seem half as important. The goal is for you to become less overwhelmed with your current life. To find some peace and happy times each and everyday. To help you calm and build your strength. To come back to you.

Do you realize it is not the outside world that is our foundation, but instead it is within each individual person? So how can we have strong family and community foundations before we strengthen the individual? Life truly is a journey of self exploration, which will become more apparent as you progress. The wonders and adventure ahead of you are truly amazing, this I know. So spend some time on your foundation, come back into you, find you and become strong again, and just watch the magic appear in your life.

I have deliberately set this chapter up to provide the positive first. A place for you to find some peace and happy times in your life. As I have said, balance is essential and for too long have you spent all your time thinking of the negatives. Spend some time bringing the good into your life, work hard on that, feel the benefits and strength in knowing you are doing this for you. Enjoy yourselves for a change.

Activity - Clearing

This chapter pushes you to take charge of how you feel, rather than just saying "well, that's life." Doing so may trigger some old beliefs about how people are supposed to think and behave, to be released. Remember that how you feel is always the key to removing anything that you are unhappy with.

It's All In The Word

Our thoughts reflect our beliefs and our words reflect those thoughts. Then why is it people think, say and do things saying it is only a joke, that they do not mean it?

When you complete this chapter you will be able to:

- Become aware of the power and meaning of words
- Use thoughts as a tool to locate your hidden beliefs
- Remove the control that mass and societal beliefs have had on your life
- Stop hurting yourself with jokes about you

Is it really possible to say crude things and makes jokes about fat people, the opposite sex, your friends or family, and it not be a direct reflection of a belief?

Are not the majority of these jokes about yourself? Is it really possible to spend much of your waking time verbally demeaning yourself to others, perhaps even calling yourself stupid or lazy, and not really mean it?

If a person did not believe this in the first place, why would it even enter their mind as a thought?

Activity - The Power Of Words

Every single thought and word is a direct reflection of what we believe from deep within us. Think on the implications of that for a moment. Think about your thoughts and words. Think about your jokes, for they are very real. Think about the hurt you feel inside at firstly being viewed, then treated this way. Over and over. It is so very degrading to ourselves. And we wonder why we hurt?

Begin to notice the thoughts and words you use, many are habit or mirror common social and cultural norms. Take the time to become aware of the myriad of thoughts racing through your mind each day. By consciously deciding which to keep and which to remove you can then begin to view your world differently.

Carry a notepad and jot down your thoughts for a week. Read every word literally, and notice how they make you feel. Notice how you use words without thinking of their real meaning or the implications of their use. Become totally aware of every thought you have and word you say. Always view their meaning in the literal sense. After a week, go through your list and highlight the one's whose meaning is not what you wish to use or say again, to you or other people.

Clean out your vocabulary, and the vocabulary of those around you. Do not accept other people's cruel misuse of words! Learn to feel the words you think and hear. Form your own understanding of words, how we use them, and how they have been misused to cause hurt and harm. Make your own decisions about what you choose to do with words and thoughts. Listen to what you feel, to see if you need to clear or merely change your mind about words.

Saying One Thing And Doing Another

Some people really do say one thing, but then act in the

totally opposite way.

What about the person who views and portrays themselves to the world as being a positive, optimistic person? What are the thoughts and words they use? Do they focus on the good in us and the world, or highlight the negative, then say we need change?

For example, I know many who wish to live in a world filled with love and hope. They are seen as the inspirational ones because they spend a great deal of time and effort telling people how to change the world. But, on closer inspection, their ideals are based on fear mongering, not love and inspiration. Is it really positive to say we need to 'demand' peace, shout it to all and fight for it? How can it be uplifting to highlight negatives as a means to scare people into thinking and wanting change?

Activity - Increase Your Awareness

Think of 10 people you know, closely, casually and perhaps in the media or entertainment industry. Notice when people say one thing and do another. Don't assume anything, instead watch and listen to their words and actions.

When you find it easy to notice, turn your attention to yourself. Become aware of your thoughts and words, and compare them to your actions. Are they in line or opposing?

Write about each person's words and actions, think on them then form your own understanding, and make a decision on who you wish to be, and become that person.

Examples of saying one thing & doing another include:

- Parents who punish or hit their children saying "it's because I love you."
- Relatives who arrive with hugs and declarations of love then spend the entire visit pointing out your faults.
- Movie stars who talk about the importance of family values during an interview, then are taped yelling at their children.

- Restaurants owners who support environmental fundraisers, but do not recycle one of their 1000's of glass and plastic waste products used each week.

Whether you are consciously aware of your own inconsistencies or not, you know and feel them inside, and they do impact on you, how you feel, your family, and the world. Who is the person you choose to be?

Altered Word Meanings

Many people have altered their personal meaning of words. Just look at the varied definitions of love for an example. Children are beaten in the name of love, and wars are fought in the name of love, but fighting isn't love to me.

We may be able to tell our conscious mind that it is love to feel pain of separation, or positive to tell people their faults, but inside we know and feel the real meaning of the words. That's why it often doesn't feel good. We think and say things, then use excuses to prove we didn't really mean it. If you didn't mean them, you would not think or say them because there would be no foundation to create from.

By spending just one day being consciously aware of each thought and word, thinking of the literal meaning, you will grasp an understanding of the possibility of their impact. You will then notice the affect your beliefs have on your words. Your thoughts and words are a direct reflection of what you really believe. Use that as a tool to access your seemingly hidden beliefs.

Mass Beliefs And Terms

We humans created mass beliefs and terms to reflect them. Because they are common we automatically assume them to be correct and to be believed. When I questioned their validity, I experienced great joy and release at being able to choose my own beliefs.

It takes time, has to get worse before better, takes hard work, seeing is believing, there are hundreds.

Talk to some friends and come up with your own list, It's actually fun. Then ask why? Why do I have to believe them? Why does it have to get worse before it can get better? Why do I have to experience pain before happiness? Why is it good to suffer? Why do good things only come to those who wait? Is there one valid reason to hold any of these beliefs?

How can we decide to go against the truth? Isn't that what you're thinking? Society has mass beliefs, norms and universal laws because they reflect the truth. This is a common belief.

I turn that around totally and ask what is truth? My truth is not yours, and yours is not another person's. Each of us operates from varied beliefs and perceptions, so of course what we each see is different, even when looking at the same situation.

To say what I know is the 'truth', is to judge my belief as the correct one and your belief as incorrect. Truth is a judgment, nothing more. So why keep the term at all?

Activity - Let Go Of Mass Beliefs

I have found mass beliefs and terms serve to restrict us. They each have some purpose of negating our wants and desires or controlling the community. Whenever I investigate any common belief, the result is that I find no valid reason to hold it as a belief. That realization allowed me to virtually dissolve most of them automatically, by choosing not to hold 'their' restricting views, and create my own as I go along.

You will find much of your mind chatter comes from these mass beliefs. It is like a watchdog sitting on your shoulder, always on alert to remind you of what society believes, and how you must conform to that.

By deciding to let go of outside mass beliefs, your mind is free for purposeful thoughts about creation.

Make a list of all of the mass beliefs you can think of. Ask friends to join in your investigation. Go through the list one by one asking "why do I need to believe this?" and think about the implications of each.

When you can clearly rationalize each mass belief you have written down in real life terms, you can decide which to keep and which to remove permanently. Remember that a conscious decision to remove beliefs does not actually release them from your subconscious.

Activity - Create Your Own Mass Beliefs

Once you can see how strange mass beliefs are, have some fun by making a list of a whole set of new mass beliefs, ones that are the exact opposite of those in the list you created.

You don't have to think about what sounds right or wrong, just create an opposite for each.

Have fun imagining people sharing, believing and living by these beliefs. How different would the world be?

Then ask yourself why can't I keep these new exciting beliefs? Who said I can only believe what someone outside me said to believe? Who made the rules? Ponder this topic and find your own answers.

Our Beliefs - Our Choice

Our beliefs are our choice entirely, with the only requisite being they make sense and we agree with them. A belief that does not feel right cannot be taken on, no matter how hard we attempt to do so. Therefore any and all beliefs you create are naturally perfect for you. If I desire to believe things happen quickly, or I can create anything I desire, why shouldn't I? I can create any belief within me I choose, by searching out its current one, doing the clearing then replacing my new belief.

Do you spend your time thinking and talking of doom and gloom, or future hopes and dreams? What do your words reflect about your beliefs?

Now is the time of deciding to use thoughts and words as a tool, for understanding ourselves, learning, and for creation.

Experience

I was standing in the checkout line, amongst probably 100 other people this afternoon. As I looked around at all the faces, expressions and activities in progress, then saw more interactions outside, I began to see the bigger picture.

It dawned on me, the magnitude of what was happening with and around me. All these people, all these spirits struggling with the same learning and challenges, all searching out their paths and growth.

When you complete this chapter you will be able to:

- Understand the 3 types of experience
- Allow yourself to openly feel and experience every single experience you have
- Know your life plays and the role you play in them
- Decide which plays to end and which to keep
- View your life and experiences from the bigger picture

How many spend all their time attempting to survive each day of humanism, with no idea where they have been or where they are going? How many have found the answers they seek about what the purpose of living is? What do people believe living is about? What stage of their path are the multitude?

I have heard many thoughts on this topic, from it being karma punishment from something I must have done in a previous life, to we eat, ... and die. No wonder enthusiasm for living is low, how could it be anything else when definite purposes are not known or felt.

It is easy to break down our individual experiences into the now moment, create situations and circumstances we like to be part of, but what of appreciating the plays, the dramas of our lives. How many of us take note of that and experience it in its entirety rather than get past it as quickly as possible, or undertake actions to avoid or escape it.

Experience The Experience

If all experience truly is neutral, and life is a process of creating specific experience we choose to learn from, isn't it time we got on with that and stopped ignoring what is happening to us?

A wise friend recently spoke about personal expression. He suggested we do not stifle our expression, instead we live and experience it to the fullest. Be proud of experience, enjoy and delight in it.

His words are so special I quote them directly. "Do not stifle your expression, love self/hate self, just live it, fully. If you're going to hate yourself, then go the extra mile. Soon you will laugh at your RANGE of expression, for you are entitled to BE everything. If you wish, then you can test as much of 'everything' out, that you can cram into a life. You are entitled to pay rent, you deserve food, and shelter. Unless you wish the experience of home-less-ness."

If you feel like crying, do it. If you feel like laughing do it. If you find yourself surrounded by misery feel that misery, listen to its story and what it has to teach you. If you are experiencing a drama of poverty, become it, feel its entirety. Experience and feel it all. To live is to experience!

Activity - Experience And Feel

We go though our days trying to rush through the experiences that come up, and then wonder why they keep repeating.

They keep repeating because we are like a living zombie. They will keep repeating until we finally live the experience so we are then finished with them.

We don't notice what is happening or allow ourselves to feel things, and if we react and get upset by something, then we stop ourselves as quickly as possible. Who told us that there was something wrong with feeling the experiences that we have?

Start this activity gently so you don't get overwhelmed. Pick a simple event, on a weekend when you can control your environment. And bring yourself back to the 'now' and let yourself feel it totally.

Using a trip to the grocery store for example, feel the crowded parking lot, feel the sun or raindrops falling down on you, smell, see, feel, and listen to everything while you walk around in the store. Notice every sensation in your body, listen and feel them all. Then write about it. Spend the next week gradually increasing the number of experiences you allow yourself to feel completely. One by one. Until you are comfortable and able to feel all of your daily experiences.

Activity - Emotions

Learn how to let yourself feel your emotions. For example, someone says something that hurts your feelings, which you would normally laugh off. Stop yourself, and then find a quiet space where you can sit and think and feel. Let yourself feel it completely, wonder why it upsets you, the reasons behind it. Just like you do with a release, let the feeling come up totally, acknowledge it as a natural one, then listen to the story it shares.

You will be amazed at what comes up, and how they do, just

to show you something to be healed and released. Remember that whatever you feel is perfectly natural! Stop burying your feelings!

The Make-up Of Experience

The world book dictionary describes experience as 'what happens to a person; what is seen, done, felt or lived through; all of the actions, events or states which make up the life of a person'. Many people believe experiences are something that happens 'to' them, how they have no part other than watch and be swept along in one experience after another, that we have no choice other than to make the most of experiences that come along.

Let's look at the make-up of experience more closely. I go to the store for groceries. Dependant on my beliefs of this activity, I may perceive it as enjoyable, a waste of time, or merely a chore. Would not the actual events then be determined by my actions, which are determined by my thoughts, which are determined by my beliefs? Would not this experience be completely different for everyone who undertakes it then?

Activity - Become Aware

Still using the grocery store as our example. Notice one of your thoughts while shopping one day. Perhaps that you can never get a car space near to the entrance, or that they never have one of your favorite items. Find something that you regularly experience.

Now do your shop in the usual way, then when you get home write about the experience, being annoyed at having to park miles away, or the disappointment of not getting your favorite item. Make sure you include your feelings.

Now go into the experience, feel it all, follow it to the belief that created the thought and experience, understand then clear it so you create the opposite belief (parking is easy wherever I go, my store keeps every special item I like in stock just for me).

Now go to the store again and notice how different your experience of shopping has become because of the change in your beliefs and thoughts. If you want to, you can become consciously aware of every single odd thought or experience you have that does not feel good, and remove them and create the opposite experience. Watch how your life changes then!

We Play Roles In All Experiences

Another example. I am poor, I do not have sufficient income for the basics such as food, amenities, and accommodation. No 1 experience is lack of physical money in my purse.

No 2 experience would be my taking on the actor role within this experience. I would behave as an impoverished person, perhaps not eating so the children have sufficient, skimping on necessities, always watching every penny in my wallet, always worrying about this lack of money and feeling fearful of events to come. I experience a poverty personality.

Is experience really something that merely happens 'to' me, or am I involved in as big a part as the event?

What if because of my perceptions and beliefs I had acted or reacted differently, would not a different experience have occurred? Is not experience outcome dependant on the person undergoing it then?

What if using the poverty example, we change the situation, seeing the person given money. Did this change their behavior or did they still keep playing the role of the poor person? Did this person continue not eating, watching and worrying about every penny, keep feeling as an impoverished person? Yes, because it is the person's beliefs that determine experience outcomes.

Activity - What Roles Do You Play?

Just like children who play house or mummy and daddy and take on a role to play in their pretend world, we take on and act out roles in each experience. Here are a couple of easy scenarios for you to think about.

The working mother, who gets up early to prepare lunch for everyone, drops the kids off at daycare, works 8 hours, collects the kids, goes to the grocery store on the way home, cooks a healthy dinner, does housework, then collapses in bed, just waiting to do it all over again the next day.

The poor person described above is an easy one to imagine.

Then there is the student, the father, the caregiver, the sick person. If you think about it, you can easily imagine the role taken on in each experience.

To make it easier at first, think about 3 friends and write about the role they play in an experience, add all the detail you can think of. Ponder the experience for them and come to your own understanding and conclusion of roles people play in experiences.

Now, think about your own roles. What are you? A mother, father, caregiver, worker, sick person, rushed person, anything that you can easily think of. Watch yourself for a whole day and notice how well you play your role for that experience. Become fully aware of how it can seem like adult pretend play.

The Experience Personality

To experience requires us to become that experience personality. A poor person becomes the personality of poverty, a mother becomes that personality, a worker and provider that personality. The personality goes about creating events and circumstances to match. Rather than being dragged along by uncontrollable events, I in fact perpetuate each experience by my actions resulting from my beliefs. One who believes, therefore acts poor, cannot act or become rich while still holding onto that belief.

Does your life create your experience, or do you become the experience of your life? Does the experience create who you are, or is it because of the person you are that creates the experience?

Are you beginning to see that experiences themselves are neutral, it is how we play out our actor roles within experiences that determine their outcome? That rather than experiences happening 'to' us, it is actually we who formulate their outcomes. What we believe and focus our thoughts on, becomes our world of experiences.

You complain that you are poor, you fear and worry and hate all the experiences being poor creates. Yet look at your actions. All you think about is being poor, you act out the experience of being poor, your dress, your mannerisms, every part of you depicts the experience of being poor. You create this experience. The experience is not dragging you along, you are creating it piece by piece. It is you who perpetuate it. You become this experience, and undertake it fully.

Activity - What Is Your Experience Personality

Expanding on the roles you play, take it a step further to become aware of how you go beyond role playing to actually creating events to perpetuate the play.

A working mother may wake each day thinking how busy and horrible her day is going to be, she may tell herself that no-one appreciates her, deny offers of help from her husband or children, instead preferring to do everything herself.

She may have 'named the play' life is hard, she has to sacrifice herself for the care of her family, and that her work is never done. But you see, she may come home and do 3 loads of washing each night, then fold and iron the tea towels and sheets, and spend time lining up shoes and bags and clothes for the morning, and a dozen other things. Can you see how she has a part in making her life more difficult?

With the intention of being kind to yourself, because really, we don't deliberately and knowingly make life hard for ourselves, we just do what we think we are suppose to, without question, discover your plays, the experiences, and now the personality you take on to perpetuate it. Discover a full understanding of the concept and what those around you and you do as far as life plays. Know that you do this so you can CHANGE every single play that you decide you do not want to keep living.

Psychological Experience

Let's add another component. We have the physical experience (1), the role we become within that experience (2) and how we create our own reality (3), now let's add our minds psychological involvement as a further experience (4).

Again I will example with the poor person. We can easily see the first 3 experiences; the fourth becomes their psychological experience. What does their mind do? Does this mind activity create a greater picture of the combined experiences? Think about your own mind's psychological activity when faced with a problem.

The poor person's mind is on full alert, thinking and questioning and searching for answers to escape this situation. It is like a computer on overdrive. The poor person's mind experiences fear, insecurity and all the other relevant components. The poor person's mind undertakes the greater experience that the previous 3 facilitate. The working out of what to do, the experience of being so fearful they become immobilized, unable to undertake any action other than watch and become more fearful. All the feelings and emotions of being stuck in the drama of this play.

We tend to focus on the physical experience, yet this is one small part of the whole picture.

> The mind creates beliefs,
> which create thoughts,
> which lead to actions and events
> creating situations,
> which become physical experiences,
> which then undergo psychological experience
> in the form of investigation.

Activity - Your Psychological Experience

Take the experiences and plays you have been investigating, for other people and for you, and include the possible psychological experience of each. Write and understand each fully, form your own conclusions about the components of experience.

The Bigger Picture

Therefore experience begins and ends within the psyche. The only problem seems to be that in the process of searching for psychological experiences, our minds run wild and get far too carried away with the undertaking.

The poor person's experience is not then being without physical money, it is the greater experience of the challenge of this event. The poor person's experience is a combination of thought, acting, reacting, becoming, analyzing and experiencing 'all' the components this situation creates. Not merely the physical experience of not having money in a purse. The poor person's experience is a psychological one.

Other examples include the experience of fighting with a loved one. We feel and become the actor in this experience well, we blame and come up with all manner of explanations for its happening. What of the greater psychological experience? The actual event of being a mind experiencing all the different emotions and thoughts and behaviors of being involved in a fight with one we love.

The experience of giving birth. We most definitely feel the actor part with this one, pain and emotion and all of it. Again, what of the psychological experience of undergoing such surges of emotion and adrenaline and activity?

The experience of moving home. I'm sure we all remember the incredible number of different activities required, from organizing a truck, purchasing boxes, packing, disconnecting and new amenity connections, notifying people. Just imagine the heightened psychological activity of considering, planning and organizing such a mammoth series of events?

Can you now see how our psyche is continually experiencing growth at an amazing rate? How each event in our lives creates a major impact on our psychological learning and development? The more complicated the event, the more heightened the psychological experience is, therefore the growth.

We are indeed a mind sculpture, a psychological experience in motion.

Activity - Your Bigger Picture

To cement this concept, imagine taking a snapshot of some event in your life. Write down all the components, events and experiences, from all aspects. The physical experience, becoming the actor in the event (the experience personality), how you help create it and the psychological experience. Spend some time analyzing the entire picture, watching for the hidden components. You will be very surprised viewing in this manner.

New Concept Shock

Taking a snapshot of our lives and the experience personality we have become is a new experience. We don't like looking at ourselves, especially when it involves issues we are not happy with. You may feel very uncomfortable in your stomach right now, and nervous about something. That is alright. Relax and allow this experience to occur, your ego is naturally scared, but all will be well. You are grasping a new perception of who you are.

You may be feeling very uncomfortable about what you see in your life that is now realized as your own creation. You may be confused as to what and who you are exactly. You may feel loss of identity. You may be unsure as to what is now real. What you see before you physically or what your mind is thinking and creating. Your ego has had a shock, it fears and feels unknowing, something the ego does not like.

Several immediate repercussions occur when we grasp a full realization of this concept. Firstly, a sense of increased wanting of the experiences you wish for in your life, the ones you haven't felt the ability to manifest. The nice things that you now feel able to allow yourself to want. When I first worked with this new concept, I began having dreams of magical events, the things I had put away as unattainable became things I strongly wanted. I would wake up in the middle of the dream and float back to sleep as a part of them.

Secondly, I found my whole perception of accepting the situation personality changed. I didn't want to fight with a loved one, or be the person doing so. It was like I put my foot down and said no, I won't do it. I began to clearly see my role personalities and did not like what I saw, and wanted to change many of them. I could see experiences and my role in creating and perpetuating them. Automatically analyzing whether I wished to be that role or have that experience. I began to step back and watch the experience from a psychological focus rather than a physical one. I began to understand the bigger picture of the human experience. It was overwhelming. A movie began running of all the situations currently in my life, all on top of each other.

Then, I felt a strong feeling of not wanting to be part of

certain experiences. This can almost be felt like a panic to make them go away, or seeing them in a more heightened and fearful way. I wanted to claim control of what was happening. I became scared of what I saw in my life. I felt a desperate need to take action on what I felt was the most critical event in my life. I needed to quiet and organize and undertake action to change.

So many, almost too many different thoughts and new perceptions came rushing to me. I desperately wanted and needed to clarify in my own mind, who and what I was, an understanding of the big picture, and a plan of what I now would assimilate and use this new information. I was indeed undergoing a very strong psychological experience from this new concept.

I was undergoing a shift in perspective, from what had always seemed safe, to the unknown. All fear reactions were ego based. For me personally, the answer to settling down my ego was to sidetrack it. I ended up becoming involved in other activities and issues for a day or so, with little time for ego to think of fears. By the time I came back to this topic, ego had taken in this new information and was settled. Then I realized how I had always known I was a psychological experience, and enjoyed that part of being human. There was no change in me the person, and nothing to fear.

Life Is An Experience

Adding another piece. What if to be human is but a mere experience? Think on that for a moment.

It does not matter what experience you create, for it is all for the having. It is only our minds who have decided good/bad etc. and our mind fears the experiences that it views as unhappy.

So a mind experience creates a physical experience, and then complains about it. Sounds silly doesn't it?

Could all the physical experiences merely be to see how our minds cope with them, for a mind experience and nothing more? This in affect facilitates a mind experience of being in charge of a physical experience? A mind experience entirely.

Let me clarify. All around us, the events in our physical lives are experiences, add to that the separate experience of our minds thinking and feeling about those experiences, being an experience for the sake of it.

So the mind (experience) creates physical life (experience) to have as an experience. It is all one big experience no matter which direction you look at it from.

The ramifications of this concept on our sense of self are incredible. I can, step by step come back to a much larger picture of who and what I personally am.

I can take a snapshot of my life, I can see clearly what that experience may be for my mind to have. I can realize that I am creating the experience not it creating me. I can make the conscious decision whether I wish to continue with that experience, I can think of experiences I would like to have now, that I know I create them. I can see myself as an experience in motion and therefore view my entire being with a new perception.

Take your time with this chapter, allow it to gradually assimilate and blend as part of your knowing, see it as one of the most positive things you can learn to decide that you can create any life experience and situation of your choosing.

To Change or Not To Change

That is indeed the question. We humans seem to set up lives of discontent, misery and hardship, complain bitterly, but then go onto do absolutely nothing to escape them. As if we don't believe there is anything we can do, but accept and live with our life situations.

When you complete this chapter you will be able to:

- Want more and not feel guilty about it
- Remove the inner voices that tell you why you can't be happy and why it's wrong to think of you
- Recognize how you feel about your life circumstances
- Decide that you want a good life and remove the obstacles that prevent it

Because our life situations make us unhappy, we think that doing anything about them relates to our personal desire to be happy. And to wish for a self-benefit is selfish because it disregards the best interests and needs of our loved ones.

I am coming to believe that the topic of happiness is to be treated in the same manner as love. As with love, it was to ponder all our beliefs and social norms, to understand where we start from, then go about looking at all the various issues, forgetting the search for love all together. Then as we work through them, releasing our fears and developing understanding, love makes itself known by itself, without our input.

Activity - What Is Your Situation?

Do you like your job, how does it make you feel, do you like the person you become when undertaking it? What of your home life, relationships with loved ones, do they make you smile or avoid going home to face? How do you feel about each aspect of your life?

Remember that whatever you feel is perfect as it is your experience. No judgment or guilt is involved when acknowledging feelings. It is natural that a person undergoing difficult situations would feel unhappy.

To recognize that feeling is a perfectly normal occurrence is to give yourself permission to do so. Every experience is about consciously having the experience of feeling it. When we prevent this, we become blind and numb to what is felt so we don't know if it is enjoyable or unpleasant, but we still do feel the impact of our physical and emotional experiences inside where it is stored until we finally experience and release it. That is why we feel so full, and can become overwhelmed easier. It is time to experience and let it all go.

So, go over your life, and discover how you really feel about every aspect (use the same life topics that you did in the meditation chapter). Take the time to ponder and write of each, allowing yourself to feel and experience how they really feel to you. Feel, listen for your stories then release the held onto.

What Do We Want From Life?

Allowing ourselves to, for perhaps the first time recognize

that we do feel deep unhappiness about certain things in our lives, then go onto question what we want from life may start the alarm bells ringing. Making you feel very uncomfortable and emotional.

Some hidden mass beliefs are responding to the prospect of being questioned. I speak of all the things you were told as a child. Being a mother involves sacrifice for her child, a man's role is to provide, it is selfish to think of yourself first, there is no such thing as happiness, you don't count, you don't deserve to be happy, this is what life is about so accept it, etc. To even contemplate pondering your unhappiness, or think of your self and needs may go against all you believe you have the right or ability to do.

Your ego child has had a big fright and may need some care and attention from you. Even needing to distract and distance from continuing with this topic for a few days, to allow her/him to calm and be ready to look at each aspect without fear.

She is known well to you by now, so do what you feel is best. Continue, spend time reassuring her, or put aside till you are feeling calmer.

Activity - I Want

When you come back to work, ponder what you want from life, do you even know? Think about what life means to you, find all your beliefs regarding it.

A Common Belief

"Happiness is not the purpose of life, instead it is to be of use to mankind, to be honorable and compassionate and do something to make the world a better place." Author unknown

This is what the person who shared that saying with me said. "That's the thing Jan, I don't think life is meant to be fully understood. Too many people with different views on it. I think life is just meant to be lived and appreciated for what it is. We have to consider others and the affect our actions have on them first."

What do you think of these statements?
Why?

Our Actions Affect Others

A husband and father may wake each morning feeling the dread of having to get ready and go to a job he thoroughly dislikes, he may work more than one job and be constantly tired and deflated. He may feel working is all his life involves. Yet he forces a smile on his face and does not let his family know how he feels. Why?

This man sacrifices his own happiness for his family. The ability to provide for their material needs is his primary role in life, one he will not fail, and willingly given at his own expense. They are everything to him, and he does not want them to feel guilt so hides how he feels.

The thought of leaving this job, or ceasing the second or third ones is not an issue. He will not put himself and his needs before his family. He believes in his role strongly, and honors his commitments even though they make him unhappy. He chose to be a husband and father, and this is what that life entails.

What about people who are desperately unhappy in their marriage, or when marriages turn lifeless? Everyone is unhappy, feeling from inside that this is not how relationships and families are meant to be. Yet they stay and do nothing.

How many times do we hear of people remaining in marriages until the children are grown and leave home, then immediately divorce? It seems many people remain in unhappy relationships for the sake of the children, not wanting to create hardship for them.

There are many life situations where taking action will

affect those we love, so we make the decision to accept what we have as how life is, and make the best of it that we can.

Because:
Inner talk

One thing I always find amusing, is how people will freely tell me of their unhappiness, complaining and saying they want more with their lives. Yet, if approached about it at another time, they defend their state of unhappiness. It's not that bad, I created it to learn so it will cease on its own when I'm ready. They go about telling me all the good things about their previously perceived unhappiness.

People who have the belief that it is not right to feel happy or question life status quo, do feel the pangs of unhappiness, but their inner talk quickly defends its creation by telling them they are wrong. We begin by recognizing something as not feeling right, discover that feeling, then go onto validate its existence.

Activity - Question

You may need to sneak up on yourself for this one, so initiate a conversation with friends, test out how many say they are unhappy then when you raise that again at another time, how they defend their misery.

Keep writing each day when things make you feel unhappy, note the event, your emotion and the reasoning. A day later go back to your writing and see how you feel now. Hopefully you have become determined enough to not allow your inner talk to tell you that it is fine and your unhappiness is not warranted. If it does come up, feel and listen, question and ask for the full story, and release the belief that tells you that you are not allowed to say you are unhappy or to be happy.

Note down your inner talk whenever you can, then go in and discover its story and clear it once and for all.

Listen as the silence comes, and you can sleep without the constant thoughts in your mind. Your mind is now free to attend to other things, like creating a special life for you.

What Is Happiness?

I have always known what unhappiness felt like, but I wonder if any of us really know happiness. Recently a friend made some interesting comments about it.

"We are continually looking for happiness but I don't think anyone truly knows what it is. It's a bit like the hunt for the holy grail. An unhappy housewife, she can't see that she is happy because she is totally bored with her life so to her it's not happy. I think we need to know what would truly make us happy. I mean, what really is happiness for everyone? It's different for each of us I think. How can you achieve something that you really don't know what it is? What is true happiness Jan? It is just a mindset. It is what we think we want. It's kind of like you don't know what you have till it's gone."

For me personally, happiness is something that sneaks up on me. I was going along merrily with my work, knowing I wasn't happy with my life as yet, but not concerning with it as I felt I would discover its meaning eventually. Then out of the blue, one day, someone said something that made me realize. Hey, I do feel happy. I like this feeling. But I hadn't even noticed it previously. I discovered that as with love, happiness is not something we consciously decide we want and create. It is about an experience of a feeling that naturally occurs when we remove whatever blocks it, such as a belief that we do not deserve or one of the mass beliefs we have taken on.

Happiness came to me when I faced and healed the things that made me unhappy. What else would I feel other than happy once I removed the need to feel unhappy? Now days I am filled with happiness and joy. I delight in it at will. To me, happiness is feeling that inner spark, that love energy from my own being.

And when I am living what is natural to me, without restrictions from fear beliefs, whatever I do is great fun.

Perhaps happiness is one of those mass things we are meant to search for, in the same way we hear, that unless we have love in our lives we are not complete. Well, I surely know the love one is false. Perhaps by continually searching, people miss what is right before them. Allowing ourselves to feel and know what doesn't feel natural and comfortable, may be the path to discovering happiness. If it is happiness we believe in and seek.

Activity - What Does Happiness Mean To You?

What makes you smile from the inside out? What makes you grin like a Cheshire cat? What fills your body with delicious love energy? What is happiness to you? Form your own understanding and concepts.

Life Is Always Greener On The Other Side

That comment always puzzled me, I didn't realize it was meant to be a contradictory one, demonstrating that wishing for more is a pipe dream. I've since heard people speak of their search for the greener pasture, but when they reached it, yet another one looked greener, and so it continued. They came to realize that to think that a different life to the one they have now will make things better, is a fallacy. All lives are the same as the one they have now. We have what we have, so either we can live with want and feel dissatisfied, or we can accept and make the most of what we do have.

Those people who think leaving their families will make them happy are fooling themselves, I have been told. How could they be happy when their actions hurt the ones they love?

Perhaps their only issue is trying to recapture their youth, another fallacy. Or wanting what they can't have. Or being just bored men and women wanting to put some spice back into their mid lives.

To me, it does seem all this self talk people undertake, certainly stops them wanting more in life. One comment struck a cord in me. "All lives are the same as the one we have now." This I know to be a valid one, but for a very specific reason.

Our inner beliefs create our perceptions, which in turn create what we think and how we act. Therefore it makes sense that altering circumstances is irrelevant to the outcome because it is the beliefs not the circumstances which control the event and our subsequent happiness.

If we change ourselves, by way of work on our beliefs, then our perception, thoughts and actions follow along automatically. Our life changes automatically. It is impossible to change and improve our lives while still holding onto those old beliefs, yet that is not realized and people keep running to escape, doing all the physical things to fix their lives, then feel deflated when situations keep repeating.

For example. A person who believes they are not loved, leaves a sad and loveless marriage. They search for love wherever they can, usually the wrong places, they might think they have found it, but very quickly come to realize it is not so. Changing the physical circumstances did nothing.

If this person searched out their own inner beliefs of not being loved and lovable, healed and replaced them with 'knowing they are loved and feeling the love that comes when they are free to be themselves', they have no need to go out searching for love, it fills and surrounds them, and comes to them.

The difference is, that the person who has worked on their beliefs will no longer need to remain in a loveless marriage, if that is how it continues after their work, and probably move on. They have had the experience so no longer require it because they are ready for its opposite. Love and happiness is now available to them.

Activity - Get it

Have you dreamed of how everything would be perfect if you changed jobs, found love, or won lotto? What would be different about you that would make any of the previous sustainable? What are the situations you wish to change in your life, and what are the steps to create those change?

Pick one small simple topic that you want to change. Use it as your experiment to try and document prior, then again after you have felt, learned and released whatever created it. Become fully aware and knowledgeable about what creates the things in your life! Learn how to do it for yourself at will, firstly with very small things to make it easier while you are learning.

Dreaming And Wanting

Do we think our dreams of better futures are just that? Fantasies to have and enjoy, but to be remembered as make believe? Things that we have no control over? That if dreams are meant to be they will come true on their own, they are outside and nothing to do with us?

And this is the one I felt the most after hearing. "But you have to keep in mind that dreams don't always last and you eventually will wake up."

What of all those special chance thoughts and ideas that pop into our head? What of the visions we have of possible futures? Do we really think they cannot become real?

I recently had the experience of documenting my own vision quest. All the visions of my future that I would visit and feel. I clarified then wrote, like a school project, all pretty and special.

As I clarified then wrote my thoughts and feelings, I had the magical experience of wonderful new knowing that flowing through me, which I added as I wrote. It was indeed a very special document to participate in.

And why is it wrong to want? Why is it that to want is

selfish and greedy? Who put such notions into our heads that we don't deserve such things? It is up to you entirely whether you decide to keep these beliefs or create new ones for yourself. What if you released then replaced them with a knowing that you are special, and can create anything you desire?

Activity - What Are Your Beliefs Of Dreaming?

This topic is addressed in detail within upcoming chapters, but for now, discover your own thoughts and beliefs of dreams by thinking of one and listening to the mind talk that tells you how it is not possible.

Change Can Be Worse

Many people are scared of change. The mere thought of leaving their comfort zone and security of home, into the unknown, can make them ill. Therefore remaining is seen as better than the possibility of worse happening.

Creating change is viewed as a struggle, hard work, a fight. This may be because they are still in the mindset of the belief they wish to escape. The only way to escape an unhappy situation is to not require it further. This is accomplished by removing the belief itself. And the person finds new circumstances automatically fall into place around them. Yet, the belief that 'change is something to be feared' stops us attempting inner change, to create the outer one. So this is the belief to be looked into, not the fact of what it refers to in their physical life.

Activity - What Are Your Thoughts Of Change

Put yourself in the situation of writing a list of the things you wish to change in your life then listen to the fears of how it could be a big mistake. Where did this belief come from, what does it mean, how has it sabotaged your life? Feel, understand and release.

Pity

If we remove the subject to hold our pity parties about, there would be no excuse to have them. We would have nothing to moan and groan about.

This topic is discussed in several chapters, including Self Importance and Difficult Lives. So all I will say here is to remind that our pity parties are part of our experiences.

We use them to gain comfort and care from others because we feel it is lacking. We use situations to set up the need for people to feel sorry for us, or come to our rescue. We set up difficult lives to get others to come to us.

Therefore the issue is not what is happening in our lives, but instead why we need the pity of another person, and why we feel the need to hold onto situations that do not make us happy.

Activity - Are You Ready To Let Go Of The Drama?

Most people have no awareness that they throw pity parties, and how this activity sabotages their life success. Watch someone who struggles with life issues, listen to how they share their horror stories, and how you feel sorry for them. This is a pity party.

No judgment! There is a good reason people began holding pity parties, but there is also a good reason to go beyond needing them as you will discover in the upcoming chapters.

Ask yourself this question. Do you wish to stay with the unpleasant experiences that lead to the pity parties where you do get a lot of sympathy and attention, or are you ready to let go of those experiences all together?

To Think Of You Is Selfish And Greedy

Another obstacle to thinking that we have the right to change is our belief of ourselves. What are the things we have the general rights to as a human being? What do you believe you deserve? Why?

Again, people prevent even contemplating change because they think to do so is to be self-centered, selfish, and greedy.

To hold this belief means you view everything you do that is in your own best interests as selfish, and bad. How do you expect to be able to have a happy life if it is wrong to do so?

This belief makes us think of the horrible affects our actions will have on those around us. How, that by doing something for ourselves results in everyone else suffering. We are not allowed to want anything for ourselves that affects anyone else.

Again, the belief discussed prevents the change and can be viewed as an independent topic, not related to the issue of what to change. They serve to keep us bound in acceptance of what does not feel comfortable.

Activity - Are You Allowed?

Are you allowed to be happy? Are you allowed to live a successful life? Are you allowed to be loved and cared for, and to be surrounded by nice things and to be pampered and to have an easy life? Are you allowed to care for you?

Listen to your feelings, thoughts and stories that come up. Understand, heal and clear them all.

Acceptance Of The Situation

Now is the point where people often form conclusions and decide to accept their life situations and find a way to come to terms with the fact that this is how life is.

There is no point in rocking the boat and making it more difficult for themselves. It is better to calm down and take each day at a time. Being happy with what they have instead of wanting more. Life can be far too short to keep on wanting more, so perhaps it is about enjoying each day as it comes and making the most of now, to be happy.

Activity - Do You Want To Accept Or Do You Want More For Yourself?

Are you ready to accept your unhappy life situations, or have you reached the point of deciding that you have to have more?

Feel, understand fully and make sure that you smile when you think of whichever decision you reach. Then you know that it is the right one for you. If you make a decision and do not feel warm and fuzzy, then you have not faced all of the issues preventing your life success, so stop, feel and listen. Keep doing this to heal and release your obstacles until there are none left.

Me

Just writing this makes me feel great sadness within. I can imagine and feel my own response if I told myself that my life is set in stone, that I can't reach for the stars, that I don't deserve or have any control in it, that my dreams and visions are just fantasy. That I should give up and be content with what I have.

Perhaps that's what has always driven me because I felt it so deeply. There must be, and is more to this living experience. There has to be because otherwise it is too sad to continue with.

If I feel unhappy about something, or it makes me feel very uncomfortable, I can't just ignore what I feel. To do so is to ignore my own being, the opposite of what I have spent these last 3 1/2 years striving to discover.

And here is the point I need to make clearly. What I just wrote refers to me alone. I cannot be happy when I don't want more for myself. It is my journey to keep reaching and searching for answers. That does not mean that my life is to be filled with sadness, only that I personally cannot accept and blindly remain in unhappy situations.

Other people have the path of discovering what makes them comfortable with their lives, what makes them feel content and satisfied to accept what they have. To stop searching and looking to the outside for happiness that only comes from within.

I suppose what I am trying to get across, is that you do not have to live a sad life. You do not have to accept 'what is dealt to you'. You have choices. You have control. Find what feels right for you. Listen to your smiles and excitement when things make you happy.

Hopes/Dreams

What are our hopes and dreams exactly? Are they really deep desires from within that we feel driven to create in our lives, or mind goals that we never really believe in, to watch pass us by so we can say life did us wrong?

When you complete this chapter you will be able to:

- Stop hiding behind false hopes and dreams
- Understand and let go of your mind hopes and dreams
- Get ready to let your real dreams come true

What Do We Hope And Dream Of?

I hope to feel better soon, I hope to do well at school, I hope that my children grow up to be responsible adults, I hope it doesn't rain today. They sound rather like things we 'hope' and pray to escape, or things we don't wish to experience. Yet we treat them like wishes, for something or someone to fix it for us.

I hope to feel better soon. Isn't that statement merely saying I feel one thing, and will use a belief in fate or karma or good luck to change it? That I do not have any responsibility in neither its creation, or resolution? Same with 'I hope to do well at school', this could refer to a job interview, a doctors test, any situation. I want to do well, and 'hope' that I do. Well, isn't it up to me how well I do, isn't it my responsibility? Or 'believe' that I will in regard to medical testing? To hope is to pray that something out there creates the situation I wish for. To hope is to remove any personal responsibility for its creation.

Time to think carefully of all we 'hope' for, and accept responsibility. Time to let go of being the victim in this life. We and we alone are responsible and create it all.

Activity - What Are Your Hopes?

Think of your hopes, feel how you use this word to hide from responsibility and having to do something. Thinking about being responsible may raise fears, good. Feel and listen to them, find their reasons and remove those.

Spend a week noticing and writing down the thoughts and comments you or those around you make in regard to hopes. Go over them one by one, and think them through so you can recognize how they take your power away.

Then make the decision. Is that what you wish to keep doing? If it isn't then do the work. Stop, feel, listen to the story, understand and release.

Dreaming

The form of dreaming I refer to is the verbal one. A mind one, far removed from floating and feeling. When we speak of our dreams, calling them desires. We tell the world what we dream, how it can be better, and our part in making it so.

I dream of having my own business, I dream of having plenty of money, I dream of being loved, I dream of being happy.

To dream is to claim a want for something. To dream is to

fill self with grand schemes and fantasies, never expecting or undertaking what is required to fulfill them.

I dream of doing magical things with my life. I dream of creating this perfect business, yet I expect it will create itself without any input.

It is like we create their idea just to have something to say and think we want. Pipe dreams because we think we are suppose to have them, not because we necessarily want them or know what we want.

Activity - What Are Your Dreams?

How do you use the word dreams? What are your dreams? Do you expect them to come true or are they just to have something to sidetrack your thoughts?

Make your list of dreams, feel and understand them, then decide if you want to continue to change the meaning of the word dream into one that means it can't come true? Or if you want to have beautiful dreams of a perfect life, knowing that you can have it?

Feel, understand and release.

Dreams Are Cop-outs

I will share my dream of the world being a peaceful place, I will speak with others of the same dream, we will tell even more people of our dream, saying we can change it.

What does that actually achieve though? Anything other than making ourselves look good by having such a noble dream?

Do we actually do anything towards this dream of the world being peaceful? Do we act in peaceful ways towards those around us, encourage others feeling peaceful within themselves?

Let me clarify. Recently groups of people dreamed of peace in the world. They spent a great deal of time gathering and talking about how this is a wonderful thing to do, how they will change the world. They sent out their message via emails. The world is in trouble, look what is happening, we have to 'demand' peace before it is too late. They held rallies 'demanding' peace. We can read those words and think, but these people did have a noble desire. They did have a noble dream.

But I ask you to think more carefully. Anyone can say words, anyone can say a noble thing and others will praise them. But, if they really wished it to become they would have taken action. They would have worked to bring peace into their own life rather than still fighting with their families and neighbors, they would have taken some action towards peace. Many I know filled themselves with grand words and claims of ideals, yet did absolutely nothing. That is the difference.

I recently read some beautiful words by Gregg Braden about creating peace (2003). "Here's what we are asking, and please pass this email to everyone you can. On April 20th, 6pm, 2003 New York time, we ask that you join with as many people as you can and do three things.

1. "Feel" the emotion of peace prevailing in the Middle East. This is where the real magic is.

2. Imagine Israeli and Palestinian children responding to this call, using the power of their spirits to activate the healing energy that will bring peace to everyone in that region.

3. Sing a song that you all know: "Let There be Peace on Earth." Music has a power that cannot be denied, and this song says it all.

That's it. Imagine if millions respond to this request. We believe that it may activate their souls to create the peace that evades the politicians. It's the children we need to encourage now, and the rest of us will surely follow."

Can you now see the difference in using fear or hope vs. the power of love and believing? Can you imagine people all over the world picturing peace and the impact of that?

To have a dream is fine. Yet to claim it as special, and you special for creating it, is to merely use it to make yourself feel and look good to those around you.

We hold onto our hopes and dreams, never expecting or believing in their realization, never seriously taking action to make them manifest. Then we watch as they escape us, another way we say life did us wrong. Woe is me!

Take a good look at what you are doing with your life. Is this really what you want to be doing, are you being the person you want to be? Are you still waiting for that 'there must be more' dream to materialize? Well wake up! You and you alone are responsible for dreaming and creating this life. It does not happen TO you. It happens BY you, and you alone.

Where do we think we are going with this living gig? It seems like we are heading to some imaginary dream, we feel proud to have such marvelous dreams, yet they aren't real dreams, we don't live them. We use them to hide behind.

My Dream

I had a special dream, held onto it for many years. I wanted to establish my own business here as a massage therapist, doing what I loved to do.

I kept trying all I could to make it so, set up at a local hairdresser, did the advertising, told friends. But it was all half hearted, because I was filled with doubts. I didn't believe it could be so. I didn't put in full effort, instead imagined and came up with ideas, but couldn't take action on them. I had even allowed the situation where my overseas credentials were not accepted here in America, so I ended up without a license.

Everyone encouraged and felt sorry for me. I was trying so very hard yet fate and bad luck kept getting in the way.

This dragged on for some time. Then one day I went by the hairdresser and saw a sign, that of a new massage therapist. And the dream flew away with the wind. It was gone for good.

So, after all this time of dreaming, yet not being able to manifest that dream, it was time to recognize it for what it was. A fantasy dream. And let it go. A sad, but good thing for me to do.

Activity - Find And Let Go Of Your Life Dream

Find your mind dream, just like mine above and discover if it is a real dream or just something you don't really put much effort into or expect to happen.

Know that the more time and effort you spend on your mind dreams, the less time and effort you spend on the real dreams that are waiting for you to decide to have so they can become real.

Conclusion

The act of hoping and dreaming for something in our future, is exactly what we will experience. The verbs 'dream' and 'want'. The experience of desiring something not had, not believed in as having.

I dream and wish for love to come into my life. I spend much time praying and hoping it will come soon. But what do these actions mean in real terms? I do not believe in love, as demonstrated by my not feeling lovable, deserving, wanted. But I hope and dream how that situation being the opposite.

I think perhaps all the things we ponder are those yet to be experienced and known from within. Our way of heading towards future experiences.

If I believed in having love I would not still 'want' for it. Why want what I already have? Therefore to want something is to believe in not having it, it not being possible.

Why would a person with plenty of food hope to have

sufficient? Does the person who knows love in their lives think about wanting or what it means to have love, no. Does one who has been to college wonder what it would be like? The experience of having something in our lives results in knowing its meaning from within, so why think on what it would be like to have, unless you are yet to experience it?

Notice what you think about, recognize if any regard true experiences already had and understood. I very much doubt it. But, this is a great clue on our journeys. That what we think of as our goal and are preparing for that through the non-experience of it. The non-experiencing is where the learning experience is formed to facilitate the creation to have it.

Hopes and dreams are magical, once we let go of hiding behind them.

Change your dreaming to intent. Think, feel, make the decision, then use intent to create it. Don't just float in fantasy land, dreaming but never expecting.

To dream is to create an idea in our minds, that is all. It is up to us what we do with that idea once formed.

While hopes and dreams are of the mind's desires to escape life situations, passions are heart and spirit desires, which when felt bring life and love into our world.

Passions/Heart Desires

What are they exactly? What do we do with our passions, those things that make us feel alive, from the deepest part of us?

When you complete this chapter you will be able to:

- Discover your passions and how they fit in your life
- Review your life circumstances and refocus its direction
- Make your passions a priority

Do we listen and follow them? Do we have time for that? Or is our time spent buried in the money making experience, supposedly for necessities of life? Do we think these passions are frivolous and a waste of time?

How and why do we choose our occupations? Our pass times? What of community service?

How many different passions/causes do we each have? Why do we have them? Are they to fill some wanted need within us?

Before I came to America I created within my mind a list of all the pass times I wanted to undertake. Water painting, drawing, photography, and several others. 2 years later, while I have dabbled somewhat in them, I am yet to spend real time doing any. I have great difficulty 'wanting' to do anything. It is confusing to me.

I do have many interests that I would like to pursue, yet I don't. I have many interests that I would like to share with others, yet I keep coming back to having to make a living, then find myself unable to progress with what I desire to do.

It is passion and letting it lead, that creates drive, inspiration and motivation within us. Yet it is also passion that is lacking in mine and many other peoples lives.

Our focus is on the dollar, the need to earn sufficient then spend it as quickly as it comes into our hands. As we keep chasing the unreachable, there is no time left for our passions.

Passion is that special feeling from within, the warm fuzzy smile from the inside out, the excitement of being or doing something loved. Passions are our innate desires which, when experienced can't help but make us smile.

We feel alive, we feel excited, we smile and laugh. It feels good to do what we desire. To spend time beyond our physical life fears and hurts, allowing our passions to lead the way creates the magic in our lives. Passions are of the spirit realm.

Activity - Find Your Passion

Think of something that makes you smile from the inside out, how long has it been since you undertook it? What is it that to even think of doing, beings a grin to your face? What is it that makes you FEEL?

What events can you add to your activity cards, that make you feel alive?

Life Direction

We come into this life with certain wants and needs regarding experience. We set up our lives very cleverly so as to see they are included, often much to our dismay. It is possible to look at our experience choices and analyze their reasoning, also to direct ourselves towards newly desired experiences.

Life has countless experience opportunities, from being a care giver, receiver of care, healer, requiring healing, rescuer, needing rescuing, teacher, student, giver, receiver, controller to being controlled etc.

Each life direction we take, whether it relate to work, personal, family or community interests, fills a specific experiential need within us. We create our realities and situations, therefore one wishing the experience of being a healer, creates through their desire, people needing healing. Therefore we can look at our lives and current direction, making a conscious decision as to whether that is the person we chose to be. Specifically, paying close attention to our inner feelings and desires.

How often are people spending their entire living time working at jobs they dislike, undertaking activities which give no joy, participating in family dramas that make them feel ill, living lives that feel restricted and unhappy?

We can carefully look at each aspect of our lives, make a conscious decision whether this is a situation we wish to continue in, or finish whatever work is required and move onto another experience. Remember everything happens for the learning that comes from experience. Until that is completed, we remain within our often referred to nightmares no matter how hard we attempt to escape them.

Activity - Your Dream Life

You have spent much time working with your dream life, now is the time to see it from another perspective. What makes you happy? Go back into every aspect you listed, update what is currently happening in that area, then stop and feel. Are you happy with this experience continuing, or not? You may be surprised at what you discover.

Some examples may include: unhappy and unpleasant

family or work circumstances, no time for yourself, no desires or passion, feeling something is missing in your life.

Look at each topic honestly and openly. If your marriage is abusive or unhappy, why do you remain in it? Is that healthy for anyone, including the children? Who is benefiting from this experience? What would a happy outcome be? Realistically, is that possible?

These are difficult issues to ponder and draw conclusions about, this I do know. Yet, what is the purpose of remaining in any situation that is not in your best interests? Other's interests are not met unless yours are. That is the natural progression.

For example, a selfless mother spends all her time and energy providing for her children, at her expense. Do you honestly think her children actually receive the care she desires for them when she is unable to care for herself? When she cares for herself automatically, her and her children's life experience alters dramatically, her children then receive much benefit.

What of a seemingly trivial one, animals. How many animals do you have? Is there time for the care and love you would prefer to give each? Are they trapped indoors 24hrs a day, destroying and making your home smelly? Do they fight and squabble like children? Are your animals causing you distress? Do you spend more time attempting to care for your animals than yourself?

Yes, the topic of animals seems minute compared to other situations in our lives. Yet it is one we live with every day in our homes, and sometimes they cause great worry and distress to us.

Honestly though, is it logical that a dog lives on furniture that is made for humans 24hrs a day, when you have a perfectly good backyard that only needs to be fenced? What of cats natural desire to run and lay on fresh grass, climb trees and feel fresh air? I am aware of cat laws, but I am also aware that if you chose to have animals, surely part of that decision is arrangements to ensure as natural a living existence for the animal as possible. Just as a fenced backyard and dog door would delight your dog, a form of fencing with roof (as encouraged in Australia) would see your cat purring. I actually saw a cat on a lead the other day. A 3 foot lead tied to the back steps, yet this cat rolled in the grass and purred and was so very happy to spend a short time outside.

Activity - Make Your Passions A Priority

Now that you have spent some time re-analyzing your current situations think of your passions. What, from merely thinking of it, makes you smile from inside? What makes you feel passionate?

What can you alter in your life to allow your passions the freedom to be felt and expressed?

The Fight to Be Me

As I look out my window into the misty drizzle so refreshing after the heat, one lone bird feeds on a freshly mowed lawn. It struts proudly while walking about pecking for worms and bugs. This one lone bird lives all that it symbolizes. Freedom and peace. It is a white dove, the first I have seen in America.

When you complete this chapter you will be able to:

- Know what you fight for
- Decide if you want to believe that you have to keep fighting or have all that you want
- Recognize your own goals and clear any obstacles that prevent you reaching them

Freedom and peace are believed to be the right of all people. It is what we fight and search for life after life.

The term fight relates to how we feel rather than just physical fighting. It is the feeling of having to stand up for something. Throughout time, man's history depicts heroic events whereby the simple man fights for what he believes in, his right to freedom and peace, demonstrated by his unfailing will to do anything to achieve this.

Man has always aspired to survive, and fight for that right.

To claim it as ours.

We see it in the eyes of the mother fighting to provide food and shelter for her children, to protect them from harm and fight all those who go against their best interests. The struggle and fight parents of children with disabilities willingly take on, the father who protects and provides for the welfare of his family, against all odds. Those who fight oppression and slavery, discrimination and abuse, and government control.

To be human is to fight the elements for survival. To go forward and break the barriers of new harsh lands, droughts and floods, high seas and hurricanes. To not let any situation beat us. To be human is not to sit back idly and be defeated. It is to fight for what we believe in.

We create lives and situations just so we may engage in this fight and gain strength of character along the way.

History can easily tell us of this belief. Search them out for yourselves, read of the heroic demonstrations by your fellow man. Some examples might include the wagon trains heading west, groups of ethnic families who traveled into new lands, exploration and world discovery, each full of individual tales, each full of adventure, each full of courage and unending strength of will.

What of current world events? Refugees fleeing war and corruption, those engaged in war because they believe in their cause. The residents of one small town in old Russia refused to admit defeat and run, they stood their ground, willing to die for their homes and freedom, and they did.

What of our own life events? Parents doing everything they can to protect their children, working 2 and 3 jobs, to secure college tuition costs, fighting every single day for their right to a better life, fighting for their children's future so it will be better than their own.

This fight I speak of comes in many forms. It may be for peace and freedom, or the right to survive, the right to stand up and be counted, the right to be respected, the right to count in this gigantic world.

Activity - What Is Your Fight?

Let yourself think about your own personal fight, the one that drives you. Watch movies about similar situations. Let this feeling be triggered fully within you. Find, feel and write about your need to fight for your life. It does not matter what comes up, if you feel it then accept the story you are told.

My Fight

The movie Braveheart was my trigger to realize my fight. Of love lost and the pain carried, of fighting for survival, for freedom to have peace and control over your own life, of knowing the fight can never be put aside until the goal is reached, to die for what you believe in, never faltering. An honorable story.

I found it interesting as I watched this movie, based on life centuries ago, to find I had the same beliefs and sense of the need to fight for survival. I had the same need to stand up for what I believe in, to not be silent and submissive, that I also held the same feelings towards politics and those in authority. I had beliefs related to those who held power using it for their own gain, rather than for the common people. I felt and held the same beliefs as this character William, played by my fellow countryman Mel Gibson.

Without any memory of engaging in a similar need to fight for survival and freedom, I found myself knowing exactly how he felt, why he behaved as he did, why he couldn't give up the fight, why he died holding tightly to them.

Of course my current life situation has not included anything remotely related, yet I know of these things. I go about my life undertaking actions related to the same feelings as this character. Living beliefs based on the same issues. How can this be so? Does it really matter?

I had no belief of other lives, but the more I delved into

myself the more information came forth to explain the feelings and knowledge I had which did not match my present life experiences.

You do not need to deliberately look into other lives, just allow and accept whatever you feel as okay, and listen to the stories that are shared with you.

Many Experiences Over Many Lifetimes

This adventure we call living comprises experiencing all situations and possibilities, in one life or another. They all come together in being part of the person we are now. They all form our feelings and memories and beliefs, to create how we view ourselves and living.

Having to fight for survival in the depth of winter snow, or scavenging for food during drought, of being abused and abandoned, of loving and losing that, everything I have experienced, combines and adds up to the person I am at this moment. I have indeed experienced many situations of fighting for what I believe in.

It is not just that to fight is to demonstrate strength and will, it is feeling the need to have to fight in order to achieve desires. Feeling that unless we fight and demand our wants, they cannot become. It is the need to stand up for ourselves, and claim ourselves as worthy. Hence we create repeat after repeat in order to experience this fighting for self.

Activity - What Are Your Opposites?

What might be the opposite we aspire to achieve? Perhaps to learn that we do not need to fight any longer. We do not need to stand up and be counted, demanding what we want. Perhaps it is experiencing the knowing that all we have fought for is ours already.

Imagine that? Every issue we fight for is now ours. Food, shelter, safety, material needs, money, freedom, peace, to be valued and respected.

What do you fight for in your life? What if I told you they are all yours for the asking right now? No more fighting and demanding. The battle is over! How does it feel? What opposition surfaces?

List each issue you struggle for, whether it is money, health, rights, acceptance, safety, future, all of them. Think of each struggle you encounter in your current life. Think of each issue where it feels like 'you against them'. Discover and heal them all.

Reaching The Goal

It is interesting, that from pondering the issues raised with fight and struggle, I have come to realize that I deeply believe in what I know and do, yet not in myself. That for me to go out and share what I know, via this book and group work, I need to feel that I am successful. Walking my talk so to speak.

Until such time that I live my words fully and become successful with this game of life, to me they are mere conjecture. What a contradiction. I have and do believe and live the person who has undergone all I speak of. I am a very different person who began this work, no longer fearful, wanting others approval, stressed and upset by events, my whole perception has changed.

Perhaps this issue is related to my perception of success, and what I desired to achieve with this work. To find peace, happiness and contentment in my life, that would lead to living a life that I experienced fully. When I began this work more than 2 years ago, I had no concept of anything I have written about here, all I wanted was to escape my own personal nightmare. I wanted to find a better life, driven by the belief that there must be something better. I had no idea it would relate to how I felt about myself, nor be a journey of self discovery. Only that I hurt, and wanted that feeling gone. I wanted to find what was missing in me and my life, to make sense of it all.

Each time I released, thereby escaped some dreaded experience and feeling, I would find myself on a high of excitement. It is still a thrill to feel. Each time I understood something about myself, and why I was who I was, I felt comforted and reassured. Piece by piece I learned first hand exactly who I was, and why. Then I had the choice of remaining as that person, or selecting who I preferred to be. The real me.

It has been like peeling the layers of an onion, one by one. With each layer came new insights and knowledge, and amazement at it all. Especially this last year as I began evaluating the psychological aspects that are included in this book. There really is a reason behind all this. There really is a path and purpose to everything. There really are connections between people and events.

As unreal as this whole experience seems, I am in awe of its complexities and concept. To live is to be part of this amazing web of creation, linked and inter-linked with all other life, from all time. We are each a storehouse of information, of feelings and experiences had forever. We indeed have it all within us. A timeline of life in each being.

I am not the person born into this life as an empty slate as psychologists thought. I brought with me every aspect of who I have and will ever be. I am life eternal, living it all, right here at this very moment.

I am the experience of living. I am living an experience of life.

This journey commenced because I wanted to escape, I set specific outcomes to measure my success, and expected those to be reached before I would feel successful. I focused on the goal, not the journey.

Success is not about achieving, perhaps it is another mass belief term I took on. What is success? Who determined it to be so anyway? Success is a judgment term related to personal expectations of self, nothing more.

We can't fail life, there is nothing TO fail. It is all an experience to be had, no judgments or expectations involved. Except within ourselves about ourselves. And what and how we determine it should be. More mass beliefs.

Does it really matter whether I spend the weekend relaxing and pottering around the house? Or racing around filling my time with activities? Who cares, beside me? Who judges what and when we should do things besides us? Why did we take on those mass expectancy beliefs?

Yet, from within me I feel there is still more to this living than I have reached. Not so much events, but feelings of satisfaction, of achieving, of doing what I believe living is. Or is that merely another mass belief? Perhaps I expect that feeling content and happy will tell me when I am on track. Perhaps we know and feel unsettled from within so we keep seeking more.

I do have things I wish to achieve in this life. I do have many goals and aspirations. I do have experiences I wish to explore. And most importantly, I do wish to have the experience of physical life being easy, especially the fundamentals of survival and necessities.

And I come full circle, for that is the fight I still undertake. The fight to be capable of acquiring the basic necessities and skills of physical life. I still fight to live. I still believe myself to be failing living life itself.

Activity - What Are Your Goals?

What is your picture that will say to you "I am there and finished". Discover the life that will be yours by listening to the story of the life that will feel right to you.

Think about it, feel it, is it a real 'have to have' life or 'want to have' life? If it is a want to have then it is sabotaging the life you have to have, so feel, understand and let it go. It will feel very different to do this, but know that if you follow your feelings and listen to what you know to do from inside, then you will come out of it just fine. Letting go is very sad, and makes you feel like you are giving up all hope of ever having it, but it is the opposite.

When we have an expectation of how something 'has' to be, then we cannot see, enjoy or experience what we actually have.

This may clarify. I hold the belief that when someone loves me they will of course behave in a specific way. But everyone is and expresses themselves differently; no-one can know my particular expectation.

Someone may love me dearly but I will think they don't unless I see one particular behavior. When I let that expectation go, I feel like no-one will ever love me like I wanted and needed and am very sad during the process. But after I completely give up and let it go, I find that I can now see the love shared with me, and it is just perfect.

Grumpy Days

Ever have those days when everything that possibly can, does and will go wrong. When it begins the moment you wake up, late, progressively becoming worse with every single activity you attempt.

When you complete this chapter you will be able to:

- Stop reacting to grumpy days
- Find and heal the real issues that make you grumpy

You head off to work with hair that wont behave, car wont start or runs out of gas, the kids and animals are all screaming for attention, your late for work and your boss is not impressed, waiting to point out a mistake he's found. Seeming like each task you undertake merely serves to bury you deeper into this jinxed day. Then end the day by burning dinner.

My day began when I woke up to a howling cat, walking over and round the bed like a caged animal making this mournful cry. I had wanted to finish some personal work this day and knew it was not possible, when I refilled my printer cartridge, it didn't work so that money was wasted. My computer won't save this piece for some reason, nor read my floppy disc. And it is only lunchtime. What a lost day.

Your senses are heightened, head pounding, tolerance and patience tested. Grumpy is an understatement for your mood, growling and shouting at all who come near.

What is going on? Do you assume its one of those days when the world is against you, going about blaming everyone and everything but yourself? Do you become more and more angry and upset?

We can easy feel moods coming on, then either attempt to put them aside and pretend they do not exist, or ride the angst they create. Either way, the mood and events are felt and not easily shaken, so why not put them to good use.

Perhaps we attempt to avoid noticing, then facing their reasons because we fear another bout of self condemnation from ourselves. We have heard it all before, over and over again so why do it again. It is much easier to blame the world and be an angry person, than look inside at what we dislike of ourselves.

To me, I feel this unexpected mood today as a waste of my day. This day is it, the now, and not how I wish to be spending it. I had planned it as a productive and pivotal day. So I feel flat and disappointed at myself for creating such a day.

When I found myself yelling at my cat each time she meows, I realized it was time to stop, slow down and get to work.

I allowed myself to feel the disappointment and annoyance at what was happening. Very quickly I found my answer. Depression and becoming full of self blame. Telling myself how useless I am, how I can't do anything right. Highlighting all the aspects of my life that are not how I wish them to be. Pointing the finger of blame at myself, reminding me how useless I am.

And those thoughts match exactly how I physically feel lately. Bloated, fat, nothing to wear, embarrassed to be seen by anyone, embarrassing to myself.

Allowing myself to flow with this feeling is difficult. I don't want to hear all this again, I thought it was cleared already, and now I will have to feel the sadness of it all over again. I would much rather curl up in bed and sleep, making it all disappear.

I do not want to face knowing that I have messed it all up,

that all this work has been for naught. I do not want to face failing the most important thing I have attempted in this life.

I know too well that this moment is what it is all about, not tomorrow or next week, not the goals and planning. This one moment in time that I am living is it.

And I am messing it up, just like I do with everything. I have had so many opportunities and help in this life, yet I keep sabotaging it all, I cannot allow myself to succeed and be happy. How sad.

Sometimes it's about feeling then going straight into the release technique, but other times you need more information first so you can grasp a new concept before doing the release.

I have left this pondering session in tact so you can see that it's perfectly normal and fine to let it all hang out and wallow in your own misery sometimes. To feel the experience as it happens (without judging and stopping yourself) while you watch where it leads you.

You can see by the next chapter that I was setting myself up for a more in depth concept.

Activity - Why Do You Have Grumpy Days?

How many times do you yell at your spouse or children when in a bad mood? Watch how you behave to your supposed loved ones, is that really the person you wish to be and portray to the world? Is that really how you wish to make your children feel? That your mood is their fault?

Next time you have a grumpy day, stop and allow yourself to find what is really on your mind, what are you so dissatisfied with in your life, and with your self?

Take the time to feel and listen, and heal your self, rather than blaming your moods on other people.

Failure & Success

What is it to be a failure? What are the key elements that create in us the personal need to judge ourselves so harshly as to have failed? When is it that we take on the belief that we are no good to ourselves, or anyone else in the world? We are failures as people.

It is one thing to not complete isolated things, yet another entirely when failure becomes a pattern in our lives, therefore becoming our personality.

When you complete this chapter you will be able to:

- Discover why you think you are a failure and how this belief sabotages your life success
- Heal all beliefs and implications of the failure personality
- Be a successful person

What Are The Specific Traits Of The Failure Personality?

Someone asks our help, and we agree yet do not comply. We fail to provide the necessities for our families and children. Leaving them hungry and going without basic needs. What of the example we give by our actions, of not being able to hold down a job, care for ourselves, addictions, being disorganized, in debt, lying and cheating to get by.

What of the people who had faith in us, the ones who gave all the encouragement, motivation and skills they could. With pure love, because they believed in us. We let them down terribly.

Activity - Your Failures

What are your failure personality traits? Write down each and every thing you fail to accomplish, from the mundane to extreme. Not keeping your home clean, paying bills on time, doing what you said you would, making something of yourself, everything. Think about and feel them all. You will be surprised at how enmeshed your personality is in failure.

Failure Beliefs

It seems our whole purpose in life is to create and recreate situations where the belief 'we are a failure as a person' is validated, to ourselves and the world. From the smallest action upwards, we make ourselves fail. A self-fulfilling prophecy.

Such hatred and dislike for self this creates. To keep reminding self what a waste of a human being and life we create, how bad we are, and deserve all the punishment that comes our way. The belief of failure is indeed a deeply hurtful and punishing one.

Activity - What Are Your Failure Beliefs?

How have you set yourself up to fail? Make a list of the beliefs you have of yourself about being a failure, then look at them carefully and imagine, document and become aware of how you create this self-fulfilling prophecy. What do you do to sabotage your life because you believe that you are a failure?

Getting Caught Out

One way this belief is highlighted is by being 'caught out'. When some circumstance prevents all attempts to hide the fact from ourselves and others, that we failed, and are a failure as a person, and living a failure of a life.

We then feel the intense embarrassment and are ashamed of the person we are, especially that another witnesses this. Perhaps who believed in and gave to us, and we let down.

For me personally, being caught out allowed me to finally acknowledge and feel my failures. I had and do fail with all I do. Its not merely a matter of saying, no you were doing your best, or there is no right or wrong, the fact is that I have failed, many many many times, in various lives.

Activity - Have You Ever Been Caught Out?

Who caught you out? How did it feel? What did you do about it? Sometimes it is beneficial to allow someone to catch us unaware, and then be forced to actually face the responsibility for failing. We can then feel, understand, heal and release the belief that creates failure.

Cover Ups

People are rarely aware of my failures, or are quick to give responsibility to bad luck, or the outside world, to feel sorry for me. I know better. I create all in my world, so my failures are mine alone and it is time to own up and take responsibility for them.

Activity - How Do You or People Cover Up Your Failures?

This one may be a little hard to notice, so keep it to remember when the topic does come up. Just becoming aware that this happens will allow you to notice how you cover up other people's failures and they yours.

Do you want to live with your head in the sand or be real? Your decision.

The Failure Mindset

It feels as though this deep sense of failure relates to letting other people down. Those who believed in, helped and supported, trusted, or were dependant on me. It feels like I failed to be the person we both knew was my potential.

When we view ourselves as failures, we become apathetic and unable to see how we affect others. We live self centered lives not feeling other's deserve the punishment that comes from being around us, that our actions don't affect them. We isolate ourselves from everyone and spend a great deal of time working to hide from knowing and accepting the failure we really are. From ourselves and those around us.

Believing we are failures creates a life cycle of failure from every aspect.

I am a failure and nothing I can do will ever make up for or eliminate that act and fact. I promised to do certain things, I took on responsibilities, I accepted gifts, I chose to do things. Yet, I failed myself and all those involved, by not succeeding.

I am a failure as a person and a life, so why bother attempting anything.

I create desires and wants, then go about making sure they fail, repeatedly validating my failure label. We continually go about punishing ourselves, without ever knowing. And will continue to do so until we understand.

Activity - Are You A Failure?

Ask yourself this. Do you feel successful with everything in your life? If not, why? Every time you embark on an activity, which does not succeed, how often do you feel sad and disappointed by that? What is the impact on you?

Make note of each action and reaction, begin to notice the self sabotage, and what you feel when this happens. For example, I wish to start my own business, so I plan and set it all up, but something always goes wrong and it fails. How do I then feel, a failure perhaps. Do I then go about justifying why it was expected to fail, telling myself all the things wrong with me, why I deserved this.

Activity - Take Responsibility

We also take great effort in gathering support for our inadequacies, to aim the blame elsewhere. We cry on friend's shoulders about our sadness and lack of being able to do that which we desire and attempt so hard.

We gather them as shields to prevent self acknowledgement and responsibility for ourselves and our actions.

The goal here is to feel that deep sense of failure in yourself. The despair and sadness, the apathy. If this is difficult to reach, keep thinking of and feeling all the failures in your life, how sad and hurtful they were. Feel the deep sadness of being a failure.

Allow yourself to wallow in this self-pity, feel every aspect of it, almost as if from the victim perspective. Feel how everyone would be better of without you around, how you negatively impact on other people's lives, how you let them down constantly. How you are just not worth it. Allow yourself to feel every aspect of this sadness at discovering who you are. A failure.

At this point we aim to release this feeling, but that can be difficult due to the need for self-punishment. Releasing this sadness at self, prevents punishment. If this is the case with you, finish reading the chapter then perhaps the order to release will present itself naturally.

Activity - Feel The Guilt

Once we have allowed ourselves to find and feel the self-pity for being a failure, we can go on to experience the guilt. We have indeed let many people down for no good reason. They did not deserve the consequences of our actions.

Perhaps it is guilt at disappointing someone who cared and had faith in us. The teacher who went out of their way to be of help, to guide and motivate us. The one who held the faith in us, the hopes and dreams.

How can we ever make amends for what we have done? To all those we have impacted on. This I do not know.

Activity - Feel Your Need To Blame And Punish You

Feel your want of self punishment, how you deserve everything you get, and more. Think of each situation from your list and the resultant punishment experienced. Listen to how you justify it, actually enjoying handing it out to yourself. Wanting it and more.

Activity - Deserving

Think of all the pleasurable things you'd like in your life, then why you don't deserve them. All the punishments you feel are deserved instead. Feel your wanting to aim this at yourself with great passion and anger.

It is interesting that these are the precise thoughts behind binge eating, smoking, drinking and all other harmful activities.

How often is it that when you feel badly of yourself you head straight for the chocolate or snacks? Now do you wonder why?

If you do any harmful activities see if you can use feeling to discover why you do, then go through the process of understanding and releasing.

Activity - The History Of Human Failure

What about the impact humans have had on our planet, and our fellow man? We have ravaged, destroyed, abused, controlled and manipulated everything we could lay our hands on. What of the actions of our politicians and business leaders? How they perpetuate the continual downward cycle of this beautiful planet and her occupants, seemingly for their own glory alone?

Let yourself think about man's history in its entirety, the shame and sadness of it all. What a waste. When you feel perhaps anger, resentment or merely sadness, then realize we are mankind. Each one of us is our history, our governments, each act we so dislike is us. There is no-one else but us. We are responsible, you and I.

Now that adds an entirely new perspective doesn't it? Can you see how our resentment and hatred of those in power and their actions, are in reality aimed at ourselves.

By me hating and blaming him or her, and allowing that to swell and strengthen, I am merely aiming it directly at myself and no-one else. To blame and hate outside is to blame and hate self. To judge wrong outside is to see the reflection of myself and judge self.

So you and I are the ones to accept full responsibility for the state of the earth and its people. There is no-one else to use as a scapegoat.

Think of some specific earth situations, feel the remorse and guilt at being part of this creation. The rubbish dumps I contribute to, the destruction of rainforests just so I have paper. The pollution coming from the factories that produce the items I wish for. The animals dying just because I wanted to own land. Think and feel all of it, and your sadness at the world you created.

Investigate and come to your own understanding and concept about the responsibility and failure of mankind, then take responsibility for your part in this. Write, feel, understand, release and come to your own conclusions and decision of what you wish to do in the future.

Activity - Break Free

Now, here is where this concept gets interesting. If I believe I am a failure, I will create failure as my life experience. Therefore to change that scenario I need to locate and release that failure belief.

Taking that further, if we as a race believe we have failed this earth and her people, that is what we jointly will create as our experience. Is that what we wish for? How can we possibly expect to create earth change when it conflicts with our belief, and what we deserve?

We humans have indeed created one almighty self fulfilling prophecy. We create our own misery and possible destruction, just because we took on the belief that we as individuals and a race are failures who do not deserve to succeed and survive. Is it time yet to end this?

Just as with the development of money throughout time, we now feel the story in its entirety, that creates this sense of failure and disgrace at what we have done to the earth. We know and feel it all from within.

Perhaps we can think of all the different topics involving time. Discovering the story and feelings from each, then combined. That would certainly create a deep sense of not deserving to live and depression in people wouldn't they?

Simple lifestyles, housing, family, money, love, work, community, friendship, honor, respect, loyalty. All the things we had, but took for granted. All the things we misused and abused, and wanted more than because we weren't satisfied. All the things we now crave in our lives. We have indeed come full circle.

If you think about it, all time comes to this point, bringing all experience to this one point. We have undertaken countless repeats, we have undertaken situations from all perspectives and situations. We have indeed had all the experiences in all the various ways possible.

Yet, as we feel and know them all, only blame, sadness and remorse is felt. Why?

If we needed to experience them all, in just the manner we have, why do we blame ourselves for them? Why do we judge one as better than another, or more beneficial?

Find your complete history and self belief of failure, keep searching and releasing until you can read this chapter and think deeply about all the topics raised and feel absolutely nothing.

Become the opposite of failure by changing your self beliefs.

Self Importance

The issue of self-importance is rather complicated, as it includes such things as belonging, value, worth, being loved, being equal in importance to all around us, virtually every concept covering our place of value as a living entity. Everything just got mixed up in our minds.

When you complete this chapter you will be able to:

- Fully understand the concept of self-importance
- Know why you had to make yourself important
- Let go of the need to self-validate
- Value yourself
- Understand and have compassion for you

In the greater scheme of things, all that lives and exists on this planet is of equal importance. Each is a grain of sand making up the entire beach, yet if one little piece were missing, a necessary interaction would be lacking and the entire beach composure changed. All are necessary and of equal value.

The World Book dictionary describes importance as meaning having value or significance. It speaks of having social position or influence, of important days and events vs. non-important days and events. The word importance seems to represent opposites, that to not be thought of as important automatically equates to non-importance. Important therefore is a judgment word, to create a position of one thing having greater value over another. Making it necessary for proof of importance to be commonplace.

What of all things being equal and having equal importance? Is one life really to be thought of as more important than another? So one is treated differently or more favorably over another. Which child is more important? Is my life of more value than yours? Is this tree or dog more important than those? Why do we have to make such judgments regarding importance of everything, prior to determining how we react or behave towards them? Is my desired bank balance more important than the expense of medicine to keep my pet pain free? So many of our daily actions relate to which we give greater importance to. Us or them.

Activity - What Are Your Beliefs Of Importance

What is important to you? Who is important to you? Make a list of how importance impacts on your thoughts, actions, life and activities.

Be honest, ask other people for their thoughts, find at least 5 major things you do that are controlled by this word.

Belief Insertion

An interesting repercussion has arisen from the mass use of importance as a belief, combined with our taking on all the negative beliefs of self from the outside world and the necessity for survival. The more we were told we were nothing, of no value or benefit, the more we felt the need to hold onto some sense of self value, to justify our living. We just had to be worth something, we had to. So we held on to that hope that we each were of some value and worth to the world, that we were important. We held on ever so tightly watching and waiting for proof that we were right. That we did matter, to something or someone. It seems that the stronger the negative beliefs came at us, the stronger we held onto and felt the need to prove our self worth. Each triggering the other, for the outside merely mirrors self-beliefs, which mirror what the outside told us.

Activity - What Is Your Story?

Did you feel important to your parents, relatives, and teachers? Think about it very carefully and find your childhood story of importance, so you can begin to grasp this concept.

We Made Us Important

We indeed became so carried away with self-importance as a necessity to validate existence, that the effect was we took it to the extreme, feeling ourselves more important than all others (matching the literal meaning of the word importance). Someone had to validate us, so we took on that role.

Then, to validate this over zealous sense of self-importance, we hid it from ourselves. We cry 'poor me' whenever another treats us as we do not expect or feel matches our worth, we cry 'it hurts' when another does not love us as we believe we deserve to be loved. We take on such false ideals of pain and hurt, when in fact it is resentment and anger that others do not live up to validating our self-importance as we have magnified it to represent.

We do something good that we feel proud of. What is our first response? To share it with another, wanting their approval to validate we are worthy. We crave recognition and acceptance. As if without their validation of our importance, it doesn't exist.

Thinking and focusing on ourselves is self-importance. If I

did not view myself as fat, why would I even think of it? If I was confident of myself, why would I continually engage others to tell and show me I am? If I had no concerns of me, and was not always on guard for my interests, why would I spend so much time thinking about me? If I knew myself to be an okay person, why would I be so concerned at what others thought of me? The amount of time and energy we undertake in self-focus equates to our heightened sense of self-importance.

We feel sad, depressed and unhappy. Our first reaction is to find someone and tell them how we feel. So they can fill that lack within us - feeling ok. So they can tell us we are worthy and special.

Another whom we love does not love in return, and tells us. What do we do? Moan and groan and complain of their poor treatment of us. We become angry at their actions and sometimes react bitterly towards them. All the while validating it is their fault. Is it really another's responsibility to love us, does everyone have this requisite? Do we love everyone we meet?

Jealousy is another form of self-importance. For if we did not perceive another being thought of or treated as more important than us, we would not care. We think that if another is treated favorably, that must be at the expense of our value. It seems, we become resentful and hateful towards everything that stands in the way of our achieving what we desire and love, even ourselves. He does not love me so I blame his actions. I sabotage success, so I hate myself for it.

Our beliefs of self and our value, and importance have become the focus of our every waking moment. Time spent undertaking activities to get others to prove they care about us is major way of validating our existence as important. We hand out all the sob stories, create all manner of difficult situations requiring rescuing, work very hard to please others so they will praise us. All to hear those magical words of comfort and care. We visit places and friends, who we know will eagerly fill this need. We crave attention.

Activity - Your Need To Be Important

What do you do to get people to prove that you are important? Go through each sentence in the above section and make a list of all the thoughts and activities that apply to you. Find them all

Fear Of Not Being Important

The thought of losing the wanting and acquiring confirmation that others care, feels uncomfortable. As though no-one will care, and that experience will never be felt again. Feels very sad to never experience another's caring again.

Just thinking of all the situations and events that are such a big part of our lives, focused on receiving another's response, that would no longer be, is overwhelming. A big part of who I am and display to the world would disappear totally.

Who then would I be?

Having the perfect body, dressed and groomed immaculately, smiling sweetly at the perfect moment, being the dutiful mother, partner or worker, being the one who has the answers another seeks, being known as the kind and considerate one who helps any and everyone out, always offering help, showing off our achievements to everyone who will listen, seeking out the company of others who are not as knowledgeable or whom eagerly offer praise and compassion at every opportunity, undertaking any specific activity for which we know others will notice and respond favorably to, telling everyone of our problems, acting the role of the helpless victim, creating situations where we need rescuing, always seeking others advice, and all the other actions we undertake with the conscious aim of acquiring attention. The list feels endless.

These behaviors are so incredibly defeating and demoralizing, yet we undertake and continue them without realizing. We think that by claiming our importance by way of self-importance makes ourselves feel more valued, when the opposite effect is achieved. Undertaking these behaviors does not make us feel good, instead they often are the ones we dislike and condemn ourselves for harshly each day.

Even the mere thought of acknowledging this false self-importance raises great fears. If we do not see ourselves as valuable, who will? No-one. Then what happens, will there be no logical reason for our existence?

So we hold on tight, and dismiss all thoughts that we think ourselves too important. What others say is wrong. What I am reading here is wrong, I do not think myself too important, to the contrary, I dislike myself and think myself unimportant. I do not undertake any of the actions spoken of so I will not listen to this.

Writing this chapter is not aimed at making you feel guilty, or badly bout yourself. Instead it is to trigger thoughts of this issue. As I have personally found, self-importance did create much misery in my own life. By allowing myself to discover an understanding of this concept, I am learning so very much about what is behind my own actions and reactions.

Because we do not feel special and an important piece of life as a whole, we use our minds to create a false sense of importance, which we then go about validating constantly. This belief and resultant behavior does not make us feel that we belong, it does nothing to increase our sense of value or importance at all. Instead, it perpetuates mirrors reflecting our lack of importance. It continues the cycle of lack of self worth and distancing ourselves from belonging in the world.

Activity - What Are Your Fears Of Not Being Important?

Again read through the above section and write down each feeling, thought and act that applies to you. Discover your feeling about letting go of thinking yourself important, and write them down.

Self Value

Self-value, although seemingly believed to relate to importance, is another word all together. Self-value and worth do not equate to importance. You, and I and he and she, and all the other human beings walking on this planet are important and of value. To be and feel valued, we do not need to invalidate another's value, or that it comes at the expense of another's importance. We are all equal. I do not have to stand up and shout to the world 'I am important', to be so. In fact, that very act creates cycles that validate our lack of importance.

You are so incredibly special, yet you have no sense of that. You are the nut that holds the wheel on tightly, without you the world would not be spinning as it is. You are as important as the air that we breathe. Without your life force spark on this planet at this time a great emptiness would be felt. Without your presence, thousands of people's lives would have missed an important aspect.

Think of it. Every single person you have ever interacted with during your life, even the ones you pass by on the street, are effected by your presence. As you are of theirs. Each interaction creates a chain reaction, of inner thought and action within minds, which then radiates outwardly as each then takes the experience with them, to effect all others they interact with, and it continues on and on.

A smile. A simple act you do without notice, effects the world. You smile without thinking at a lady you pass by. You do not know she is feeling sad or lonely. You do not know the effect one single smile can create. That she felt it and smiles from within. Then takes it and smiles at another, who then takes it and smiles at another, who then takes it and smiles at another. One single smile becomes a hundred smiles. Can you see the magnitude of reaction from one single smile? Can you see the magnitude of reaction from one single action of yours? Now take that initial action away. Think of the loss of all those smiles in people's lives.

Not all interactions are pleasant ones I know, so lets consider those too. I go to the store and am treated with disrespect by another. I feel and react to it. This event mirrored my own sense of self, it triggered my thinking and perhaps using this as an opportunity to look into a feeling I was not happy with. It gave me the wonderful chance to realize and then find a belief of self that I am not valued, to be worked on and healed. If this person, and consequently all the others who mirror to me, and you, and everyone else on this planet, did not do so, how could any of us find hidden beliefs of self? Think of all the people you trigger in this way, and how they would loose that without your presence.

Think of some simple casual interactions experienced recently, and the effect they have had upon you. Can you remember how they made you feel? How you then took that feeling away with you and used it within your other interactions? Can you see how we, as human beings have awesome and very special repercussions on each and every person we come into contact with? How each of our existence is so incredibly important, valuable and necessary for the entire world's functioning.

As we reach a point of being secure in ourselves, our belonging and value within the scheme of life, we no longer need any validation what so ever that someone cares. We have no need for our belonging and value and importance to be reinforced. We know from within, so all thoughts of self disappear naturally, and we are free to merely be.

You DO belong. You ARE important. You are of EXCEPTIONAL value. Without YOU, the world would not function. You ARE necessary.

Activity - You Are Important

Let the above section trigger all your feelings about your value. Discover, feel and know them all. Take time with this one.

Replacement Belief

This forms the basis for our replacement belief, making our fear of releasing this false sense of self-importance possible. Now begins the work of searching out each and every belief regarding our not being good enough, bad, not deserving, not belonging, all the beliefs creating the need to keep telling ourselves that we 'were' important, that they were wrong, that we do deserve to exist.

When we begin our releasing work, the replacement beliefs came naturally because we are the adult telling our inner child the correct story, making releasing the easiest part of the process.

As we proceed with deeper issues, such as this one, full understanding and logical thought is required before we can do the work. The new beliefs have to be formulated from scratch with new ideas and thoughts.

The real brain work then begins, for we can find an emotion and belief, yet need to develop a replacement that is logical, believable and acceptable prior to being able to release. We know when this has been achieved by how we feel, almost like a click and sigh of relief, then happiness at solving the riddle. Then I often laugh at myself, for the new belief was right in front of my eyes the whole time.

Listen to your feelings when telling yourself you are valued. What is the resistance? Why is that statement wrong? Let yourself feel it for the last time, because as you do you will release and replace it with a new belief.

Think and feel what surfaces, feel the self anger and hatred, feel its sadness then listen to its story, follow its lead until the pang comes from the original belief inception situation. Reread the release chapter if necessary on releasing emotions.

There may be several different beliefs involved, so be careful to only focus on one at a time. You may find as one is released another quickly surfaces. Great, a mass release creates fast and amazing results. You may find several days or weeks are required to find them all. Whatever or however you undertake this process is perfect, do what feels right to you. Keep going until you can say any statement regarding your value, worth, belonging, importance to life as a whole etc. and feel nothing.

Me

I was undertaking my own personal work of self-importance while writing this chapter. But rather than just sharing the answers I found, I share my process of reaching them.

Basically, working through this concept involves thinking of the issue, then allowing whatever is felt to surface, be understood then released. By following the path diligently over several days, your triggers and answers will come as mine did. It does not matter if your methods or answers are different, remember what feels right to you is the perfect way to go. And that whatever your experience is during this, feeling is valid, no matter how strange its experience or story. Even if you are not able to complete the work of this chapter, it does not matter. Go on with other chapters, then when it feels right, return to this one. No defined order of personal work is better/worse than another.

The majority of my own self-dislike behaviors relate to things I did not do, things I failed to do even when I wished to. Yet, I would always end up doing something instead which I felt was for me, at the expense of another. Things that were perceived as selfish. I would find myself stalled, unable to do an activity I wanted to for another, with the result being something aimed at me, even when I did not intend this at all. This could be feeling depressed and reading a book or sleeping, instead of taking my son out, or lazing around the house and not organizing some important financial matters. Everything always seemed to be aimed at me, which I disliked so very much. The end result would be an ever increasing feeling of lack, defeat and failure of self.

Perhaps it is the self-importance behaviors that perpetuate self-dislike generally. Watch yourself for one full day, note down all the thoughts of dislike for your behaviors. Then relate those behaviors back to self-importance. How many of them were about your need to be the focus of attention, whether your own or someone else's? Reread the 'What am I?' chapter before continuing as its concepts are expanded on next.

Beliefs Of Non-importance

As I laid in bed ready for sleep, I allowed myself to feel. My 'me' component told the story of receiving the days idea from spirit and how nice it felt to look forward to doing something that wasn't self focused. Then the disappointment and despair as something unknown prevented it being carried through. 'Me' felt very disheartened and disappointed with self, combined with a strong sense of failure as a person. 'Me' had no idea or interest in what caused the activity block.

I then allowed myself to keep feeling, to see what would surface. This time it was ego. I felt this block very strongly. Deep, intense emotion. Beginning as a thought and feeling, then spreading to my stomach, ribs and throat. I couldn't locate its story so once it was strong, I worked to release it with breathing. Then something amazing happened.

I felt as if an opening occurred in me, then out of this tiny hole, I was dragging some lump out, bit by bit. It was much bigger than the allowed space it resided in, so was difficult to grab and pull out. I felt the lump's emotion, it was ego's deep feeling, yet I was not it, and it was not me. It was very separate as if a foreign matter and emotion.

This emotion, as exposed, began telling its story of who and what it was. This emotion comprised every situation within my life whereby I was told I was not valuable or deserved. This emotion was all the unfelt and unsaid responses to each treatment. This emotion comprised all the reasons I took on self-importance as a belief.

This emotion was the time my grandmother told me I was no good, and didn't deserve to be on this holiday with her as I was not as good as my cousin. This emotion was the hurt and anger at being thought of and treated in such a manner, unexpressed. This emotion consisted every single event like this that had occurred, it had been stuffed inside and hidden. Not able to be felt or acted upon during the experience. This emotion consisted of all the unsaids and unthoughts. This emotion is packed tightly with all I have held onto, so much and so many events. This emotion is to be felt and experienced incident by incident, then released. So many different stories, so many different events to be felt and released. Feeling like they would never end. Then I slept.

Listening To 'Me'

When I woke, I still felt the pang in my stomach, an uncomfortable-ness that I couldn't shake. So I allowed it to surface more and be felt. Rather than feeling the previous nights emotions from ego, it was the 'me' part having its say. Release and resolution was not possible until the entire situation was understood, and a clear knowing of the new belief to be inserted, so I listened. Previously I have done work on why humans dislike the human experience, and how 'me' felt the sadness and anger at all control being taken away, yet having to be the one to take responsibility for another's actions. Although along the same lines, this was different.

It was about the hopelessness 'me' felt, that no matter what it wished and truly aimed to do, control could be whisked away at anytime. Me had no say in, nor understood the blocks, only being affected by them. Anger of not being in control was felt strongly, so listened to. I then realized that 'me' could regain control by being the controller of the situation. Rather than allowing blocked feelings to flow, 'me' could instantly recognize and act on them. Directing ego to locate and heal the issue at hand, thus giving 'me' great sense of control. (The releasing technique)

But, there was more, this pang was still too strong. So later that afternoon I allowed it to surface yet again and listened. This time it spoke of not wanting to be part of all this. That it had no control anyway, ego saw to that. It had no desire or want or like of the situations it was forced to work hard in figuring a way out of. Ego was the one creating the situations and want of their experience from fear beliefs, not 'me'. To 'me', this whole experience was rather unpleasant and it had had enough.

I hadn't realized that it was 'me' who took on the worry and fear of life events and situations ego created. Nor of the incredible responsibility to clean up ego's mess was taken on also by 'me'. No wonder it felt so miserable and disheartened.

Full and complete feeling of 'me's' anxiety over current situations I was experiencing was allowed to be felt fully. Physically I felt ill, emotionally I jumped at shadows, very fearful indeed.

My experience was the same daily roller coaster ride common to many people. The dislike, despair and lack of control for things we do which we do not wish to, the depression at being stuck in this experience without any idea of how to escape it, the strong dislike for this experience and the wishing and hoping it would just end. I could feel each and every issue mounting in strength like a wall growing and enclosing me. I kept breaking out in a hot sweat. I knew the end desired result, just not how to achieve the release and change of belief.

A Conversation With 'Me'

The day went on without resolution. Emotions kept heightening without understanding. Then finally I gave up, I could already feel 'me's' complaining, so I decided to consciously hand the floor over to 'me' and listen fully. The following is that discussion.

"Here I am looking around at all the turmoil and disorganization in my life. My home, finances, work, lifestyle, mind, everything, is one big mess. I did not create this, nor wish for it. I had no part in it what so ever. Yet I am buried in it, without seeming escape.

I don't understand why or what is happening to me, I don't understand how to fix it, all I know is I just want to curl up in bed and hide from it all. Forever. Its not fair! Why am I the one who has to fix it? I didn't create it. I want no part of it. This is not how its suppose to be, nor what I deserve. I wish I had a magic ball to make it all disappear. It's not my responsibility yet the responsibility is placed on me. As always! No-one listens or understands how hard this is. No-one cares or wants to help me. If I come up with ideas and strategies to fix it all, if I come up with thoughts to motivate me into changing it all. They are futile, everything I want to do I'm unable to. It is not fair!!! I hate this living experience!!! What is this all about???

I have to make money to pay for necessities of life. Yet every time I organize something, those dang fears of ego get in the way. Every time I focus so incredibly hard to come up with ideas, they are overruled by ego. I keep working on understanding myself, I do the searching, I do the feeling, I do the releasing, I do it all. But for what? Where does it get me? I feel like I've been thrown out to the wolves to fend for myself, without any options I can use.

So much for me belonging and being a part of this world. This world has abandoned me. Completely. Who is around for me? Who is around to help me? Who gives a dam what happens to me? No-one! So why should I care what I do? Why should I keep banging my head against this brick wall? Why bother with anything? I'm not angry with ego, I do understand why ego fears and all that. I do understand its all for a reason. But hey, enough's enough. Give me a break! Literally!!!"

'Me's' Self-importance

Then it clicked. This tantrum was a grand performance of self-importance. 'Me' actually thought itself more important than the other parts of myself. That 'me's' issues alone were more important. And 'me' complained bitterly of lack of control. What a joke.

When we meet another with problems, do we listen and offer help? Yes, because their problems do not affect us directly. But, what do we do in regard to ourselves, when the problems do affect us directly? We claim poor me, this is such a hard life, give me a break. Without any thought or regard for the reasons behind the problems, the fears and hurts ego has taken on, for us. We focus on their effect alone. We complain and hate all the weaknesses of ourselves, our ego, we try our hardest to ignore and make them vanish, we disown them. We dislike the other parts of ourselves with a passion, then go about thinking of our self as so much higher and mightier.

Activity - Discover Your Story

It is quite easy to experience what I am speaking of, for yourselves. Think of an issue that troubles you, one single thing. Think about how miserable it makes you, how trapped within it you feel, the annoyance at yourself for the behaviors perpetuating it. Think and feel clearly.

When you do feel the frustration and annoyance of the event, think about its cause. Think about the level of fear that must be behind the fact that you cannot undertake a simple act required to alleviate it. What hurt ego must be experiencing, and trying desperately to get your attention with, so you can help heal it. For it is you, the 'me' part of yourself that is required for the healing, ego can only highlight issues, the rest is up to you.

So, all this time we have complained and berated ego so savagely, it was us, the 'me' part that was letting the team down.

Self Importance

When we think about it, ego does a magnificent job of telling us constantly what is going on, all the fears and beliefs and hurts. Yet, instead of listening to these prompts, we were wrapped up in our own self-importance and thought of ourselves alone. We went into the 'poor me' syndrome of complacency, and did nothing for ourselves. Then because we feel there must be blame, we blamed ego for the whole thing.

"Me" Carries The Fears

I was still missing some piece, and I could feel it strongly in my stomach and throat. "Me' does have a valid point of view though, someone needs to be concerned and be aware as situations happen and are being created. Perhaps this is another self-important role 'me' took on to justify its existence.

My stomach is churning still. I really do fear all the situations in my life, and feel like I have no control even though I have done much work and know to the contrary. Somehow this learning missed 'me'. I began asking myself questions, trying to understand what I was feeling physically. Why be scared of situations? Why always feel I'm going to get into trouble? Why was I feeling as I was.

Then one of the strongest emotions I have felt in a long time surfaced. Deep and profound fear. My body shook, my shoulders tightened, my stomach wanted to be sick, and I wanted to curl up and hide from the world forever. The more I tried to reason the possible answers, the less I felt. So I spent several hours resting and sleeping with this emotion. To no avail. What on earth was so terrible that happened to me? Why was I so scared? I imagined all possible scenarios yet felt nothing. Eventually I gave up, and sidetracked my mind by doing something that required my concentration elsewhere.

As I lay in bed on the third night of this concept, my mind was questioning. What was this about? What was I blocking so strongly? I decided to allow my dreams to help and relaxed.

Then it came. I felt and experienced the events of my life clearly for the first time. Previously I had thought it uneventful and ordinary. From a small baby, my life's theme showed itself to me piece by piece. The emotions were very strong.

Although I had always known and complained, I had never experienced them it seems. Never realized what a nightmare I had indeed lived of abuse and unhappiness. The explanations of why I withdrew, why I couldn't stand up or speak out for myself, why I didn't have frames of reference for happy normal situations. All the major events jumped out at me, I felt them personally, yet also in context to each other. It all became very clear. I knew who I was and why I was that person. No wonder I was like I was, no wonder I stalled and didn't achieve what I wished to. For the first time in my life, I understood the person I was. I understood ego.

Understanding Yourself

The next part is hard to relay in words as we can each only experience it for ourselves. The act of understanding oneself fully for the first time is very humbling. In knowing why one acts as they do, removes all dislike and blame for it. It is not that pity or sadness is felt, more understanding for itself, finally. I knew and understood and accepted who I was. All the different parts of myself. I merely was.

Although these thoughts did not occur, I will say them so you get an idea of the ramifications of this experience. There is no longer any sense of one part of me being the victim and the other the controller, all parts are accepted and equal. I feel a complete calmness for the parts that comprised my entire being.

I no longer feel scared of my current life situations as the victim. I can be anyone and do anything I please. I know why I don't understand or know how to do things, they have never been experienced so do not have a frame of reference, I can see and feel everything about me, I understand myself totally.

Finally

The work of the last 3 days was tiring, which I feel now. It is a strange calmness, no panic, no focus on myself. Perhaps I am feeling little because all the previously constant thoughts and mind chatter of myself have gone. It is empty without being empty. Rather than any thoughts of blame or anger at myself when I think of and go about my life, I now feel compassion and understanding. This work has not eliminated my fears and blocks, merely opened the way for real work to be undertaken, with many wonderful opportunities to look forward to.

I am ready to seriously make plans, which I believe in, to create the person and future I choose. I am ready to take charge of my life. I am not helpless anymore.

Working Through This Chapter

1. Read the entire chapter each day for several days
2. Write down your discoveries for each section
3. Grasp an understanding of the concept of self-importance and how it is a natural thing we do
4. Plan specific time to do the releasing work
5. As you begin reading, feel and listen for the first thing to come up on its own, release and heal it
5. Keep planning specific time, read and do what naturally surfaces, one topic at a time
6. When you can read each sentence in the chapter slowly, and deliberately without feeling anything, and have come to a clear understanding of self-importance, then you have finished

Health & Well-Being

Health and well-being, I wonder what that really means? Is it something we have control over, or are our physical issues a natural consequence of life?

You may wish to refresh your healing and releasing skills prior to doing this chapter as they are the key to health success.

When you complete this chapter you will be able to:

- Understand the bigger picture of health
- Decide to care about and for yourself
- Create your own journey towards health

What Are People's Beliefs Of This Topic?

I have always enjoyed good health, and not taken much notice of my body. Accept to think of it as I do my cars. Something that keeps running well, despite the abuse and neglect I give it.

I smile when I think of the different cars I have owned. A Toyota Cressida, which drove 4 hrs through the bush with out passing one house or car, then only after I arrived at my destination, stopped and refuse to start again because the alternator was not working. Then a week later on the return trip, driving those same 4hrs before breaking down, because faulty repairs meant the entire system attached to the alternator fell off. Or when I ran out of gas, miles from the nearest gas station on a very hot summer day, yet even after stopping, the engine started up again on its own and ran until I drove the 5 miles to the gas station.

Even my current car has been amazing. I have driven all over north eastern America, without regard for its condition, yet it kept going and going. And recently when a tire split and was bulging all the way round, the only indication was I slid slightly when breaking, for 2 full weeks before I got it checked.

My body has been just as faithful and loyal to me. I grew up eating sugar, by the spoonful when very young, and from a teenager until recently, my basic diet consisted of chocolate bars, I remained a size 6 with clear skin though. During my first pregnancy I gained a mammoth amount of weight. I literally had no neck, and my upper legs more than doubled in size. I binged night and day. Yet, within 6 weeks of my daughter's birth I was trim and back to a size 6, with a flat stomach and no stretch marks.

I have never eaten vegetables, apart from potatoes, corn and cold carrots. Rarely ate fruit until the last couple of years, and paid no attention to my nutritional needs at all. I must add that my children were both fed natural home cooked food and still love their fruit and vegetables. Presently, it has been more than 12 months since I have eaten regular food, often going several days without anything. I have given no notice to my body needs, except when cramping and excessive reactions from lack of nutrition, and then would only eat some bread or similar to quiet my body's complaints. I do not exercise like I enjoyed before leaving Australia, swimming and walking at least 5 miles daily, yet my fitness level is still good, my heart rate and blood pressure excellent. Basically, my body, just like my cars, takes care of itself no matter what input I apparently have.

Please do not misunderstand, I like everyone experiences

the repercussions of my neglect. My skin is very dry, I look tired and drawn, and my energy levels get quite low. But basically, not the expected impact. It seems then that for me personally, health and well-being has been taken for granted, and not thought about because love was my life lesson, not health. So that has been my reality.

Other people I know have very different health and well-being issues. My son, who was always thin, stopped gaining weight totally at 13, after a specific incident. He grew nearly 2 feet and remained the same weight, now fully grown at 5' 11" and weighing a mere 100lbs. It does not matter what or how much he eats, weight eludes him. His stamina and fitness are severely affected. His body is not happy at all. I have always believed that when he finds his special place in the world his body size will normalize and he feel well-being. He has no thoughts of his health, apart from having to experience it. No sense that he has control of what and how his body behaves.

That belief is similar to others I know. It is like they encounter chronic illnesses, go to a medical doctor who verifies yes they are sick, diagnoses specific conditions and prescribes medication. That they, themselves have no part in their own body's well-being. They appear to start with one diagnosis, then progressively acquire more and live with dis-ease as if it is a part of their lives.

We have been taught well, not to interfere with the medical profession. Leave the diagnoses and treatment to the professionals and merely do what we are told, without any thought to self-intervention possibilities. I am not against doctors at all. It is a personal choice what to do and believe.

People generally seem to accept dis-ease and physical symptoms as a natural part of life. As though luck plays a major part in it. Some, like me are rarely ill, while others undergo one bout of illness after another. The overall incidence of general conditions seems to be increasing. Back problems, allergies, asthma, obesity, arthritis, reflux and constipation.

What part do our mind and beliefs play in health and well-being? Try these exercises. Think of 2 things you could do tomorrow, one you really enjoy and the other you dislike thoroughly. (Yes, this is from the feelings chapter) Feel your body reactions to each, there is a definite feel and difference isn't there? Now, think on one of your recent aches and pains. What was the mind relationship? One lady who's back was always knotty and aching, when asked what was on her mind realized it was the same as how her back felt. All twisted and knotted.

What of the man who suffers severe acid stomach/reflux, complaining his life is already too stressed to deal with this added discomfort? Acid = stress. Or the person, whose first idea of what would make their day happy, is going to the bathroom each morning? All the while holding on tightly and not wishing to let go of their fears and beliefs. And they wonder why they are constipated?

I have not undergone detailed research into common symptoms, apart from reviewing one particular book to see if it matched my conclusions. You can heal your life by Louise Hay has a list of symptoms and suggested mind emotions to correspond. All those I have personally discovered have, when checked, matched her list. She suggests affirmations to replace thoughts, while I help clients delve into their emotions and beliefs to be permanently cleared with Greene's Release.

When a client spoke of a sore neck, I would grin at their puzzled expression when they asked how I knew so and so was being a pain. Upon presenting with cold symptoms, people always know exactly what topic is causing such confusion in their minds. Some do not like being found out for being angry, when I ask of it because of sinus infections. Or not wanting to see or hear with the corresponding organs.

I do believe that all we believe and think corresponds not only with our life situations, but also with our health and well-being. I watch as different moods I personally have, manifest within my physical and heighten when I deny my feelings and expression. It is held onto in our physical bodies.

There is much that our body and psyche know that we do not. One amazing story relates to my father. When traveling interstate, a speed hump somehow was incorrectly made and when driven over, he being the driver felt its force strongly. He jumped up hitting the roof of the van, all the cupboard doors opened and food and belongings fell out. That same day, several other campers had the same experience. It was a freak event, as each person was only driving at approximately 5 mph.

My father's spine was injured from the jarring and a hospital visit was required. The tests revealed his injuries easily, but highlighted another surprise. He had had cancer, which was successfully removed and for several years, all checkups remained normal. Including the one, less than 3 months prior, so much so further testing was not required for another year.

The tests undertaken for injuries from the accident revealed that his cancer had returned and was nearing a dangerous size. If he had waited until the scheduled testing it would most likely have been too late for treatment. Which by the way was again successful. A freak accident saved his life.

What about accidents, operations and serious illnesses? Accidents are just that, no-one has any control over them. Are you so sure of this? Think carefully. My girlfriend recently had a series of potentially serious accidents. She fell of a high ladder, down her cement front steps, and while carrying boxes down to the basement. When I visited, her legs and arms were covered with cuts, grazes and bruises. I cannot remember all of her injuries, only that they were not serious. I am not my girlfriend, so do not know all that surrounded these incidents. Yet I do know at that time she was feeling unwell and run down, but kept pushing herself to the limit with chores she insisted required her attention. I told her she was scaring me, to please look at what is happening, and please stop and take care. She did and didn't have any more accidents.

Just this week, while carrying 2 large bags of trash out before the truck came, I overbalanced and luckily did not fall down our full flight of stairs. At the time I did not think any more of it, and continued on with my day. Later that evening my foot began hurting more and more. I had apparently sprained several ligaments underneath and on top of my foot. They were very unusual places, but extremely painful.

The next day I thought about my mood and thoughts at that time. I was rushing to beat the truck with recyclable trash, that I wasn't happy about having. Empty coke bottles that I had neglected to dispose of so the pile had became too large, and of products I am not happy about using. So I was unhappy with myself about 2 different things that morning, both related to the trash. I was displeased with myself, and while thinking those very thoughts I suffered an injury causing unwanted physical pain. A big coincidence?

When we think carefully about accidents we do have, most can be related back to our thoughts and actions. Rushing, not paying attention, not caring or considering ourselves.

Operations are interesting. One person may take months and recover very slowly, like myself. While another bounces back instantly, more lively and well than ever. What is different about the mindset of each person that predisposes them I wonder? This is similar to general illnesses. While some people keep going and ignore all distress and pain, others make it a drama for attention. Moaning and groaning and taking on the role of the needy sick person, wishing another cared how they felt and would demonstrate that in actions, while a very few take personal responsibility and care of themselves when unwell.

Serious illnesses force people into action. Less than 3 months after a stressful situation began, I was in hospital having my gallbladder removed. Gallbladder is thought to relate to holding onto resentment and situations, not dealing and resolving them. Now I can laugh at how silly I was.

Much is known of cancer, so I will not delve into this issue. Instead group all serious illnesses together. What causes their inception? Why does one person get ill while another doesn't? What part does a person's mind play in such events?

What of considering our general well-being. Do we facilitate the everyday things our physical requires? Like, go to the dentist when we know it is needed, get those new glasses immediately, rest when our body first shows signs of fatigue and distress, follow directions when taking medication, or take that which will alleviate discomfort. Do we provide any good care to our own physical bodies? Adequate and appropriate nutrition, rest, exercise, relaxation and maintenance. Why does it then surprise us when our physical part shows signs of neglect and wear?

What Are People's Reactions To Physical Issues?

When I sprained my foot, I ignored and had one very restless nights sleep. I had not iced, bandaged, taken anti-inflammatory medication. Why did I neglect my own needs like this? I do know better.

My girlfriend who had the repeated accidents followed the same direction. She ignored all physical issues and kept going, not caring for physical injuries at all. How many times have we all heard the 'I'm tough routine'? I don't need sissy medicine or bandages. What about people who will in no way care for themselves when unwell. Waiting and demanding another do it for them, as a way of proof of love. Then there are the ones who go to the other extreme. Telling everyone who will listen of their sickness or injury, playing the sympathy role. Or making their health the main focus, with every action relating to 'getting' well. This one got my attention when I was working as a physical therapy technician. The knee people. Such hard working and dedicated people, yet the rewards did not match their efforts. They would tense up their entire bodies, just for a leg raise, they would walk and swim and exercise dutifully, just to get their knees well. Forget walking or doing anything for the mere pleasure of it, every aspect of their lives revolved around healing their knees. The slower they healed, the harder the person worked and focused on it.

I had put of writing this chapter for some time, because I

didn't know how to tackle it. When I began tonight, I thought I'll flow along with what comes and see where it leads me. Now I can clearly see why it took me so long to write. Health and well-being is indeed a diverse and complex topic. After reading what I've written so far I'm sure you are feeling the same as me. It seems so complicated, where would one start clarifying thoughts, creating well-being, repairing the damage created, or becoming healthy again.

What happens when we begin to consciously think of our health and well-being. I am still a smoker, but have known for some time that I will quit, and in the same way I did with chocolate. One day I realized I hadn't eaten chocolate for weeks, and was surprised. It happened naturally on its own, as I no longer required the fix its chemical reaction gave me.

Seriously though, what does happen when we begin thinking about the impact on our health of what we do? When we take that focus of thought? If I go over my unhealthy habits and recognize them as such, am I then predisposing myself to that new belief? Smoking has never affected me, and I do not believe it will make me ill, yet to suddenly look at it from the perspective of harming my physical, it might begin to do so.

If I now look at all I do as unhealthy, might I then begin to demonstrate the side effects of my behavior, which until now have been minimal. What would be the effect of looking at the negatives of our behavior and health, or would that create more issues and problems?

To think of what we want, is to create the experience of wanting. To think of the negatives of a situation is to create self blame as the experience. Your body will reflect what you think of it and yourself. However you view your physical is what will appear, so if you see yourself as fat that is what will become, if you see yourself as old and wrinkled that is what you and the world will see. If you do not like what looks back at you in the mirror, it will become the physical reflection of your perceptions of self.

Your body will reflect the state of your mind. Unexpressed

feelings are held onto by the physical. Stress and worry translates to physical tension. Taking on undue responsibility for others is as though carrying the weight of the world on your shoulders. Restricting self can become restricted physical movement. While a happy inside is reflected to the world in sparkling eyes and a smiling face.

Your body will reflect the care you give it, which comes from liking and naturally being able to care for self. Much of our daily action involves some form of self punishment, eating poorly, ingesting toxins and chemicals, accidents, neglect. Your body will reflect your beliefs of health and well-being. If you focus on being unwell, that will be your experience. Being unwell. It is entirely up to you. If you do not like the state of your physical and want change, then create it. If you are satisfied with your physical state, so be it. Why is it that people do not care of their own health and well-being?

Discovering Well-being

You know and have felt yourself as spirit, 'me' and ego, all the intangible parts. Now it is time to discover your physical part, or so we believe it to be in this living experience. Take your time thinking deeply on the following sections, feel and listen to what surfaces, then undertake the clearing work for each thing discovered.

Activity - Your Body

What do you think of your body? Ask all the why questions related to your answer. Find out why you dislike your physical person this much, why do you blame and punish it, and why you have no desire to care for it.

At some point you will feel your physical body's emotions and story. Why does your mind override your physical needs?

Why is it the mind that totally controls what the physical gets, such as nutrition, care, rest, etc?

We are a psychological process in motion creating a physical experience, yet we forget to participate 'in' the physical and disregard its input. Feel, listen and notice the excitement you feel within just from the thought of feeling all your physical experiences of every motion and sensation from them. Listen to the stories your physical has to share with you. If allowed, it willingly shares the reasons for what it is feeling.

Activity - What Is Your Story Of Illness?

Re-read the Experience chapter, think carefully about your need to be unwell, what is it you are trying to experience, what do you gain and how do you perpetuate the ill personality?

Investigate what and why health is an issue for you, and then do the learning to change your reality. All it takes is belief. Whatever you believe will become. But most of all, remember that what you physically see before you, both in your body and life, is a direct reflection of your mind and your beliefs. That is your lead to follow.

Health As A Life Lesson

For some people, health is a constant issue that needs to be resolved. The following is to help you create your own journey into health.

Care About And For Yourself

Every life lesson comes with its own theme to learn. Money teaches value, love teaches us that we are love, and health teaches us to care about and for ourselves.

This may seem trivial, but seriously, it is time for you to heal and find the love to care about and for yourself, so you may go on to live a long life that is happy and healthy.

Do not go overboard and make your journey about 'wanting' and 'having to have' health, so it becomes a search to escape a nightmare situation. This is fear based, so be careful to clear anything that keeps you in this drama.

Instead, make this journey about a curious and open search to find your story of health, invite everything to do with health to come up and be known to you so you can resolve this issue. Remember that every feeling that comes up is your trigger to investigate, understand, release, heal and create its opposite.

When you complete your adventure you will feel peace, and care for and about yourself naturally without thought. You will instinctively do that which is in your own best interest at all times.

Activity - Emotionally Care About Yourself

Here are some questions for you to ponder, investigate, heal and form your own concepts about. Take your time!

- Why is it wrong to care about you?
- Why don't you deserve to be cared about?
- Who didn't care about you?
- Who taught you that you didn't deserve to be cared about?

Activity - Physically Care For Yourself

It takes time and effort to care for yourself. But, you do it for your family, your home, your work, and even your car, so why is it so hard to care for you? Perhaps you never learned how to do it, or that it was an important thing to do.

- Are you important?
- Do your physical needs matter?
- Do you know the components of physically caring for you?

Activity - Review

Reread this chapter slowly (the part prior to health as a life lesson) and put a mark next to every single word, sentence or paragraph that you feel.

One by one, work through the issues that were triggered, clear them out completely, once and for all. Understand what they mean, to you and other people, form your own concept and belief about each one.

Only when you can reread the entire chapter again, and feel nothing but peace and happiness, have you completed the objective.

Activity - Physical Well-Being Is Emotional Well-Being

When you do not allow yourself to feel emotions, your body will do it for you! Your body is expressing your emotional distress! This section will show you how to change that.

- What upsets you or makes you sad?
- What hurt and heartache do you still hold inside?

Search out every single sad emotion within you! Write a list then find and remove every single one of them, investigate, listen to the story and release them forever!

This may take some time, so do not rush this process as it is very important. When you feel nothing but joy, then you have finished, so go and do the 'Me' chapter to clear out the physical part of the emotions that is still there. Finish it completely.

Activity - Daily Emotional Well-Being

Now that you have cleared your stored emotions, keep your container empty. Each night, before you go to sleep, stop, feel and listen. Then release every single sadness or hurt from this day, then the physical part also using the 'Me' chapter information. Keep your container free for your happy emotions and experiences.

Feel

Your body feels your emotions because you don't allow yourself to feel. Why? Change that right now! You cannot go on allowing your body to feel for you! You cannot keep treating your body like this! Your body is important! Treat it that way! Your body allows you to physically be here, living this life. Your body is your temple

Highlighted to stress the importance, so think about each sentence very carefully. Listen to what you feel, release, and heal yourself and your body.

You Are Important

You are so important yet you have no concept of that. Your body is sick because it is trying to get you to see how important you are, and to treat yourself as important.

You are so incredibly special, yet you have no sense of that. You are the nut that holds the wheel on tightly, without you the world would not be spinning as it is. You are as important as the air that we breathe. Without your life force spark on this planet at this time a great emptiness would be felt. Without your presence, thousands of people's lives would have missed an important aspect.

Think of it. Every single person you have ever interacted with during your life, even the ones you pass by on the street, are effected by your presence. As you are of theirs. Each interaction creates a chain reaction, of inner thought and action within minds, which then radiates outwardly as each then takes the experience with them, to effect all others they interact with, and it continues on and on.

A smile. A simple act you do without notice, effects the world. You smile without thinking at a lady you pass by. You do not know she is feeling sad or lonely. You do not know the effect one single smile can create. That she felt it and smiles from within. Then takes it and smiles at another, who then takes it and smiles at another, who then takes it and smiles at another.

One single smile becomes a hundred smiles. Can you see the magnitude of reaction from one single smile? Can you see the magnitude of reaction from one single action of yours? Now take that initial action away and think of the loss of all those smiles in people's lives.

Activity - Know That You Are Special

Listen to what you felt when you read the above section. Let yourself feel it all. Do the work to feel, listen, understand, release and heal.

Activity - Feel Everything

Teach yourself how to feel your way through life. Let yourself feel the good and the bad, feel the sensations, the adrenaline, the joy of it all.

Use the feeling chapter to help you become one with feeling, so you are fully open to experience it all, and you body will never have to do it for you again.

Activity - Caring For You

What is it to care for you and do that which is in your best interest. Below is a beginning list of suggestions for you to investigate, feel, release, heal and form your own concepts so you may begin to care for you. What do you think is involved with caring for yourself? Add to the list.

- Good food
- Having plenty
- Filling your life with love
- Experiencing the best of everything
- Putting yourself 1st, not 2nd or last

Activity - Physically Caring For You

What are the components of adequately caring for you physically. What do our bodies and minds need?

I have begun the list below for you to add to, investigate, understand, release, heal and create new experiences.

- Stimulation
- Exercise
- Good food
- Grooming

Activity - Get To Know Your Body

Your physical body is a very special expression of you. One that you probably have never paid any attention to, because it is about you.

If you take the time, to let yourself learn how to physically feel your body at all times, you can then make it a part of your living experience, to combine with your thoughts and feelings.

All you need do is sit and feel it, then have a conversation and ask some questions. What does your body feel like? Does it feel tired or invigorated, what about how it feels when you use it, or snuggle up on a comfortable chair, what about when it is hungry, or tired? How does your body feel when you dress it up? If you learn to feel and listen to your body, it will share some wonderful insights and what it wants and needs, just like if you sit and listen to your thoughts, you know what is best for you.

Activity - Become The Expert

This chapter has introduced many thoughts about health and well being. Some things you already knew were related, some you had no idea of. Use this book and chapter to create your own journey into health and well being so you can become the expert on the subject. Then write about it all, in detail. Come to your own conclusions and form your own concepts.

You may listen to other people's thoughts, or read about concepts, but **do not** use any one else's input to sway your new conclusions, which may not match common thought at all. You know far more about your body, and your health than anyone else, because they are yours and they are about you.

It is your body after all.

The New Me

Sometimes it really feels like I wake up not knowing who I am. As though I am changing so very fast, I can't keep up with myself. As fast as I clear what has always been familiar, I must learn who I am without that before the next round of changes comes upon me.

The new perceptions come like waves, one rolling in after another, changing all I perceive and believe, changing my entire belief system.

I am discovering who I am, moment by moment. I question and ponder what living, life and this journey is about. I question who and what I am. Searching for a new base, something that feels familiar.

This section covers some of my personal pondering, questions, and concerns as I walk into this new world as a new me. Then of what I discovered.

Walking This Morning Was Very Pleasant

Clear blue skies, birds chirping, a happy dog trotting along. Peace was all around me. But was it truly peaceful, or merely that I was not at that time privy to the countless dramas unfolding behind closed doors.

When you complete this chapter you will be able to:

- Release your built up emotions
- Discover your story of life

We can shut ourselves off to others suffering, hide behind our blinkers and not watch the news or read a newspaper, yet suffering is all around us. It is the human condition.

Why all this pain? Does the end really justify the means? I asked myself these questions recently. How can it be beneficial or needed that the children must suffer so? I couldn't believe such pain was justified.

I was reliving and feeling as a 3yr old, the utter disbelief and devastation of all the pain combined from one life. How could it be right any child feel so? Made me very sad, not wanting to be part of this living gig. I desperately wanted to leave and never come back or have any part in it ever again. I truly wanted to end this whole learning experiment we call the human existence. I was so angry for the hurt and suffering all the dear children faced, for in feeling my own I combined and felt theirs.

For the first time I believe, I actually felt for the dear little one that was me. She hurt over and over and over again and I wanted it to stop. It was not right.

I then began to seriously ponder, what is the point of living? What is the real meaning of life? What is spirits goal with all this?

Surely not an existence of endless suffering and pain. There must be more, so I dug through every logical thought within me, building the pieces one by one.

Activity - Heal Your Self

Let this chapter trigger your feeling the sadness of your life and lives. Open to feel and hear all of the stories, write and understand where you have come from and why you became who you are. Then feel and heal your self.

My Knowing

Suddenly I felt it click, I instantly calmed and knew my reasoning was falling in line with my inner knowing, which then flooded me with the missing pieces.

We are each spirit, one spec of special energy within this vast expanse of life. Each more special than we can imagine, and surely do not feel. People say this is a journey of self discovery, a search for the holy grail. Well it is, an almost endless search for true self, driven by vague memories and beliefs of there must be more than this. True self is spirit.

How do we find this spirit? What will happen when we do? How does spirit relate to this 3d existence of pain and torture?

Think on it, how every time profound learning occurs, after

a seemingly heartbreaking event, how we feel the sense of calm, of knowing, of real self. From this basis I came up with a theory of the meaning of life.

After several years of countless lessons, I have come to the realization that they do indeed build upon themselves. That makes sense, as the child learns to crawl before it can walk, so we are gently led through our inner mind growth.

We start of completely led and controlled by our mind/ego, full of fears and emotions and the most negative beliefs of ourselves and living. Gradually, step by step we may take the challenge and work on our lessons; feeling, experiencing, releasing, then replacing these beliefs one by one. Each one then becomes, enabling for us to live that particular topic without fear. One by one they grow, and we slowly come out of our shell. The fear of confrontations lessens, bitterness for a parent replaced with understanding, the beginnings of being able to speak out for oneself. The simple knowing experienced gradually builds upon itself till we discover profound understandings of the way of life.

Yet we still jump from a new found sense of calmness and knowing, to the most heart wrenching fears, making us shake with terror. The process is indeed a long and tedious one, not for the week minded.

Then one day, as if by magic, we suddenly notice we are calmer, more outspoken, independent, others are asking what has happened for we are a very different person from the one a few weeks prior. The change of balance has come.

Our mind/ego fears are no longer in full control, we are now stronger in our sense of self and knowing, no matter what appears before us. Our minds are able to ponder and accept more readily and easily complexities of existence

What is happening? Well my friend, your spirit is an incredibly special light that devised a way for it to be able to live fully within this physical existence, but for it to do that, our basic mind had to become compatible with its flow of high level knowing. I am not saying our minds can ever cope with all spirit knowing, but I am saying they can be upgraded for want of a better word, to the level where free flowing information from spirit knowing is enabled.

Why the suffering? Why such a difficult existence for mankind then I hear you ask? Questions I asked and found answers to that enabled me to change my entire outlook of this.

Everything in this physical existence is experience. Just that. Nothing more, nothing less. So as the child learns to recognize and know the different textures of grass and water and heat and cold, developing concepts of understanding, so we have undergone the experience of different emotions and events. Fear, love, hate, want, loss etc.

The learning from each event more profound than the last. Fear that teaches us we are safe no matter the situation, love that teaches us connecting with others, hate that teaches us to look within and see it is self hatred we feel, not hatred for another, I could keep going on. But there is a common theme as we progress, which when built upon itself becomes the foundation of the realization of who we really are. Strong emotions are part of and necessary for the drive to discovery, yet once we learn more of ourselves they can be put aside and neutralized.

That common theme is self knowing. Spirit knowing. For this exceptional journey into physical existence is but a mere play, a physical and time restricted one. There is more than we can imagine. The child who experienced devastating loss learns there is never separation in spirit, and experiences that profound event of spirit connecting, the owner who grieves for the loss of her dog learns of the beauty of the love they shared, spirit love, the man who attends his ill wife learns the joy of sharing and loving without fear or restriction, pure spirit love. The woman who experiences abuse learns of her own strength, the man who is betrayed learns faith and trust, the soul mates who journey together through many lives of hardship and pain learn of the commitment and never ending love of another part of themselves, their soul love. The woman who experiences hatred from not speaking out the truth learns faith, that complete spirit faith in the support of another has always been there.

Everything comes back to spirit. That life is eternal and special and magical, if we only open our eyes and see past this play, that it is indeed a learning game, of return to spirit living. Spirit waits anxiously for our readiness for it to have control and flow freely within this 3d experience. True spirit living, that is what I now believe this is all about. The great experiment to see what the human spirit is capable of.

Knowing all I do, and remembering and experiencing all the pain and suffering of memory after memory, even through the eyes of a hurt child, I would do it all again. I chose and would choose again to experience that life and love and loss and end, for the mere sake of learning that spirit is never ending, all encompassing, eternal as is love between spirits.

Part of all this is the fact of being linked to each other's experiential paths. Being the ones to do the pushing or triggering causing pain to another, feeling that pain as deeply within ourselves. This is a deep lesson within itself to undertake. Yet I know it is one of the dearest to me, for only those of true spiritual love connections commit and agree to undertake such sadness, to fulfill what another dear one asks of them.

It is very hard to watch the suffering of those around us within their plays. Hard to distance and not interfere and fix for them, the human want to prevent pain in another is strong. Yet, we have to believe and have deep faith in the knowing that this is their choice, they desire the profound learning and mind growth in readiness for spirit living, from this experience. Who are any of us to deny another such?

This lesson is an ongoing one I am finding, having to consciously be reminded and think of my inner thoughts all the time. Perhaps it is merely another deep spirit lesson, to be able to just be there for another, a shoulder, and connect truly in spirit with them to aid in the strength required at this time. For to feel another's spirit energy with you in times of need is the greatest gift able to be given and the greatest comfort. This I know. Perhaps another part of this lesson is in allowing another to be there for us too.

The world as we know it is changing fast, sometimes it seems it is about to explode with all the pressure of the events going on. Hard times are indeed before us. Yet with this also I am able to smile, just as I feel happy for one who is experiencing a deep lesson. The entire world is taking part in this awesome return to spirit. The human condition dictates that we do not seek change unless forced to do so. We sit in our misery until we cannot take it any longer and give up totally. Only then does the journey of self discovery begin.

I equate that with what is happening within the world now. We all agreed to take part in this, we all planned it well. I do not know what will happen, but I do have strong faith all will be well. After the pressure builds and bursts, much devastation possibly. That is where the special spirits come in. Have you any idea just how many people around the world are being called into getting ready, just for such an event. Preparing through growth of inner strength, moving around to where they will be needed, gathering in groups of soul families, changing their interests and occupations to what makes their spirits sour, learning the old ways of simple living and loving...there is much wondrous movement.

Activity - What Is Your Story?

When you are ready, ponder and write your own story of life. Find your peace and understanding.

Me

How do I value myself? Do I treat myself as important and of worth? Do I see that I am cared and provided for?

When you complete this chapter you will be able to:

- Feel love and compassion for yourself
- Release the emotions that you have held onto

Perhaps it is that we never took on the role of self-caregiver, which in itself requires us to see ourselves of value to receive this care and attention.

It's easy to see this one. Look at yourself, look at your home, your car, your life. Are you treating yourself as valuable?

What do you think of yourself? As an individual, a family member, a member of society. Are you of benefit to the world you live in? Do you feel proud to let another meet and see the person you are, the life you live? How would you describe yourself to another person? What are your best characteristics, and your worst?

This reminds me of a study course I took a while back. On the last day, the lecturer had us write our name on the top of a blank sheet of paper, each person wrote something about us, then folded it over so not to be seen.

When I got mine back I was shocked, the comments of what these people thought of me beyond my comprehension. They were not simple statements, but instead detailed, expressions of overwhelming admiration of my personality characteristics.

We do things without thought, and often receive compliments. But that relates to what we do, not who we are as people. Perhaps we really don't know how to view ourselves as the world does, and have no idea what others think of us. I wonder if there is a way to find out, that is if we are game.

If I had to write of myself right now, I don't think I could find one redeeming quality I would feel comfortable listing.

I know people do not like being around me, that I am seen as an offence. I undertake many activities to push people away, because I know who I am. But I am human, and venture out into the world, trying to find a space where I can feel comfortable and welcomed, because I want to belong. Yet, it always comes full circle and I retreat back into where I belong, by myself where no-one sees this horrible person.

We all know well, that inner voice which is so precise and timely in its critique of all that we do. We have heard all our faults and weaknesses. We have heard them all many, many times.

This is the place to be reached in order to clear this one. For me, it was someone close's dislike of my person, which triggered me into feeling it. I can't say its an easy space to get into, complete self hate and condemnation, or that it is pleasant, for it definitely is not. Your intent to clear this major belief will provide a way for your discovering it. And it must be cleared in order to move forward.

Activity - Clear Your Self

Write the story of you, what is good about you, and what is not. Listen and find all the negative things you and then other people have said or thought of you.

Listen to how you feel. Follow the feeling and find your story, release and heal each thing another person said to you one by one. Then do the things you think of yourself. Remember to do each topic individually, at different times.

Activity - Clear Your Emotions

We not only hold onto painful memories and beliefs, but painful emotions too. Releasing the memory and/or belief does not remove the emotions.

Think about the sadness of realizing that you and others don't like you, feel, then wait, and see what comes up. If there is a story, follow and do the releasing and healing.

When you find there are no more stories left, you will feel something strange in your body, an actual physical thing. This is your bag of sadness, like a big balloon of sadness stockpiled from all time.

It is often located between your breast bone and belly button, coincidentally very near the region called the solar plexus which relates to opening.

Just like you surround, grab and blow out your fears when releasing, you can do the same with the contents of your bag of sadness. Find the right way to open and release it, perhaps by your usual releasing method, or feeling a space open in your belly button to pull them out, or imagining a flower in your stomach which opens to release the contents, anything that feels right for you is perfect.

Keep feeling, grabbing and removing the contents, then perhaps go back and check over the next few days for remainders. You may find other emotional bags to remove also.

Dare To Be You

How incredibly simple this all really is. How could I never have realized. What silly human beings we truly can be sometimes. Laughing

When you complete this chapter you will be able to:

- Be free to be yourself

All we need do is be ourselves. Our real selves. If we feel happy, smile, if we feel sad, cry, if we dislike our job or relationship, leave it, if you don't like doing something, don't do it, if you do like doing something do that, if you wish to say something to someone, say it.

It really is that simple! Do whatever whenever you feel like it. Without the second guessing yourself, and doubts and fears, all of it. Do what you wish to do!

When we do what feels right, without restriction and holding back, we feel so incredibly free, like we literally remove those bricks off our shoulders. The other aspect is that we can sit at the end of the day, and judge ourselves. Then, all we can do is smile, and feel good about us. We did good!! We are then satisfied with our days, because we lived them fully and honestly to ourselves, we did exceptionally good.

We actually feel proud and like who we are. It's a natural opposite of how we complain and berate ourselves for all we do that we don't like. Perhaps that is why we berate, for if we didn't we would have no idea those activities were not preferred from inside us, meaning what we wished we had done, the innate instinctive ones. So when we do follow our hearts and do what feels right, we can only feel good about ourselves, the world, and living. .

Activity - Get Use To Being You

At first, being yourself feels a little strange. You do and say things that come as a big surprise, sometimes making yourself cringe.

The trick is to let it all hang out, knowing that the lovely surprises will far outweigh the embarrassing moments. And when you behave in ways that you do not like, investigate and remove the need to do them.

This way you encourage fun and spontaneity while monitoring and correcting unwanted behaviors

What I Have Achieved

Who am I? What am I? These are questions I have been asking myself today.

When you complete this chapter you will be able to:

- Appreciate yourself

I see the world, my place in it, and me in a very different light now. I see what really is. I see what I create and become. I see all that has been, and is yet to be.

I see me, for perhaps the first time ever. Without hatred, or blame, or guilt, or fear. It is alright to BE me. I like who I am now and aspire to be. I like this journey I am creating for myself. I enjoy being myself. I am not scared to be me any longer.

So I sit, and ponder all that has been prior to this one moment in time. All I have known and experienced, all I have learned and unlearned, all I have achieved.

And especially the strength within me, that has led me on this special journey. My spirit essence. What a special thing to be connected to, what a special thing to know IS me, CREATES me, LIVES this life with me.

I sat down one day after realizing I wasn't that horrible, incapable person I had always believed, and wrote of the achievements throughout all my lives. The strength and courage and persistence that I AM.

I sat down and told myself the story of me.

Activity - What Have You Achieved?

Spend some time pondering your journey, and the story of your life. What is the story waiting for you to hear?

Everything Is Created With Love Energy

Step outside and watch for something that catches your eye.

Is it a beautiful tree, plant, or birdsong you hear? Perhaps a sky filled with sparkling stars, or a moon shining down upon you. Or even the laughter and smiles of children playing. Find something that brings a smile to your face.

Did you know that you created it?

When you complete this chapter you will be able to:

- Experience the beauty and wonder that you create in the world

Take a tree for example. One person may see beauty beyond words, another sees a nuisance that litters the ground with branches and leaves, and yet another may not even see the tree.

Or a bird. I may not see it, but I hear a magical voice singing love to the world, another person may put their hands to their ears, another shoo the bird away.

Or even the rain. Do you see gentle drops of water, renewing and refreshing all that is touched, the inconvenience of getting wet, or perhaps the annoyance of not being able to spend time outside?

Each of us views the world through our own unique eyes.

Each seeing a different thing. Our perceptions and world view create what we see.

So go outside to look, listen and feel the world you create. Feel the magic and beauty of your very own special creation.

See the tree, and wonder at its beauty. Each minute leaf and shape, the magnificent colors and textures, take your time noticing it all. Then FEEL the knowing that that beauty comes from within you, and is only so because that is what YOU made it.

The beauty that fills the world is there because it is what you see with your perception.

You create all the beauty before you. Enjoy!

An amazing experience eh? I remember the day I realized this concept. Sitting in my car in a parking lot waiting for my son on a hot September day.

As I gazed at the nearby trees I saw something different about them, so I looked closer to investigate. The more I looked the more beauty and wonder I felt at their magnificence of being. Such perfection to be found in an everyday object.

Then when a sparrow came to rest on the tree, somehow the picture became more perfect. Thousands of tiny feathers, perfectly formed and colored, those indescribable eyes, then the sound arising from that teeny creature.

This picture of perfection grew and magnified as my gaze increased. More trees, more birds, people of all variation. Black skinned, brown skinned, tall, thin, wearing strange outfits and hair. Each item I focused my gaze on revealed such wonder from within me.

I felt a warmth growing in my chest, I felt love growing and expanding out into the world. I felt the world reflecting this same love energy right back at me in all I saw.

At that moment I was forever touched. It became clear. Clear that every single thing comes from love energy. Just as that newly born infant touches our hearts with perfection and love, so it is with all before us.

Each thing is created a new, each time we think of or gaze

upon it. A new with our new perception of that moment.

If we take the time, we can take the journey into this wonderland whenever we choose. It can become our every moment of living.

Have you ever stopped to feel your own love?

I can stop, listen and feel. Then become aware of a small warm place in my chest. I can breathe into this place and feel it expand in strength and mass.

This warmth I feel is pure love energy, the essence OF me, what I am comprised of.

This energy can then grow and radiate outward beyond my physical and essence of self. I can feel myself connect with my loved ones, and our joined love energy magnify even greater and expand. And so it goes.

I can become one with events as they occur, seeing beyond the physical aspects. Feeling and knowing the greater connections and sharing behind each and every situation and connection.

The strength of the bond of love that we are formed from, especially when this love does not seem a possible aspect of what occurs.

My dear friend from Australia, who was my rock and support, who then went on to undermine me to my son, causing him to doubt and disbelief the only person who was physically here for him. Great anguish was created for us all, then I realized it was his responsibility to come to his own conclusions and beliefs of me. So I suggested he develop a way to come to his own understanding, rather than just listening to one source, I suggested several for him to speak to, and handed him their telephone numbers.

Then one day, about six months later, my son came up and hugged me, saying 'I love you mom'. And I held back the tears. Our relationship is now based on love and compassion, not judgment and wanting from the other. Pure acceptance of who we each are, and both of us knowing we have chosen to travel together as companions, a lovely knowing and experiencing.

So my dear old Australian friend is no longer. Yet when I think of her I smile because I know what she gave up, a special friendship. She was the perfect one to facilitate this experience for my son, so I am forever grateful because it has changed him as a person, taught him to find his own beliefs and knowing, for himself.

I can only feel pure love for her, and all the people I now realize gave up being part of my physical life, just so a situation could be facilitated. This can be expanded into daily events, seeing the love that is behind all actions towards us. We ask and they give.

Just think of all that is involved for each situation TO occur. What lies behind, then you will know.

To see beyond the obvious of situations is impossible to describe. It is to know the reasoning of it all, to feel each minute aspect. To be overcome with the love energy creating everything. It is to FEEL creation as it occurs.

I can know myself as me, yet see all the other parts of me on their journeys, some happy, some sad, some alike, some opposing. And I can smile at all the special aspects of myself that I am. I can say to each and every one, who and what you are is perfect by me!

It feels like all the parts of me are now welcomed and sent forth with love, to undertake their various paths, all those that seem strange to me, for each brings brand new knowing and learning, and love.

Go forth and have all the experiences you can muster. I welcome them all, as I know they all come back into this one mind which joins us, for us all to know of and learn from.

Just as the person who gives up their ability to be physically close to us, does so with the greatest love, by sharing and facilitating a difficult experience for us, so does the one who takes a very different life path of beliefs. They are so loved by our heart and mind, yet that love is limited in the physical because of their differences. We cannot accept them going against us, that is how we take it. But they do not go against us, they go FOR us. With love.

It was while sharing a quiet moment with another online, that these insights became. One who has opposing beliefs to mine. "Oh God Bless us all. I wish you HEALTH. And more than WEALTH. I wish you LOVE!!!!!"

This last statement is how I learned acceptance, pure acceptance. Rather than think in terms of my beliefs when reading it, I can accept the love she shares with these very words, and appreciate how deeply she means them, from her belief system.

We see and think of everything from our own belief perspective, blind to what others share, because we cannot see what it means from their perspective, too focused on our own, and how theirs must be wrong if ours is right.

We think that because they are so very different, their beliefs in direct contrast to our own, they must be against us, for that is what their beliefs seem to say.

Now I can welcome their differences, their individuality, what they bring to this one mind, which also is mine. We ALL contribute the best we can.

But I do not feel comfortable around some of them. They are me and I only wish to love them all, but cannot love what they are sometimes, so it is hard and I try to make them come around to my beliefs, so it is easier to bridge the physical love aspect.

Could it be sometimes I see myself as I could be if I followed their path perhaps, and I so do NOT wish to end up like them? I crave my individuality, yet I crave familiarity.

There are people that I definitely do not like, their actions, beliefs, ways. They go against all I believe in as loving and decent.

But we want them to be like us, to have the same beliefs, to be a companion to share with, and feel sad when they cannot. We want company on OUR specific path.

We don't want to be alone, we don't want to walk this path by ourselves. We want someone to share this love and exploration with. A companion, one that matches our knowing and beliefs, and world view and aspirations.

One who not only is close spiritually, but physically as well. One that crosses all boundaries of the physical and spiritual. One to become one with. One we will know as ourselves and them as themselves, perfect mirrors.

I no longer wish to journey alone, I want more.

Activity - Your Creation

What do you create with your love?

Spend an entire week watching the beauty in the world that YOU create! Feel it, live it, open and share energy with it.

Activity - Your Future

What will be your future path? What have you discovered that you long for?

Is it love, deeper friendships, closer family relationships, opening to connect with nature, filling your time with activities that make you smile, fulfilling work?

What is your more?

Conclusion

I want you to stop and take a look at the journey YOU have undertaken during these many months. Remember the person you were way back then, well just look at you now! Perhaps you cannot even remember that person clearly, seems a world away from who you are now.

You possess the knowledge and ability to go on to create whatever future your heart desires. You now know what is right and best for you! Just open your heart to experience the joy of life.

Whatever you do, know how special you are in my heart and mind. Without you this book would not be, and I might not be the adventurer I now am.

Close your eyes and feel. I reach out and surround you with a hug filled with love, just for YOU!

Take care, Janet.

About The Author

The decision to flatly refuse to continue living a life of pain and heartache turned Janet Greene's world upside down. Giving up her will to live opened the door for her inner self to break through a lifetime of fear and torment and take charge.

Led by the wisdom of her inner self, Janet's 4 year introspection journey took her deep inside, beyond her conscious thoughts to Heal Her Self. She instinctively knew how to permanently heal and release her fears, emotions, painful memories and dysfunctional self beliefs which sabotaged her happiness.

As each belief was removed and she began to understand herself, Janet noticed that the growing sense of freedom to feel, and be, and express, and live life as she'd always known that it should be, became the most natural thing in the world to do.

After being led to move half way across the world to America, she began sharing remarkable insights and discoveries with herself via writing to speed up her healing work.

Janet's Books *Heal Your Self, Heal Your Heart, The Little Book of Secrets* and *The Road to Integrity*, which are the compilation of Janet's writing, each take the reader on a guided journeys to discover and permanently heal their own emotions and beliefs which sabotage their life, while *A Smile for the Children* (for the child in all of us) lets the reader *feel* how very special they are.

As soon as Janet completed *Heal Your Heart, A Journey to find your Soul Mate,* she did just that and now lives the Ultimate Dream of Love with her Buddy Soul Mate, Marc.

Marcus & Janet came together in 2003, married a year later and are living the happily ever after dream.

Made in the USA
Lexington, KY
29 January 2011